Houseplants & Succulents

by Steven A. Frowine
Professional Horticulturist and Plant Aficionado

A Wiley Brand

Houseplants & Succulents For Dummies®

Published by: **John Wiley & Sons, Inc.,** 111 River Street, Hoboken, NJ 07030-5774, www.wiley.com

Copyright © 2024 by John Wiley & Sons, Inc., Hoboken, New Jersey

Published simultaneously in Canada

For general information on our other products and services, please contact our Customer Care Department within the U.S. at 877-762-2974, outside the U.S. at 317-572-3993, or fax 317-572-4002. For technical support, please visit https://hub.wiley.com/community/support/dummies.

Wiley publishes in a variety of print and electronic formats and by print-on-demand. Some material included with standard print versions of this book may not be included in e-books or in print-on-demand. If this book refers to media such as a CD or DVD that is not included in the version you purchased, you may download this material at http://booksupport.wiley.com. For more information about Wiley products, visit www.wiley.com.

Library of Congress Control Number: 2024930163

ISBN: 978-1-394-15951-2 (pbk); ISBN 978-1-394-15952-9 (ebk); ISBN 978-1-394-15953-6 (ebk)

SKY10065020_011724

Table of Contents

Introduction

About 90 percent of all plants in the world are from the tropics. I guess most plants prefer a year-round warm, humid climate to the harsher winter weathers where temperatures repeatedly fall to freezing. Can you blame them? Fortunately, many of these same plants relish the cozy, warm homes that we spend most of our time in. I guess that's why they're called houseplants!

Of course, sometimes it helps to modify your home's climate to make it more welcoming to these plants. For example, many homes, especially during the winter, have the low humidity more likely found in a desert than a tropical jungle, so you have to add a little moisture to the air for your plants. Also, houseplants thrive when you adjust their growing environment to provide sufficient light (natural or artificial), correct temperatures, adequate ventilation, the right amount of water, and a bit of fertilizer, but these changes are all very doable.

It's my pleasure to introduce you to a vast number of gorgeous, lush houseplants and succulents to discover and enjoy. As a professional horticulturist, I was trained academically in the plant sciences, but more important for this book, I've been a passionate hands-on grower of countless types of plants. Cacti and succulents, houseplants, various members of the African violet clan, carnivorous plants, begonias, many kinds of tropical foliage and flowering plants, as well as a wide variety of other plants — you name it, and I've probably grown it.

I'm pleased to be able to pass on my experiences with these plants. I've had some successes and some disappointments, and I share both with you. I've grown various houseplants for more than 50 years, and I've never grown bored with them. There are always new ones to try, which I hope you discover in this book.

About This Book

Houseplants and Succulents For Dummies tells you, in concise, easy-to-read language, all you need to know to grow and appreciate splendid and varied houseplants in your home. This group of plants is so huge that you may be overwhelmed by the prospect of choosing and growing any of them yourself, so I share which ones are easiest to grow and which are more challenging. I also make a point of using lots of illustrations and photos to show you what I'm talking about.

My goal is to help you feel comfortable with these dazzling plants and get to know them on a personal basis. Then you'll be eager to discover all their mysteries and slow down your busy life to savor the pleasure and beauty houseplants can offer.

This book contains the following information:

>> **The common and scientific names of houseplants:** I include both names because the common names can vary a great deal, and some plants are known by more than one common name. Only Latin or scientific names are universal. I realize that sometimes the scientific names are tough to get used to, but knowing them can better ensure that you and your plant friends or vendors are talking about the same plant.

>> **Detailed profiles of each plant discussed:** This gives you specific growing information and tips for each plant.

>> **Many illustrations of important how-to information and techniques:** Sometimes pictures speak louder than words.

>> **A color insert that displays a sampling of brilliantly hued houseplants:** Seeing some beautiful plants in their full-color glory should entice you to try some of them in your home.

>> **Detailed information on how to multiply your favorite houseplants:** If you have a favorite plant, why not make more of it for yourself or to share or trade? Reproducing plants is surprisingly easy.

>> **Lighting options, both artificial and natural:** I give you plenty of options for lighting up your houseplants' lives.

>> **Online resources:** You get lots of information in this book, but if you have questions I haven't answered, there's abundant useful information on the web!

>> **Effective disease and insect controls:** Certain creatures and organisms can destroy your plants, so I tell you about effective and safe ways to control them.

Foolish Assumptions

In writing this book, I assume a few things about you and your experience with houseplants. At least one of the following applies to you:

>> You've seen houseplants for sale in the garden section of your local home-improvement store or garden center, and you've always wanted to give them a try.

>> You purchased or were gifted a new houseplant and are wondering, "Now what?!"

>> You saw houseplants at a flower show and wonder if you can grow these exquisite plants in your home.

>> You've had some houseplants for a few years, but they don't seem to be doing well, and you can't get them to bloom again.

>> You've grown some houseplants successfully and are now ready to branch out and expand your collection and your skills.

Icons Used in This Book

I use the following icons throughout the book to point out particularly essential information:

TIP

When you see this icon, you can be sure you'll find information that will make you a more successful houseplant grower.

WARNING

This icon points out some common pitfalls you want to avoid when growing houseplants.

REMEMBER

This icon highlights information worth remembering when you're working with your houseplants.

TECHNICAL STUFF

Take it or leave it. This icon points out information that may help, but it's not essential.

Beyond This Book

This book is full of tips and other pieces of helpful advice you can use as you start growing and caring for your own houseplants. If you want some additional tidbits of wisdom, check out the book's Cheat Sheet at www.dummies.com. Here you can find a list of 10 houseplants anyone can grow, 20 tips to keep your houseplants thriving, steps to turn beautiful flowers from your houseplants into a charming corsage, and more! Just search for "Houseplants and Succulents For Dummies Cheat Sheet."

Where to Go from Here

This book is set up in easily digestible stand-alone pieces. Pick out sections that interest you most and read them first. You can bounce around in the book any way you please.

If you already have houseplants but are having difficulties growing them, you may want to start out with Part 4. It gives you quick answers to common problems.

Trying to decide which houseplant you should start with? Look at Chapters 2 and 16. To get jazzed about houseplants, check out the color insert. And if you have a houseplant that's in dire need of repotting, skip right to Chapter 7.

If you're not sure where to begin, scan the table of contents or index for a topic that catches your interest, flip to the chapter, and start reading.

1
Getting Started with Houseplants

IN THIS PART . . .

Discover which houseplants are inexpensive and easy to grow in windowsills and under artificial lights.

Choose the right tools that you need to grow and maintain your houseplants.

See how to display your houseplants.

Discover the many joys and benefits of growing houseplants.

Find out the best place to buy your houseplants.

Get month-to-month growing guidelines for your plants.

Chapter **1**

Discovering the World of Houseplants

You're about to encounter a marvelous category of plants called *houseplants*, and you're in store for an exciting adventure! Houseplants hail from all over the world — from moist rainforests to bone-dry deserts. Within this group are plants that grow in the dense shade of tropical jungles and plants that thrive in the blinding bright light of full sun. Some can get several feet tall, whereas others are miniatures that can fit in a teacup. They display every conceivable leaf shape, texture, color, flower size, and color palette.

In this chapter, I introduce you to this amazing group of plants. First, I cover what's behind the naming of houseplants. Then I share some of the benefits of growing plants in your home before I wrap up the chapter by giving you an overview of what you can expect to happen with your plants during each month of the year.

Getting to Know Houseplants

One of the most intimidating hurdles that beginning houseplant growers face is interpreting the complex names of plants. Although some houseplants have a regularly used common name, many do not, and when you realize what an immense group of plants this is, you may understand why many plants are referred to by their Latin or Greek name. In this book, I always use the Latin name because that's the universally accepted name, but I add a common name when there is one.

I know the Latin and Greek names can be a bit daunting — so much so that you may wish the scientific terms had died with those long-ago cultures. But there's a benefit to using Latin and Greek for the natural-science world — those languages aren't changing! You'll start to make friends with Latin and Greek as their use becomes more familiar and comfortable to you.

TIP

Pronouncing a plant's name a little at a time makes it easier to say and understand. In the following sections, I share the names, one word at a time, of a species plant and then a hybrid.

TECHNICAL STUFF

Unfortunately, even though Latin and Greek may not be changing, plant names can change as botanists discover that certain houseplants were originally incorrectly assigned a name, or they need new names because they find that houseplants they thought were closely related aren't related. Also, botanists from different countries don't always agree on a name. Still, they tend to follow specific naming guidelines called the International Code of Botanical Nomenclature formulated by the International Botanical Congress. The World Checklist of Selected Plant Families is also a standard reference.

REMEMBER

It can be confusing and even aggravating when a plant name changes. In this book, I use the most recent name (*nomenclature*) for houseplants, but you can be sure some names will change — and may even have changed between the time I wrote this and when you read the book.

Houseplant history

The timeline of houseplant history is difficult to nail down. Certainly, growing food crops took priority in the early parts of human history. Most of the "houseplants" in ancient Egypt, Greece, and Rome were container plants grown both inside and outside people's dwellings. Examples include citrus, fig, and other fruit trees; roses; vegetables; and various flowering annuals and perennials. And Asians have long treasured plants. A Chinese poem, "The Lonely Orchid," written by Su Shih in the 11th century, expounds on the fragrance of a potted orchid.

Almost all houseplants hail from the tropical or semitropical parts of the world. Exploration during the Victorian era resulted in plants being brought back from these areas. The invention of *Wardian cases* (which are essentially *terrariums*, or glass containers for growing plants) made the process of bringing back plants from faraway places much more viable and successful because these cases offered protection from salt mist on the returning ships and provided needed humidity and moisture. The landed gentry of England and parts of Europe purchased the plants at auction houses for display in their impressive greenhouses and orangeries. Ferns and other foliage plants lushly decorated home conservatories or sunrooms and became a desirable addition to any respectable estate.

As homes throughout the world became centrally heated and the installation of glass windows let in more bright light, houseplants were offered a more hospitable indoor habitat. A reawakening of interest in the natural world occurred during the 1960s and '70s. As this interest grew, a larger variety of potted houseplants adapted to the indoor environment became available. Houseplants became a standard feature in home design magazines.

Houseplants have never been more popular than they are now. Their rise in popularity among all age groups of gardeners seems to have accelerated in the 2020s. Interestingly, the advent of COVID-19 played a part in this resurgence because as folks spent much more time in their homes, they wanted to add the beauty and comfort of plants to their living spaces. "Plants, the new pets" became a trend, particularly for millennials working from their houses or small apartments. As a result, the number of houseplants available increased dramatically. Today, the selection of houseplants in almost all houseplant buying venues — from grocery stores, garden centers, and home stores to mail-order and online suppliers — is unparalleled. What a great time to grow houseplants!

Species houseplant names

Plants that are sold as they were created by nature ("from the wild") rather than hybridized by humans are referred to as *species plants*. They usually have two names, but sometimes they have three:

>> **Genus name:** This name comes first and is capitalized. (Note that the plural of genus is *genera*.)

>> **Species name:** It comes second and is lowercase.

Both names are in Latin or Greek, and they're italicized.

>> **Botanical variety or form:** This is a third part of the name that comes after the species name. For example, an orchid that varies from the standard species — maybe it has a larger flower or a slightly different coloration — has a third component in its name, preceded by *var*. This part of the name is lowercase and in Latin. If the variety is specified as a "form," it has a lowercase *f* after the species name followed by the form name in lowercase and Latin. Botanical "form" is one step of specification beyond "variety."

TIP

The genus name is much like a person's family name, and the species name is like your given name. In other words, if my name were written the way a plant's is, I would be *Frowine steven*.

Here's an example of the complete name of a botanical variety of a houseplant: *Ananas comosus* var. *variegatus* (common name: variegated pineapple). Table 1-1 explains the plant's name.

TABLE 1-1 **The Components of a Species Houseplant Name**

Part of Name	Name	Explanation
Genus name	*Ananas*	The first name of a houseplant is the genus and is like your family (last) name. It's always capitalized, italicized, and in Latin.
Species name	*comosus*	The second name of a houseplant is the species. It's always lowercase, italicized, and in Latin.
Botanical variety	var. *variegatus*	Sometimes, there's a third name. This is called the *botanical variety,* which means this example of the species has something special about it (for example, flower shape or color) that separates it from the more usual form of the species. This name is lowercase, italicized, and in Latin or Greek.

Here's an example of a form of a bromeliad plant: *Neoregelia carolinae* f. *tricolor* (common name: blushing bromeliad).

Cultivar names

When a particular selection of a plant shows some characteristic that's different or exceptional from the standard plant of its type, it's given a cultivar name. (*Cultivar* is an abbreviation of *cultivated variety*.) This name is always capitalized, is set off by single quotation marks, and is not in Latin or Greek (it's usually English) — for example, *Aloe arboretum* 'Electra'.

Aeonium arboretum 'Black Rose'

Hybrid plant names

Eventually, humans got mixed up in the plant world and started developing *hybrids*, which are the result of *crossing* two species (taking the pollen from one species of plant to mate it with another). Hybrids of most houseplants usually contain two names: the genus and the hybrid name or cultivar name (the *cultivated horticultural hybrid name*). An example of a cultivar of a hybrid is *Aloe* 'Blue Elf'.

Orchid names are another kettle of fish compared to other houseplant names. Orchids' names, especially the hybrids, can be much more complex. This is due to the exceptional ability of orchids to be bred between two or more different genera. Most hybrids are a result of orchid breeders purposely breeding one or more genera together to create a unique new orchid that has some of the characteristics of each parent. As you can imagine, this makes orchid hybrid names quite complex.

TIP

For most of the plants in this book, I list only the genus and species. I don't mention hybrids of these plants because specific hybrids may be much harder to find where you shop for plants.

Understanding the Benefits of Growing Houseplants

Growing and studying houseplants provides the ultimate horticultural experience and pleasure. Here are some key reasons to start growing houseplants now:

>> Growing houseplants is fun and relaxing! (That may be the most important motive for working on your green thumb.)

>> You don't need to be an expert. Houseplants are easy to grow. See Part 2 for information on how to be successful.

>> You can start with beginner houseplants that can make any newcomer wildly successful. See Part 3 for a description of great plants to start off growing.

>> There has never been a wider choice of houseplants, and you can easily find the one that's right for you. See Chapter 2 to make this process a snap.

>> Some plants emit exquisite perfumes. I will mention in the text if a particular plant has an especially pleasing scent.

>> Plants don't need to be expensive; most are reasonably priced. Many cost less than a flower arrangement, and they last longer!

SELECTING THE PLANTS THAT WILL DO BEST IN YOUR HOME

Choosing a houseplant is an exciting, but sometimes confusing, decision! So many types of houseplants, so little space. In this book, I make the selection process easy for you:

- Check out Chapter 2 to walk through some of the steps for deciding which houseplant fits your home environment and to find suggestions about where you can purchase them.

- Consider starting your houseplant collection with the easiest houseplants. They're the most foolproof of all. See Chapter 16 for suggestions.

- When you're ready to expand your collection or you want more choices, check out all the other houseplants in Part 3.

>> Houseplants are available from big-box stores, specialty growers, flower shows, garden centers, botanical gardens, houseplant societies, and online or mail-order suppliers. These outlets have large selections, which was unheard of a decade ago.

>> Because of the huge diversity of houseplants, you'll never tire of them. You'll always find new ones to try and enjoy. Check out the chapters in Part 3 for some of the many possibilities.

>> If you join one of the houseplant societies mentioned in the appendix, you'll meet new friends who are as fanatical about plants as you are. The societies' magazines and online information are marvelous sources for information and gorgeous pictures.

>> Houseplants don't have to be grown in an expensive greenhouse. They'll be happy with a windowsill or artificial lights. See Chapter 5 for the skinny on how to grow houseplants to perfection in your home.

>> Plants beautify your home and life. See Chapter 4 for some tips on how to enjoy them to the fullest in your home.

>> Houseplants can live a very long time — even decades. In fact, they get bigger and better every year that you have them.

>> As they grow, you can divide and multiply them to share with your friends or to trade for other houseplants. See Chapter 8 for more tips on dividing and multiplying your houseplants.

Growing Houseplants: A Month-by-Month Guide

To be generally successful in growing houseplants, just follow these suggestions:

>> Know the environment you have to offer your houseplants and find house-plants that fit into it. See Chapter 5 for more information on your growing environment.

>> If necessary, modify your growing area to help your houseplants perform at their best. Chapter 5 also addresses this.

For the most common houseplant questions and problems, check out Part 4.

Beyond choosing the right houseplant for your environment, you must pay attention to the time of the year to know what your houseplant needs. In the following sections, I give you a month-by-month rundown of the calendar year with suggestions of what you may need to do during each month.

Note: You can't be too exact with the timing of this care schedule because the United States is a vast country with climates ranging from the cold north to the semitropics. The guidelines in this book are for the United States and other countries in the Northern Hemisphere. If you live in the Southern Hemisphere, take that into consideration. For example, January in the Northern Hemisphere corresponds to July in the Southern Hemisphere, and so on.

January

This is a period of cold, short days and low light, so houseplants don't grow much. Fortunately, some houseplants are budding up and getting ready to show off their splendiferous blooms very soon. Consider the following:

>> For houseplants such as some of the cacti and succulents, this is a time of rest, so you'll want to reduce your watering.

>> Some of your potted "forced" spring bulbs like daffodils, crocus, tulips, and hyacinths should be rooted well enough to be brought in from their outdoor cold area.

TIP

If you haven't already done so, you can pot your amaryllis bulbs.

>> Watch out for bugs. Check the underside of the leaves of all your plants and treat them right away if you see any signs of problems. See Chapter 9 for more information.

>> Keep the humidity moderate (40 to 50 percent) with good air movement. See Chapter 5 for ways to do this.

>> If you're watering with well water, warm it to room temperature before using it on your houseplants. Ice-cold water can cause forming buds to drop and may stunt new growth. This is especially true for plants with hairy foliage because cold (or sometimes hot) water spots the leaves.

>> Don't put your houseplants too close to the windows because the leaves can be damaged by the cold. Thermopane windows reduce the chance of such damage.

>> Apply little fertilizer. Houseplants don't need it yet. In fact, if you apply too much fertilizer at this time, the excess salts in the unused fertilizer can damage plant roots.

>> When you water your plants, do it in the early morning so the foliage dries off before evening. Water remaining on foliage on cool evenings invites disease problems.

>> Make sure very sensitive plants like African violets and moth orchids don't get too cold. Put a maximum/minimum thermometer in your growing area to monitor your minimum temperatures.

>> Consider having an artificial light growing area, so you can enjoy growing your plants when windowsill plants have pretty much shut down. This setup also can spare your plants from light-deficiency disorder.

February

This is another dark month, but the days are getting longer and brighter, which should cause an increase in growth. Keep the following in mind:

>> Toward the end of this month, increased light may mean you have to be careful with your houseplants that require less light, so they don't get burned. You may have to move them farther away from the windows or install a light-reducing curtain.

>> Spend some enjoyable downtime looking at catalogs and online houseplant suppliers to dream about what you can add to your collection, but don't order houseplants for mail delivery until it warms up in the spring. Otherwise, you run a high risk of cold damage to your houseplants during transit.

>> More of your houseplants that are naturally winter blooming will be showing buds, and some may be blooming — especially bulbs like amaryllis and some orchids.

- » Don't overcrowd your plants. This can create poor air circulation, which leads to poor growth and disease problems.

- » Make sure your plants receive as much light as possible without overdoing it.

- » You can sow seeds of slow-growing annuals, like coleus and impatiens, that you want to grow indoors.

- » Tubers of tuberous begonias and gloxinias can be potted at the end of this month.

- » Tall-growing flower spikes like ones on amaryllis and some orchids need to be staked. Be careful when inserting the stakes not to spear the bulb or penetrate any of the main roots.

- » If you're growing under lights, take note of when you last changed your bulbs. Fluorescent lamps (the tubes in fluorescent lights are commonly called lamps) can lose up to 40 percent of their light output after several months of use. Because new growth is starting on houseplants, this is a good time to change the lamps so the plants will receive the most light possible. LEDs generally produce their full amount of light for a longer time than fluorescent lamps. For much more detail on artificial lights check out Chapter 5.

- » Apply very little fertilizer during this month. Wait until you see new growth.

March

Finally, signs of spring arrive with longer and brighter days. Most houseplants respond very favorably to the increased light and warmth of this month. Here are some guidelines for March:

- » Be careful that the increased sunlight doesn't heat your greenhouse or windowsill too much. Apply shading if necessary. See Chapter 5 for various shade-providing options and ideas.

- » The increased light and warmth of this month means an acceleration of growth. Sprouting new shoots should be more evident.

- » This is the beginning of the show for many houseplants. Many orchids and other houseplants will be starting to bloom.

- » As the days get brighter and warmer, resume your regular fertilizing schedule.

- » March and April are usually prime times to check out flower shows in your area. They're inspiring and fun, and shows are a good place to buy a few new houseplants and related supplies.

>> More light in this month means more active growth. If you're growing plants in a windowsill that has light coming from one direction, their growth may lean or elongate. Prevent this by turning your plants a quarter turn every few days so they grow more uniformly.

April

In April, many houseplants start to flower. You'll notice increased growth and new roots and foliage as spring charges full steam ahead. You'll be busy tending your houseplants. Remember the following:

>> Many houseplants showing new growth can be repotted at this time. See Chapter 7.

>> Sometimes during the low-light periods of winter, plants become stretched or "leggy." This is a good time to trim them back to encourage fuller and bushier growth.

>> Be on the lookout for bugs. The warmer temperatures cause them to hatch.

>> Houseplants that seem to have stopped growing during the dark of the winter should be showing new growth, so resume your regular watering and fertilizing schedule.

>> If you didn't apply shading on your greenhouse last month, your plants may need it this month.

>> A gauze curtain may be needed to soften the light for houseplants growing in a south window.

>> Start summer flowering bulbs that like warmer weather, like caladiums, cannas, and callas.

>> If some of your light-sensitive plants, like African violets, have spent the low-light winter days in a southern exposure, move them to an east window to avoid sunburned leaves.

>> Try not to be too eager to move your tropical plants outdoors until you're sure there are no more chances of frost.

May

Rapid growth continues at full bore this month as days get brighter and longer. May is another prime month for houseplant flowering and another active month for you, their caretaker. Here are some tasks that need your attention:

- » More frequent watering and fertilizing is needed. More details and guidance in Chapter 6.

- » If you're in a northern climate, move some plants to a protected shaded spot outdoors by the end of this month, but be careful not to do this too soon. Houseplants that prefer it warm and don't appreciate being too chilled at night — they don't like temperatures below around 55°F (13°C).

- » Increase your ventilation to remove excess hot air and prevent fungal disease spotting on flowers.

- » May is usually an opportune time to repot your houseplants because they should be in active growth. Attend to this right after they've flowered; repotting when they're flowering is stressful for them.

- » Take your houseplants outdoors for a close inspection. Check for bugs or disease problems. It's easier to apply whatever remedies are necessary outdoors rather than in your house. Remove all dead leaves while you have your plants outside.

WARNING

Some houseplants do not do well outdoors. This applies to delicate plants and plants with hairy leaves like gloxinias and African violets. Their foliage easily burns from too much light and becomes spotted from rains.

June, July, and August

Temperatures have heated up. Some houseplants, like a few of the summer-blooming hybrid cattleya orchids, moth orchids, oncidium orchids, and slipper orchids, are in flower. These months aren't usually noted for a lot of houseplant flowering, but they're a time when your plants produce many roots and leaves to build up energy for future blooming so pay attention to them in the following ways:

- » Be sure your windowsill or greenhouse doesn't get too hot. Consider moving houseplants from a south window to an east window, where they'll appreciate the reduced light and heat.

- » For houseplants growing under lights, make sure your growing area gets plenty of ventilation because it may be getting very warm. If you have trouble keeping the temperature low enough, consider summering your houseplants outside in a protected shaded spot. They'll enjoy the vacation.

- » For light gardeners, this is a good time to clean and sanitize your growing area. Also consider replacing some of your fluorescent bulbs, especially ones showing dark bands at both ends of the tubes, which indicates they're starting to fail.

» If you plan to take a vacation, be sure to line up a dependable plant sitter. This is a serious and important job. Take time to show your plant sitter exactly how often and how much each plant should be watered. I've discovered from personal experience that a week of improper watering (usually too much) can do serious damage to your plants. Using self-watering pots can make this job easier for a plant sitter, and the plants can go longer between waterings. For more information on self-watering pots check out Chapter 6.

» This is also a prime time for insect problems. If it gets hot and dry, be on the lookout for mites. If it's wet, slugs and snails can be a plague. Aphids, mealybugs, and scale can show up anytime. If you need to spray, do it in the morning when it's cool and be sure your houseplants are well watered before you spray. Check out Chapter 9 for more information on how to handle common bug problems.

» Your houseplants should be responding to your earlier repotting efforts with new root growth.

» If you put some of your container houseplants outdoors, make sure they don't receive too much light, or the leaves can burn. Also realize that hot days can dry out your plants very quickly. Check them daily.

» Even if some of your plants don't seem too big for their pots, summer is a good time to repot them if the potting media is older than a year or so. Older media breaks down and can lose its ability to drain well. See Chapter 7 for tips on repotting.

If you have pots that you want to reuse, this is a good time to wash and store them. Soaking them overnight in a solution of one part bleach and nine parts water removes algae, disease organisms, insects and their eggs, and crusting from minerals. You can also put clay or ceramic pots (not plastic — they may melt) in the dishwasher on the hot or pot cycle.

» Potted indoor cacti and succulents may be moved outdoors for the summer months, after all danger of frost has passed. They may appreciate some sheltered shade at first, especially during the hottest part of the afternoon.

September

Cool evenings and shorter days are signs of the change in season. The cooler nights are beneficial for initiating or setting flower buds for fall-blooming and winter-blooming houseplants. Here are some other things to be aware of during this month:

» If you're in a cold climate, bring in any plants that have been summering outside. Before doing so, check them closely for pests. If spraying is called for, it's much easier and safer to do while the plants are outdoors.

>> Start cutting back on the frequency of watering *deciduous* houseplants (plants that shed their leaves) like catasetum orchids (which have yellowing foliage at this time of year).

REMEMBER

It's normal for houseplants to lose some of their lower leaves after they are brought indoors. This is just a response to being moved from the humid, bright outdoors to a drier, lower-light area. Don't be concerned unless this leaf drop continues for a month or so. If this happens, it may be a result of overwatering.

>> Remove the shades on your greenhouse in most parts of the Northern Hemisphere.

>> If you would like to try forcing some spring bulbs for winter flowering indoors, this is the time to pot them.

>> Before it frosts, take cuttings of outdoor plants you want to grow during the winter or hold onto for the next gardening season. Coleus and geraniums are some examples. See Chapter 8 for information about taking cuttings from plants.

>> Peak houseplant season is around the corner, so stock up on growing supplies.

>> Move houseplants that require a lot of light from the east window back to a southern exposure.

October

Do the following for your houseplants, no matter whether you're growing them in a greenhouse, under lights, or on the windowsill:

>> As the days continue to shorten and the angle of light gets lower in the sky, position the houseplants in your windowsill and greenhouse so that they capture the most light.

>> Be sure your glass or glazing surface is clean. This can make a real difference in light transmission.

>> If you're growing under fluorescent or LED lights, clean the tubes or diodes with a damp cloth to remove any spray residue or water deposits that reduce their intensity.

>> Lower temperatures and less light cause growth to slow on many houseplants, so reduce watering and fertilizing accordingly. See Chapter 5 for more details about desirable plant-growing temperatures.

>> Get ready for winter. Insulate your greenhouse, and get a standby emergency propane heater.

November and December

Flowering spikes show up on some moth orchids, slipper orchids, and oncidium orchids. Some of the nobile–type dendrobium orchids start to show buds. The low light, short days, and cold temperatures of these two months bring most houseplant growth to a stop or at least a crawl. Plants grown under lights have more growth than plants in a greenhouse or on a windowsill because of the additional light that can be provided. Here are tasks to complete:

>> For the Northern Hemisphere and other cold parts of the world, November is the last month to safely purchase mail-order plants before it gets so cold that there's a higher risk of freeze damage in transit. Visit houseplant nurseries to pick out holiday presents for your houseplant-growing friends (or yourself!).

>> Put houseplants that require more light, like most cacti and succulents, in a bright window, close to the lights, or high in the greenhouse to expose them to as much light as possible.

>> If you want to keep poinsettias, Christmas cacti, amaryllis, or freesia in great condition, keep them in a cool, bright room (at least four hours of sunlight is ideal), and don't forget to water them as needed.

>> Clean off your plants' leaves with a soft damp cloth to increase their ability to absorb the lower light during this time of the year. If you want to add a natural luster to the leaves, wipe them down with milk. Whole milk works best because of the fat content.

>> Water plants in the early part of the day to ensure that no standing moisture is on the leaves overnight. In cold, damp weather especially, excess moisture can cause disease outbreaks.

Chapter **2**

Choosing the Perfect Houseplants

O ne of the main reasons some people fail with houseplants is that they simply choose the wrong ones. When you consider the thousands of distinct kinds of houseplants available, you can see how people may not know which one to buy. To be successful, you need to pick a dependable supplier, a healthy plant, and the type of houseplant that fits your growing environment.

Selecting a houseplant that suits your growing conditions is much more practical than trying to suit your growing conditions to the houseplant. In this chapter, I walk you through the important questions to ask yourself and your supplier so you end up with the houseplant that's just right for your growing spot.

Figuring Out Where to Shop

Nowadays, because houseplants, especially cacti and succulents, have skyrocketed in popularity, you can find them for sale in many places. In the following sections, I fill you in on your supplier options.

Specialist houseplant growers or suppliers

A houseplant specialist is always my first choice when I'm buying houseplants. Reputable suppliers in this category were selling houseplants for many years before it was the chic thing to do. Almost all of them are houseplant fanatics whose hobby grew out of control — so they were forced to either stop buying more houseplants or start a business. They know *everything* about their plants — where they came from, what their attributes are, and how to grow them. They almost always have the largest selection and cater to both beginners and sophisticated, experienced growers. They love to help other people discover the pleasure of growing houseplants and are full of useful information.

The only disadvantage of specialist growers or suppliers is that you may not have one near where you live. Unfortunately, the number of these growers seems to be dwindling because most folks now purchase their houseplants through more convenient channels. Of course, that doesn't have to be a deterrent. It just means you'll need to do some planning and take your own houseplant-buying safari to search out these growers! I urge you to seek out these dedicated growers because they are breeding and growing the lesser-known and more fascinating houseplants. If houseplant lovers like you and I don't support these committed folks, we risk losing the diversity of houseplants that only they supply and now enjoy.

TIP

See Appendix A for houseplant societies that list specialist houseplant suppliers who are reputable and reliable. (See Chapter 1 for an explanation of *genus*.)

Your local garden center

Having a local houseplant source is extremely convenient both for buying the plants and for getting information on growing them. Today, garden centers offer more unusual and more interesting plants than ever before — and houseplants are among them. The types of houseplants on offer vary greatly from one garden center to the next.

Home centers, groceries, and discount stores

Because houseplants have had such a meteoric rise in popularity, home centers and discount stores now frequently stock a limited selection. The good news: They usually carry the houseplants that are easy to grow. The bad news: Getting information about plants at these stores is difficult. But if you're shopping for your first inexpensive houseplant, and if you don't have easy access to a garden center or houseplant grower, these are good places to start.

PURCHASING DISCOUNTED SICK PLANTS IS RARELY A BARGAIN

I know it's tempting to buy some of those plants on the back shelf at the home store that look a little worse for wear. Hey, they're a great deal! Not really. You're basically buying problems. Plants that are marked down because they're distressed have at least one of many problems, including root damage from over- or underwatering or some type of disease. You don't want to introduce any of those issues to your plant collection at home. The truth is, most of these plants won't survive, and even if you're lucky and they do make it, they'll likely be stunted for most of their lives. You're much better off starting with the most robust, healthy plants you can find. You'll have a higher chance of success.

TIP

When shopping for plants at home centers and discount stores, find out which day of the week their regular shipments come in. That's the day you want to be there to get the best quality and selection.

Plant and home shows

At plant and home shows, you can often find displays of a broad range of gorgeous houseplants. Houseplant vendors are a regular feature of these shows, so they're a great place to shop. To find a plant show in your area, check out the various plant magazines or search their websites.

TIP

When buying flowering houseplants, buy ones that are just starting to flower rather than plants in full bloom. That way you will enjoy a much longer flower display.

Online houseplant suppliers

You can buy a fine selection of houseplants without ever leaving your home. Most houseplant suppliers have websites, and some of those sites are detailed and informative.

If you already know which types of houseplants you want, you can use a search engine to look for them by type or name. eBay has become quite a useful source for various houseplants. Etsy and Facebook Marketplace are also good plant resources.

TIP

When you search online for plants, you can use both the common and the scientific name, but if you search by the scientific name, you're more likely to get the exact plant you're after because different plants may use the same common name.

PURCHASING HOUSEPLANTS ONLINE

Here are some guidelines I use when purchasing houseplants online:

- **Check out the vendor's rating.** If the satisfaction ratings are below the high 90s, check out the vendor's responses to complaints to make sure the ratings are reasonable. Sometimes customers can be unrealistic in their demands.

- **Examine the picture of the plant being offered.** You should see a picture of the *exact* plant being offered, not a picture of a group of plants. You need to know that the picture isn't just representational of what you may see when the plant flowers but an exact picture of the flowers your plant will display. Be aware that the offspring of seed-grown houseplants vary dramatically.

- **Look closely at the plant's foliage.** Do the leaves show discolored spots or holes that may indicate disease or insect damage? Is the foliage floppy and weak, which may mean that it's poorly grown?

- **Make sure the vendor accepts returns.** Ask the vendor whether they accept a returned plant if the one you receive is in poor condition or if it isn't the plant you ordered.

- **Check out the cost and speed of the shipping method.** In general, you don't want your plant to be in transit for more than a few days.

- **Try to have your plant shipped to you on a Monday.** That way you don't run the risk of the plant being held by the shipping company over a weekend if the shipment gets delayed.

- **Order when the weather is mild with daytime temperatures above freezing.** If that's not possible, make sure the shipper includes a heat pack with your shipment and guarantees live delivery. Also, avoid extremely hot times.

Considering Your Environment

When you shop for houseplants, you can very easily get carried away. The excitement of the moment may completely overwhelm rational plant selection. Few beginning houseplant growers take the time to consider their environment *before* they buy. Unfortunately, if you don't think this through before you shop, you may end up bringing home a gorgeous houseplant that's completely wrong for you.

TIP

If possible, always choose a houseplant that fits your growing area. Even though in Part 2 of this book I give you pointers on how to modify your growing area to make it more suitable for houseplant growth, you can only modify your environment so much. For instance, a houseplant that's commonly found growing in full sun in Hawaii probably won't take well to a windowsill during the winter in a low-light area like New England. And a houseplant from the cloud forest that's drenched with almost constant rainfall and extremely high humidity probably won't be happy and bloom in the hot, dry air of Arizona.

TIP

When you're considering a plant, be sure to ask the grower about its temperature, light, and humidity requirements. Check out its ultimate size. Then match this information with what you know about your houseplant growing area.

In the following sections, I help you assess your environment so you can be confident that you'll pick out a stunning houseplant that is right for you and that will thrive where you live.

Taking temperature readings

Before you bring home a houseplant, you need to consider the average daytime and nighttime temperatures in summer and winter where you live.

TIP

To determine high and low temperatures indoors, get a maximum-minimum thermometer that records this information and place it in your growing area. A broad selection of temperature- and weather-recording instruments is available from home stores, garden centers, or online. I find that a maximum-minimum thermometer (see Figure 2-1) is especially useful to determine your minimum and maximum temperatures for day and night. They're available in digital or analog.

FIGURE 2-1:
Maximum-minimum thermometer.

© John Wiley & Sons, Inc.

When houseplant publications refer to *temperature preferences*, they almost always mean the evening temperature. The daytime temperature is usually about 15°F (9.5°C) higher than the evening temperature.

Measuring your light intensity

Just as important as temperature is the amount of light your houseplant will get. Houseplants that thrive in high light need several hours of direct sunlight (preferably in the morning to early afternoon) or bright artificial light, whereas those that thrive in lower light will be happy with less direct and more diffused light in a windowsill or under less intense artificial light.

Will you be growing your plants under artificial lights? Most light setups consist of multiple fluorescent high-output lamps and LEDs, and they can provide adequate illumination for most houseplants. High-intensity discharge lamps are capable of much more light output but can be expensive to operate and generate quite a bit of heat. For most folks, the best option is going to be LED or various fluorescent bulb units. For more detail about lighting, see Chapter 5.

How bright is your light? Figure 2-2 illustrates a simple yet effective and reasonably accurate method for determining the intensity of your light.

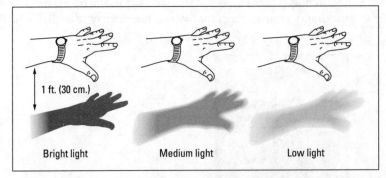

1 ft. (30 cm.)

Bright light   Medium light   Low light

FIGURE 2-2: The shadow test is a simple and reasonably accurate way to measure light intensity.

© *John Wiley & Sons, Inc.*

A more exact way to measure light is to purchase a handheld light meter (see Figure 2-3). You can choose from several modestly priced models, including free apps for your phone. I prefer the handheld models because they're so easy to use.

The most common measurement of light intensity is the *footcandle*, which is equivalent to the light emitted by one candle one foot away. This is an old English measure that's still used today, and it's what most light meters read.

Professional and very serious light gardeners use other, more exact light measurements, but, frankly, most home growers don't need to use them.

After you determine the light levels in your environment, use the following sections to identify some houseplant candidates that are appropriate for different light intensities. Remember to keep temperature in mind (see the preceding section).

Bright light

The following houseplants require a bright greenhouse, a very bright south-facing window, or four or more high-intensity fluorescent lamps, large banks of LEDs, or metal halide lamps (see Chapter 5):

» Most cacti and succulents

Orchids that prefer bright growing conditions like cattleyas and oncidiums

Most flowering houseplants

» Most herbs

» Most carnivorous plants

» Most flowering annuals

» Most citrus and other tropical fruits

» Spring flowering bulbs

» Most tropical bulbs (like amaryllis)

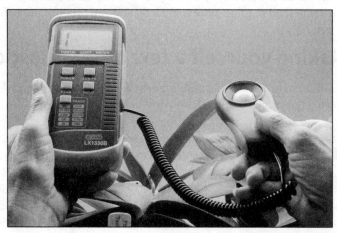

FIGURE 2-3:
An example of a handheld light meter.

© John Wiley & Sons, Inc.

Medium light

The following houseplants need a shaded greenhouse, a large east-facing window during the spring, summer, and early fall, or a four-tube fluorescent light fixture or LEDs of the same light output:

>> Relatives of African violets (like streptocarpus)

>> Tuberous and leaf-type begonias

>> Moth orchids and slipper orchids

TIP

In the winter, when days are shorter and there's lower light, the greenhouse needs to have some shade material removed, and plants can be moved to a brighter south window, or you can continue growing them under lights.

Low light

The following houseplants do well with a low level of light, easily attainable with two to four fluorescent lights or LEDs with equivalent light intensity or an east-facing window:

>> Most ferns

>> Most foliage plants, both large and small

>> African violets

TIP

Many houseplants can be grown at considerably higher light levels than are recommended if they're gradually adapted to this higher light intensity and are in a well-ventilated area. Why would you even try this? Plants grown in higher light intensity tend to grow more compactly and can produce more flowers.

Asking yourself a few other questions

In addition to considering temperature and light, you want to ask yourself the following questions:

>> **How much space do you have to grow houseplants?** If you have plenty of headroom, you can grow some of the taller houseplants, like dracaenas, palms, or scheffleras. If space is at a premium, search out very compact or miniature growers, like many of the cacti and succulents, small potted foliage plants, and compact flowering plants like African violets. Part 3 gives you plenty of choices for plants of all sizes.

>> **When do you want your houseplants to bloom?** Spring, summer, fall, or winter? In the evening or during the day? Armed with this information, you can pick those houseplants that will be in bloom in the season and time of day of your choice.

>> **Do you have air circulation in your growing area?** Most homes have adequate air fresh air, but if your houseplants are going to be in the basement or some other spot where the air is stagnant, consider adding a fan of some type to provide them with circulating air. See the ventilation section in Chapter 5 for more information.

When you're considered all aspects of your growing environment, you'll be better prepared to choose a houseplant that will thrive.

Knowing What to Look for in a Houseplant

After you consider your environment, you're ready to go shopping. You have an idea of which types of houseplants will work best where you'll be growing them, and now you just need to look at a few things like the plant's health and age. I fill you in on these factors in the following sections.

Choosing a healthy plant

Picking out a healthy houseplant is essential. Even in the best of circumstances, the houseplant you bring home will have to adapt to changes in its environment. A strong, robust plant has a much better chance of surviving this ordeal than a weak plant does.

TIP

Here's a checklist of things to look for when you select a houseplant:

>> **Look carefully at the leaves.** They should be stiff, not shriveled or dehydrated. They should also have a healthy green color. Brown or black spots on leaves can mean disease, or they may be harmless; if you find spots, ask the grower about them.

>> **Look for any signs of insects.** Most insects hang out on new growth, on flower buds, or on the undersides of the leaves. Also check under the pot for snails or slugs.

>> **Examine the exposed roots on top of the potting material.** The roots should be firm and light colored, not black, soft, and mushy.

PLANT IDENTIFICATION APPS

With the vast number of plants available, sooner or later you'll need some help identifying what you are looking at. I have been quite impressed with some of the plant ID apps, and most are free! The free one I am most familiar with and recommend is iNaturalist (www.inaturalist.org/), which identifies both indoor and outdoor plants. You simply take an image of the plant, and the software compares your image with what it has in its gigantic database to return a likely match. Sometimes, the app isn't right on the money, but it usually gets close. More than 7 million folks are using the app, so that gives you some idea of its popularity!

>> **Watch out for plants infested with oxalis (which looks like clover).** *Oxalis* is an annoying weed that spreads quickly and is difficult to get rid of after it's established. The only way to totally get rid of it is to remove all of its roots when you repot. It won't directly harm your houseplants, but it can harbor insects and is a cosmetic distraction.

REMEMBER

Make sure the plants are labeled. Labels will be important later if you want to look up information on growing your particular type of houseplant.

Unfortunately, houseplants purchased at home centers or grocery stores often aren't labeled. You can ask the sales associate if they at least know the common name of the houseplant you've chosen. Otherwise, you can look through this book until you find the houseplant that looks something like the one you bought.

Deciding between a mature blooming plant and a young plant

When you buy a mature blooming plant, you get to see exactly what the flower of this houseplant is like. Because many houseplant flowers can last quite a while, you'll be able to enjoy the blooms on your new houseplant for weeks after you bring it home. The biggest disadvantage of buying blooming plants is that they're usually the most expensive, because they're in the highest demand.

Younger plants — ones that are months or even years away from blooming — are much less expensive than their mature counterparts. The joy in choosing these plants is anticipating when they'll bloom and what they may look like.

Even less expensive, but a bit more challenging, is acquiring cuttings or leaves that you can propagate yourself. See Chapter 8 for more information. Of course, you'll have to wait even longer to enjoy the flowers on these plants.

ARE SOME HOUSEPLANTS TOXIC?

First, most houseplants are not intended to be eaten! That said, it only makes good sense that you should protect dogs, cats, other pets, and children from ingesting any part of them. Some houseplants do have leaf hairs that can cause allergic reactions. Fortunately, the list of houseplants that contain toxins is short. Sometimes the more toxic issue can be the pesticides that were applied to the plants as they were growing. Check with your supplier if you have concerns about any pesticides they may have used on your houseplants.

Here are a few houseplants that have been cited as having some poisonous properties:

- Caladium
- Colocasia
- Dieffenbachia (dumb cane)
- Easter lilies
- English ivy
- Lantana
- Oleander
- Philodendron
- Pothos
- Sago palm
- Snake plant
- *Solanum pseudocapsicum* (Jerusalem cherry)
- Spathiphyllum

If you have any concerns about the toxicity of a particular houseplant, check it out on Poison Control's website (www.poison.org/articles/plant).

SPLURGING ON DESIGNER HOUSEPLANTS

As I've mentioned, houseplants have become incredibly popular. I guess as part of this phenomenon, the demand for extremely rare, and therefore very expensive, houseplants is the rage. The sky is the limit if you want to be first on the block to own these treasured few-of-a-kind plants.

Here's a sampling of recent eBay and Etsy listings:

- *Philodendron spiritus sancti*: $50,000
- *Philodendron billietiadiae variegata*: $10,000
- *Monstera deliciosa* 'Mint': starting bid $6,999
- *Anthurium crystallinum* variegatum: $6,560
- *Anthurium* 'Circus: Peanuts': $3,650
- *Hoya carnosa* 'Silver Dollar': $1,600

Understanding how houseplants are produced

Very few houseplants sold today have been collected from the wild because it's illegal to do that almost everywhere, and the plants collected in this manner take quite a long time to recover. Instead, some are now being grown from seed or spores (for ferns). The flower color, flower size, and growth habits of seed-grown plants vary quite a bit from their parents. This can be an advantage if you're hoping for a new form of the plant to appear but can be a disadvantage if you want the new plant to look exactly like its parent.

Most houseplants today are produced by cuttings of some sort — from leaves, stems, or roots. Because the result of this method of propagation is offspring identical to the parent, the new plant is essentially a clone of its parent.

Orchids are most frequently produced by *meristemming* or *mericloning*. In this method of propagation, a new plant is multiplied from single cells, usually from a plant of exceedingly high quality, in a *flask*, which is a type of laboratory bottle. The result is that all the offspring are identical.

For more information on plant propagation or multiplying your houseplants, see Chapter 8.

HOUSEPLANTS THAT LIKE TO SHARE EACH OTHER'S COMPANY!

Some houseplants just like to hang out together. They are plants that have the same basic growing requirements — humidity levels, soil moisture, temperature requirements, and light levels. For instance, most of the foliage plants are happy together as are many of the flowering plants. Plants in the same family or groups like African violets and their cousins are a good match, and many of the carnivorous plants share the same habitat. Cacti and succulents are a natural duo.

Selecting houseplants with a sweet scent

Some houseplants offer the bonus of a pleasing scent. They can pleasantly surprise you with the appealing perfume of fruits, candies, and foods (like chocolate and vanilla). Alternatively, they can gross you out with the putrid smell of carrion (to attract fly pollinators). In Part 3, I introduce you to a selection of houseplants, and I indicate which plants are delightfully fragrant and ones that have a not-so-pleasant smell.

Introducing Your New Houseplant to Your Home

Adding new houseplants to your plant collection is exciting, but this is also a time for caution. Even though you may have been careful in the selection process, your houseplant may be harboring insect eggs that are about to hatch, or it may have a disease problem that you didn't notice.

TIP

So, to be on the safe side, keep your new plant isolated from all your other plants for at least two to three weeks — enough time to see if any insects appear or a disease shows up. If you need to treat your new plant, doing so will be easier when it's quarantined from your other plants.

To identify pests and diseases and the safest treatment for them, see Chapter 9.

Chapter 3

Having the Right Tools on Hand

E very hobby has its tools. Just as you need the right saws and sanders if you're building a cabinet or you need the right knife, grater, or pan when cooking a special recipe, you need the right tools for growing plants. The number of tools you need depends on how serious you are about houseplants and how many of them you're caring for. In this chapter, I fill you in on the tools I find most useful.

Focusing on Pruning and Cutting Tools

You'll probably use your cutting and pruning tools more than any others. Plants always have a leaf that needs to be trimmed or a dead or diseased stem that needs to be cut off. These tools are also used for repotting (see Chapter 7). Figure 3-1 shows the kinds of tools covered throughout this section.

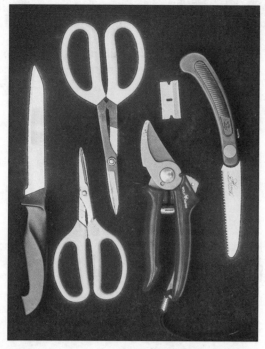

FIGURE 3-1:
Cutting tools —
from left to right:
thin-bladed knife,
two pairs of
scissors, bypass
hand pruners,
single-edge razor
blade, and folding
pruning saw.

Pruners

You need different types of pruning tools, depending on the thickness of the plant part you're removing. The following are pruners you'll commonly use:

>> **Hand pruners:** Use hand pruners to cut thick creeping stems. There are two types of hand pruners:

- **Anvil type:** This pruner has a flat cutting blade and can mash the stem tissue (which isn't what you want).

- **Bypass type:** This pruner has a curved blade (refer to Figure 3-1). It makes cleaner and closer cuts. (This is my preferred type of pruner.)

>> **Scissors:** All scissors aren't created equal. I prefer those that are designed for bonsai or flower arranging (like the scissors shown in Figure 3-1). They're extremely sharp and have large, comfortable vinyl hand grips. Some are made of high-carbon steel and hold a sharp edge for a long time. Others are constructed of stainless steel and offer the advantage of not rusting. Smaller scissors are handy for finesse work, like trimming delicate leaves and removing spent flower spikes as closely as possible to the foliage. Heavier scissors are ideal for cutting thick stems.

Knives and blades

Knives and blades can come in very handy, but choosing the right type is important. Here, I guide you through the types available.

Knives

Knives are used most often to circle the inside of a pot to remove a plant when its roots are packed into its container, especially with clay pots. (You can usually cut plastic pots with sharp scissors along the length of the pot to remove the plant.) A very-thin-bladed knife, like the type used for filleting fish (refer to Figure 3-1), is handy because it's easier to maneuver in tight spaces. You can also use scalpels (such as those used for dissection) or craft knives.

Razor blades

Razor blades are perfect for making extremely precise cuts when trimming the edges of leaves or separating divisions of plants. One advantage of razor blades is they're so inexpensive that you can throw them away after you're done.

TIP

Disposing of used razor blades prevents you from spreading disease to other plants and saves you the hassle of sterilizing them.

As a safety precaution, always use the single-edge type of razor blade (as shown in Figure 3-1).

WARNING

Hand pruning saws

Using a hand pruning saw is bringing out the big gun. This tool is most useful for cutting extremely thick creeping stems when dividing plants. You can also use one to thin out very tightly packed roots or to cut away a thick plastic pot when you're transplanting or repotting a houseplant. You can find several types of these saws, but the compact folding ones are the most handy.

TIP

I find the small-bladed, fine-toothed type of saw (refer to Figure 3-1) often used for cutting bamboo to be especially useful for cutting thick roots or dividing root-bound plants.

Considering Potting Tools and Supplies

The tools and supplies in this section make the potting process easier. For specific potting techniques and guidelines, check out Chapter 7.

Potting tools and supplies

Potting requires a combination of force and finesse. The tools and supplies in this section make the process easier and more effective.

Hammers and mallets

For most purposes, a rubber mallet (see Figure 3-2) is what you need. You can use it to pound in stakes or clamps that hold newly transplanted or divided houseplants in their pots.

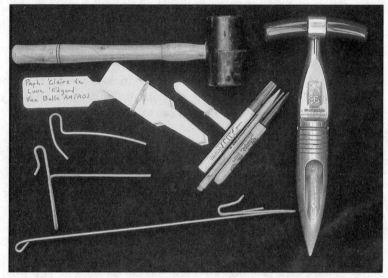

FIGURE 3-2: Potting tools — clockwise from top-left: rubber mallet, dibble, potting clamps, labels, marking pens.

Regular steel claw hammers can be useful for breaking clay pots that otherwise can't be removed from overgrown plants.

Dibbles and planting sticks

Getting the potting material to settle around the roots of a plant is important because large air spaces can cause the plant's roots to dry out or not form properly. *Dibbles* (refer to Figure 3-2) and planting sticks are used to push the potting material into these air spaces.

Torches for sterilizing tools

Dirty cutting and potting tools can spread diseases. Preventing the spread of disease by sterilizing any tools that come in direct contact with houseplant root and leaf tissue is always a good idea. You can use chemical solutions to do this (for instance, a 1:10 ratio of household bleach to water), but chemicals are very corrosive, and some are toxic. A straightforward way to sterilize metal tools is to flame them with a propane or butane torch (see Figure 3-3). Both are available in small handheld sizes.

Steven A. Frowine (Book author)

FIGURE 3-3: This compact, lightweight, self-striking butane torch is a breeze to use.

Labels

The plant tag that comes with a houseplant contains especially important information that you want to protect. Knowing the correct name of the plant is crucial when you're looking up growing information. Many times the tag includes the plant's parents' names, which can also provide helpful growing clues. If you want to enter your houseplant in a show, it may be disqualified without proper labeling.

TIP

Maintaining a list of your houseplants is also a good idea. You can assign numbers to each of your plants, and placing the numbers on the labels can make it easier to cross-reference your list when you need to look up details. The list serves as a safety net in case the label is damaged or lost. Some folks also put the plant number or name of the plant on the rim of the pot or even use a paint marker to write the identifier on the bottom of one of the leaves.

Labels are available in many sizes and colors. Which size or color you use is a personal choice — the material they're made of is a more important consideration. Table 3-1 lists some pros and cons of each kind of label.

TABLE 3-1   **Pros and Cons of Various Label Types**

Type	Pros	Cons	Comments
Metal (copper)	Lasts many years	More expensive Not as readily available	Good for long-term use Is usually thin enough to mark by indenting with a pencil
Metal (zinc)	Lasts many years	More expensive Not as readily available	Good for long-term use Can be marked on with a #2 lead pencil or engraved
Plastic	Inexpensive Available in largest range of sizes and colors	Becomes brittle (especially if exposed to sunlight) and then breaks very easily	Recommended for short-term use only (less than a few years) Will accept a broad range of markers
Vinyl	Doesn't get as brittle as plastic	More expensive than plastic Not as readily available	The best overall choice Will accept a broad range of markers
Wood	Inexpensive Readily available	Rots quickly	Because it lasts such a brief time in damp potting material, it isn't recommended

Label markers

Using the right marker can mean the difference between being able to read the name of a houseplant three years after you bought it and trying to remember what it is. Table 3-2 lists some advantages and disadvantages of each type of marker.

Clamps and stakes

Numerous types of stakes and clamps are available for holding a plant in its pot when it has been transplanted and its roots are not yet adequate for anchoring it. Refer to Figure 3-2 for some examples of metal stakes. Bamboo stakes are also available.

TABLE 3-2 **Pros and Cons of Various Label Markers**

Type	Pros	Cons	Comments
Engraver	Lasts forever Most effective on metal labels, especially zinc	Time-consuming to use Difficult to write small letters More expensive Hard to read after a few years	Handy for long-term labels that are exposed to the elements and chemical sprays
Paint pen*	Comes in a variety of colors and thicknesses Won't fade as badly as permanent markers	Takes longer to dry than permanent markers Must be cautious when using them to avoid smearing the paint before it dries	Available at craft and art-supply stores
Pencil	An old-fashioned but still very effective marker on plastic and vinyl	Not as easy to read as some other markers Can smear	Use #2 lead for best legibility
Permanent marker	Easy to find and use Available in many colors and thicknesses Makes dark, visible letters	Will bleach out in sun Can be affected by pesticides	Good to use, but after two or three years may have to be traced over to remain legible Some brands are more resistant to sunlight than others

My favorite

Identifying Watering Accessories

Mastering the art of watering is one of the keys to success in houseplant culture (see Chapter 6). Here, I introduce you to tools that can help you do this job efficiently. The accessories covered in this section deliver water, and in some cases fertilizer, gently and effectively.

WARNING

Don't water your plants with softened water! Water softeners prevent scaly white mineral buildup in home water pipes by replacing the water-hardening chemical, usually calcium, with sodium salts. Sodium in this salt can be toxic to plants.

Water breakers

Water breakers are attached to the end of a hose to diffuse the water and prevent it from washing out the houseplant potting material (see Figure 3-4). They deliver a large volume of water in a gentle way — and they work well.

FIGURE 3-4:
A common type
of water breaker.

© *John Wiley & Sons, Inc.*

You can find water breakers that deliver different volumes and water patterns, such as mist, fine shower, jet, or flood. Some watering heads can be dialed to whichever of these forms you want.

TIP

You're usually better off choosing the water breaker that delivers the finest stream of water possible. This will be most useful for the broadest range of watering applications.

Water-flow regulators

You attach a *water-flow regulator* between the hose and the water breaker and use it to regulate the water volume. The simplest ones are manual on/off valves. *Thumb* or *squeeze valves* are easier to use with precision than the on-off shutoff valves to determine the volume of water you want to deliver to your houseplants (see Figure 3-5).

Hoses

Buy the best-quality hose you can find. The better ones will not kink and will last much longer than the inexpensive ones. Better quality hoses are a larger diameter (1/2 inch [1.27 cm] or greater), have thicker hose walls — often with a reinforcing material that resists kinking — and are made of higher quality vinyl or rubber. If you use your hose only to water a modest collection of indoor plants, some of the less expensive, lighter weight hoses will probably suffice.

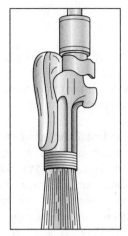

TIP

There are adaptors available at most hardware stores for attaching your sink faucet to the fitting found on most garden hoses.

Watering cans

Many of the sprinkling or watering cans on the market are close to worthless for using on houseplants. They deliver too much water too fast and are awkward to use in tight indoor spaces.

TIP

However, if you want to use one, the best type for most situations is one that holds ½ to 1 gallon (2 to 4 liters), has a long spout (so you can reach plants in the back row), and has a removable water breaker (sometimes called a *rose*) on the end of its spout that delivers a very fine stream of water (see Figure 3-6). The watering can may be made of metal or plastic, but the water breaker should be made of metal, preferably a nonrusting one like copper.

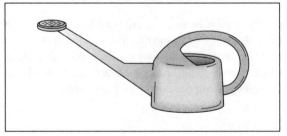

Sprayers and misters

You can use sprayers and misters for misting your plants to increase the humidity temporarily, clean the leaves, or apply pesticides. If you're going to use any chemicals in the sprayer, a plastic sprayer is a better choice than a metal sprayer because plastic is less prone to being affected by corrosive substances.

TIP

One type of hand sprayer that I've found particularly effective for applying insecticides is a *teat sprayer*. Its spray head points up instead of straight forward as on a standard sprayer. Because teat sprayers are typically used to wash off cow udders (hence the name), they're sold at farm-supply stores. Plants don't have udders, of course, so for houseplant growers, a teat sprayer serves admirably for applying insecticides to the undersides of leaves, where the bugs usually hang out.

Fertilizer injectors and siphon mixers

Commercial growers use a device called a *fertilizer injector* that injects a small amount of water-soluble fertilizer into the water each time the plant is watered. In this way, plants are constantly fed a very diluted amount of fertilizer instead of a larger amount every two weeks or so, as is frequently done. These units tend to be on the expensive side and may be a luxury item, unless you have quite a large number of houseplants to fertilize.

A much cheaper way to fertilize your plants is to use a simple *siphon mixer*. Several brands are on the market, but they all work the same. You attach the siphon mixer to a faucet and then attach a hose to the siphon mixer. A flexible hollow rubber tube is inserted into a concentrated solution of fertilizer. (See Figure 3-7.) When the faucet is turned on, the suction action created by the water flowing through the hose draws the concentrate through the tubing, so it flows into the water in the hose to be diluted as it's being applied to the plants.

Deionization and reverse osmosis units

Deionization and *reverse osmosis units* are used to purify your well or tap water to reduce or eliminate concentrations of salts, metals, and minerals called *total dissolved solids* (TDS), which can be harmful to some particularly sensitive houseplants. The units aren't cheap, can be cumbersome, and bothersome to use. So, before you consider getting one, make sure you need it.

FIGURE 3-7:
Simple siphon mixers are easy to use and handy if you have quite a few house-plants to fertilize.

MAKING FERTILIZATION A SNAP WITH A SIPHON MIXER

Here are a few tips on how to get the most benefit from a siphon mixer:

- **Use a completely soluble fertilizer so it doesn't plug up the unit.** Because some granular and thick liquid fertilizers don't dissolve completely, they can jam up the injector.

- **Use a water breaker that functions with a low volume of water.** The water flow coming out the end of the hose will be significantly reduced when the siphon mixer is attached.

- **Be sure the unit you have also has a backflow preventer.** That way, when you turn off the water breaker, but not the faucet, the back pressure won't cause the concentrated diluted solution in the hose to flush back into your water supply or into your fertilizer concentrate.

- **To be on the safe side, use the siphon mixer only for applying fertilizers, not pesticides.** These mixers aren't precise enough for pesticide applications, and you'll end up wasting the chemicals and possibly doing damage to your plants from an improper dosage of the pesticide.

- **Be careful to dilute the fertilizer to the correct concentration.** Siphon mixers usually inject the fertilizer on a 1:16 fertilizer-to-water ratio, but always read the directions that come with the unit.

TIP

Here are some things to consider before you buy:

>> **If your houseplants have been growing well, then don't worry about using a deionization or reverse osmosis unit.** Most households can get by with the water they have.

>> **If you've had water problems or just want to be on the safe side, check with your public water provider to see what the average TDS in your water are.** If you have your own well, you'll need to have a test done at a private water lab.

- If you have 60 parts per million (ppm) or less of TDS and less than 5 ppm of sodium, you're home free. Your water is of decent quality for plants.

- If your water tests at 60 to 120 ppm for TDS and you have up to 10 ppm of sodium, all except the most sensitive houseplants should be okay, but you're on the edge of poor water quality.

- If you have readings higher than 120 ppm for TDS or 10 ppm of sodium, you may have more plant-growing success if you use better-quality water. To do this, you can collect rainwater (you can buy special rain barrels that hook up to your downspout) or consider buying a reverse osmosis or deionization unit.

If you have high TDS but a small collection of plants, purchasing and using distilled water alone or using it to dilute your tap water may be your simplest solution.

If you're on the higher end of the TDS level, be particularly careful not to overfertilize.

For detailed information on selecting and using fertilizers, check out Chapter 6.

Modifying Your Environment with Humidifiers, Ventilation Equipment, and Heaters

Your home environment is designed to make you, not necessarily your plants, comfortable. Fortunately, many of your living requirements are the same as the living requirements for most of the houseplants in this book. In some cases, though, you'll need to modify your plants' growing space to better suit them. Here's a look at some equipment that will make your growing space better for your houseplants.

Humidifiers

I detail the importance of providing sufficient humidity for better health for both you and your plants in Chapter 5. To humidify an entire room, there are at least three approaches, which the following sections cover.

Evaporative-pad humidifiers

With these units, fans blow across a moisture-laden pad that sits in a reservoir of water. Evaporative-pad humidifiers are my first choice for home humidification because

>> They're reasonably priced and readily available.

>> They don't spray the room with droplets of water that can carry mineral deposits and bacteria.

>> They circulate air at the same time.

>> They increase the humidity only to about 50 to 60 percent (most have an adjustable *humidistat,* which measures humidity). This level is beneficial to plants, but not sufficient to cause moisture damage to your house.

>> They require no plumbing and little maintenance — just change the moisture pads one or two times a season.

Cool mist or ultrasonic humidifiers

Cool-mist or ultrasonic humidifiers create a high frequency vibration in the water that atomizes it into a very fine mist or droplets that can be effective for increasing the humidity in small areas, but with constant use, they can cause deposits of minerals from the water (especially if your water ins hard) on leaves and spread bacteria.

Greenhouse-type foggers or humidifiers

If you have a greenhouse or a large growing area that needs a lot of humidity, a greenhouse-type fogger or humidifier is for you. However, these units can be pricey. They're plumbed into a constant water supply that's controlled by a float (much like a toilet bowl). The humidity level can be regulated by a separately purchased humidistat.

THE MYTH ABOUT HAND MISTING

You may have heard the suggestion that you should mist your houseplants with a hand-mister to increase humidity. Don't waste your time. The fine water droplets from the mister will evaporate so quickly that they increase the humidity only for a short time. Another disadvantage to this method of humidification is that if your water has a high mineral content, hand-misting will eventually lead to white deposits on your leaves left behind from the evaporating water. Also, if you hand-mist regularly, especially in the evening when the moisture is slower to evaporate, the moisture on the leaves can lead to disease problems. See Chapter 5 for some practical solutions to increasing the humidity for your plants.

Ventilation equipment

Adequate air circulation is especially important in houseplant culture. Stagnant air can be a cause of various diseases. Fortunately, many convenient and inexpensive pieces of equipment do this job admirably. Here are some of the best choices:

>> **Ceiling fans:** These are readily available and do a super job of moving large volumes of air in a figure-eight pattern at a low velocity. Most of them have reversible motors, so they can either be set to pull the cooler air from the floor (usually the summer setting) or push hot air down from the ceiling (usually the winter setting).

>> **Oscillating and standard fans:** You can find these in all blade sizes, and most have variable speeds. All will do the job, but you're better off getting one with a large blade and running it at low speed. This will move more air but at a slower velocity, so the plants won't become dehydrated by a strong air current. For oscillating fans (the ones that swing back and forth), splurge on a better-grade model that has metal or heavy-duty gears; otherwise, they'll strip in short order, and you'll then have a stationary fan.

>> **Muffin fans:** These small, handy fans (3 to 6 inches/8 to 15 centimeters) are used to cool electronic equipment like computers. They're great for bringing a gentle, quiet breeze to a small corner of your growing area. You can find them at electronic or computer-supply stores or catalogs.

For more information on the importance of ventilation and air movement, see Chapter 5.

TIP

When plants are grown in close proximity to one another, they benefit from the humidity from the water vapor that each of them naturally emits, but there is a point when it becomes too close for comfort. Plants crammed too close together can prevent this airflow, which can lead to disease and block light to neighboring plants.

Heaters

If you're like most people, you rely on your home heating system to provide most of the heat for your plants. You can supplement that with small electric heaters or water-resistant heating mats commonly used to start seeds. If you're growing under lights, you can enclose your growing area in plastic film to help retain heat produced by the lights and ballasts (the resistors found in all florescent fixtures that controls the amount of electric current supplied to the lamps or tubes).

WARNING

Do not place your plants on top of radiators or electric heaters because the excessive heat from these fixtures can fry your plants (not to mention it's an electrical hazard). If you want to use heating mats, make sure they're moisture proof and intended to be used for growing plants.

Thermometers and hygrometers

I have to admit, and my wife will quickly concur, that I'm a nut about monitoring temperature and humidity. I have remote sensors all over my home that tell me maximum and minimum temperature and humidity levels each day. As I explain in Chapter 5, temperature differentials are important to know if you're interested in getting your plants to bloom and most houseplants thrive in higher humidity.

Thanks to modern digital thermometers and hygrometers that are simple to use and inexpensive, you can keep track of the temperature and humidity in your home with little effort:

» **Thermometers:** Different plants have different temperature requirements, so thermometers are essential and fundamental indoor gardening tools. You can buy a digital or analog model, and most are simple to use and inexpensive. Some measure air temperature in real time, and others record high and low temperatures over a given length of time.

» **Hygrometers:** You use a hygrometer to measure the relative air humidity. The most accurate ones can be expensive, but the less costly "consumer" units, which are frequently found in combination temperature/humidity instruments, are close enough in accuracy for most home-growing situations.

Chapter **4**

Houseplant Appreciation and Display

The main purpose for growing houseplants is to enjoy their unmatched beauty in your home. In this chapter, I walk you through tips that will make your experiences with houseplants more successful and pleasurable.

Caring for Houseplants in Their New Home

Bringing a houseplant into its new home can be traumatic for both the plant and you! You must get to know each other. Most houseplants you buy come from the very high-light, high-humidity environment of a commercial greenhouse. Your home environment is usually less bright and has lower humidity than a greenhouse, so the plant must make some adjustments. Helping your new plant make the transition with the least amount of distress is your goal, and in this section, I explain how to get there.

If the plant is in bloom

Flowers are welcomed features on plants, but they tend to be more delicate than the leaves, and they require a bit of extra care to maximize their longevity. Here are some things you can do to make the flowers on your new houseplant last longer:

>> **Place the plant somewhere in your home that's bright but doesn't get direct sunlight, except possibly in the morning.** Too much harsh sunlight can bleach out the flowers and scorch the leaves.

>> **Keep the plant on the cool side — not above about 75°F (about 24°C).** Flowers stay fresher longer this way.

>> **Be sure to keep the plant well-watered.** Even though houseplants stop growing much when they're in bloom, their leaves and flowers still need water.

>> **Don't let any bees or flies get into the room where your houseplant is blooming.** If bees or flies pollinate your plant, the flowers will collapse afterward.

>> **Don't put the plant close to ripe fruit.** Ripening fruit gives off ethylene gas, which can cause flowers to collapse prematurely.

>> **Keep your houseplant away from strong fumes from paint thinners, household cleaning products, and other pollutants.** These can cause the blossoms to fade.

>> **Don't spray the flowers with water or place the blooming plant in a room that is highly humid and has no air movement.** This can cause spotting on the flowers from fungal diseases. Refer to Chapter 9 for more information.

If the plant is not in bloom

Before you add your new foliage plant or not-yet-blooming flowering plant to your collection, follow these tips:

>> **Look under the leaves and at the young growth to make sure there are no bugs.** Bugs like to feed on succulent new plant tissue and hide in out-of-the-way places.

>> **To be on the safe side, isolate the new plant from your collection for at least three weeks.** This will allow time for hidden insect eggs to hatch.

>> **As a further precaution, spray the plant thoroughly with insecticidal soap.** Use a paper towel to wipe off the excess spray. Doing so not only kills any soft-bodied insects but also cleans the leaves. Insecticidal soap is readily available at most garden centers and home stores.

>> **Consider repotting the houseplant into your own potting mix.** That way you're assured that the potting mix is fresh, and you know its watering requirements.

Staking and Grooming Your Blooming Houseplants

Houseplants that flower deserve to look their best when they're putting on their show. Proper staking and grooming can make a significant difference in the way houseplant flowers appear. In this section, I offer some pointers on how to do it right.

Figuring out how to stake

Houseplant flowers and spikes (flower stems) can be heavy, and if they aren't staked properly, they'll open at an awkward and disconcerting angle. This can be a distraction, because the most interesting and alluring perspective to view houseplants is usually head-on.

Staking techniques vary with the type of houseplant. The two major types are the spray houseplants (which have several flowers on each spike) and those with single flowers or just a few on one spike. It's best to stake your houseplants *before* they flower. Doing so ensures that the flowers are oriented correctly when they open. Stick to these simple steps:

1. **As soon as the flower spike is about 12 inches (30 cm) long, insert a vertical bamboo stake into the potting mixture close to where the spike originates at the base of the plant (see Figure 4-1).**

   If you prefer, you can use a green stake, so it blends in better with the flower stem than the bamboo stake will.

2. **As you insert the stake, twist it to work it around the plant's roots to minimize damage to them.**

3. **Attach ties every few inches (4 cm or so) as the flower spike grows.**

   You can use twist ties, Velcro strips, soft string, or yarn, but don't use sharp string or wire, which can damage the stem. The most popular method is to use plastic spring clips to attach the flower stem or spike to the plant stake (see Figure 4-2).

In the last few years, houseplant growers have discovered one of the best ways to attach upright flowering stems to bamboo or wood stakes: spring-operated baby hair clips! They're available in many colors, inexpensive, and frequently formed in whimsical shapes like butterflies or dragonflies, which fit nicely with the houseplant look. Plus, they work well! See Figure 4-2.

Be careful not to attach the ties too tightly because doing so can damage the flower spike.

4. **Place the last tie a few inches below (4 cm or so) where the first flower buds are forming.**

This last tie helps support the weight of the buds and flowers.

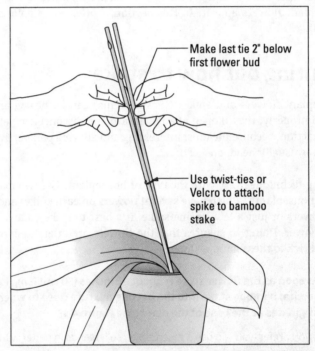

Make last tie 2" below first flower bud

Use twist-ties or Velcro to attach spike to bamboo stake

FIGURE 4-1: Staking this way helps support some of the flowers of plants with tall spikes.

© John Wiley & Sons, Inc.

Flower spikes always grow in the direction of the strongest light. After the flower spike reaches about 12 inches (30 cm) tall and the buds start to form, *never* change the plant's orientation to the light source. If you do, the spike will try to reorient itself and you'll end up with a twisted, distorted spike with flowers opening in all directions.

Photo by Steven A. Frowine

When the flowers are fully open, they'll stay that way, so you can then move the plant anywhere you want.

REMEMBER

Be sure to stake before the flower has opened so the bud will orient itself to gravity. If the flower spike is at an angle, the flower will adjust itself to open perpendicular to the angle the flower stem is pointing. If you stake the spike after the flower has opened, it will keep its original orientation and will look awkward.

Helping your houseplants look their best

After plants grow for months on the windowsill, under lights, or in a greenhouse, they can look a little rough around the edges. The leaves are usually dusty or blemished with chemical or mineral deposits or sunburn, older leaves may be wilted or dead, and some of the tips of the leaves may be brown.

TIP

When your plants are in flower and you want to show them off to their best in your home or get them ready to exhibit in a houseplant show, here are a few suggestions to keep in mind:

>> **Clean their leaves.** A simple way to polish the leaves is with milk. Dampen a paper towel with milk (whole milk works best) and rub off the blemishes. Other possibilities are Neem oil, horticultural oils, coconut oil, or commercial leaf shining products. This gives the leaves an attractive sheen that's harmless to the plant.

>> **Carefully remove any dead or severely damaged leaves.** Besides being unsightly, damaged or dead leaves can be entry places for disease. See Chapter 3 for a description and an image of various useful cutting tools.

>> **Trim off the brown tips of leaves with very sharp scissors.** The sharper they are, the cleaner the cut and the less leaf-tissue damage will result. When trimming, follow the natural shape of the leaf, as shown in Figure 4-3.

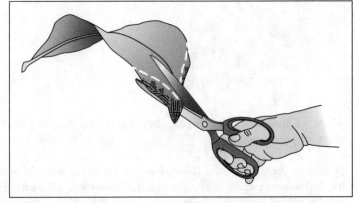

FIGURE 4-3:
Trim off brown
tips of leaves
following the
natural curvature
of the leaf.

© John Wiley & Sons, Inc.

Displaying Houseplants in Your Home

Designing with houseplants has much to do with personal style and taste. Consider your houseplants not just as indoor décor but as interior design elements. What are the tones, moods, colors, and styles of your home's rooms? For example, do you prefer a modern or a rustic look?

Some houseplants have strong vertical elements that seem to play well with formal settings, whereas others have a loose, informal growth habit. When you're deciding where best to display your plants, keep in mind color, texture, scale, contrast, and shape.

When several houseplants are arranged together, some folks enjoy replicating the shapes and sizes of their plants, and others like variety. Contrasts in foliage or flower textures and colors can create visual interest. Your choice of containers also reinforces your look. I like containers that look natural or neutral so the plants are the main focal point, but you may like to emphasize your unique containers.

From a practical standpoint, you need to group plants that have similar growing requirements, such as light and humidity. For instance, foliage plants generally require less light than flowering plants. That doesn't mean you can never display the two together when one of your favorite plants is in bloom. However, after the flowering plant is done blooming, you may need to move it to a brighter spot to give it the added light it needs to flower again. Another example is that most succulents and cacti, which prefer very bright spots with little humidity, wouldn't be happy in the same display as plants that prefer lower light or higher humidity.

Various parts of your home may be better suited to different plants. For instance, tall foliage plants seem to fit best in a spacious main living area, while small flowering plants like cacti and succulents work great in a south-facing windowsill. Other small flowering plants like African violets and some of their relatives would be happy in an east-facing window, while humidity-loving plants that do well in lower light, like ferns, may thrive in your bathroom.

TIP

Many people neglect adequate display lighting. You want to show off your plants when they're at their best, so you may need some lighting that isn't adequate for growing plants but is primarily used to highlight them, especially in the evening when you get home from work or when you're entertaining. Track lighting can be highly effective for this purpose.

Knowing some tips to best display your houseplants

TIP

When you're showing off your prized plants in your home, here are a few tips to keep in mind:

>> **Be sure to protect your furniture by placing houseplant pots on waterproof pads, like cork platters, tiles, or plastic lids from various food containers.** This prevents water damage to your wood furniture.

>> **If you place your plants on saucers, be sure they're waterproof.** Terra cotta planters are porous, and moisture will seep through the bottom of the pots and can cause considerable damage to unprotected wood furniture.

>> **Place felt or rubber pads, frequently sold in packs, under cachepots (decorative pots that usually do not have holes in the bottom), planters, or saucers so your furniture and windowsills won't be scratched.** Some pots and saucers can have rough surfaces.

>> **Display blooming plants where they get bright light but not hot late-afternoon light, so the flowers last longer.** High temperatures cause the flowers to prematurely collapse.

>> **If the growing pot is encrusted or ugly, insert it into a larger ornamental pot or basket.** Choose simple green, white, or neutral colors that don't compete with the houseplant's flowers.

>> **Place a layer of sheet moss or Spanish moss on the soil surface in the pot.** This is a nice touch for covering up the sometimes-unattractive potting material.

>> **Set houseplants on a pedestal or other elevated surface so you can view them at eye level (see Figure 4-4).** Few houseplants are attractive when they're viewed from above.

>> **Think about how you can light your houseplants to display them best.** Many people are able to view their houseplants only in the evening during the workweek, so artificial lighting plays an important part in showing them off. Track lights work great.

TIP

Use halogen or other bulbs that produce white light or light as close to sunlight as possible so the color of your houseplants will be rendered accurately. Regular incandescent light produces a yellow/red light that will make reds glow but really dulls blues and greens.

>> **Group flowering and foliage houseplants with colorful leaves with tropical foliage plants.** Vibrant foliage creates an attractive backdrop for houseplant flowers.

FIGURE 4-4:
Placing a houseplant on a pedestal and inserting its growing pot inside an ornamental container draws attention to its best attributes — flowers or handsome foliage.

Arranging Houseplant Flowers

You can make dramatic flower and foliage bouquets from your houseplants. If you judiciously remove some of the leaves and flowers from your plants for an arrangement, you won't be able to even notice that the plants have been touched.

Some houseplants — like anthuriums, orchids, calla lilies, amaryllis, and birds-of-paradise — have magnificent flowers that make stunning floral arrangements. Sprays or large leaves from houseplants with spectacular foliage, like some of the leafy begonias, philodendrons, foliage-type anthuriums, and crotons, can be arranged in a similar fashion. The key to using houseplants for flower arrangements is to keep it simple and not let their elegance get overwhelmed by too many other elements.

Understanding the three basic flower-design elements

When it comes to flower arranging, flowers and foliage come in three basic shapes: line, mass, and filler. All these shapes play a key part in the construction of an attractive flower arrangement.

>> *Line* flowers are tall and are used to give your arrangement height and width. Various branched houseplants with buds (for example, red gingers or some of the bromel flowers are used to create this effect. Also, the linear foliage of sansevieria (or snake plant) makes an arresting vertical element.

>> *Mass* flowers are round or full-faced and give your bouquet weight or mass. They're usually the focal point of color and interest in an arrangement. Examples are anthuriums, hibiscus, spathiphyllums, clivias, and gardenias.

>> *Filler* flowers and foliage have stems with many little flowers or leaves. Filler foliage is usually fine-textured. Examples are many of the spiderworts, ferns, asparagus ferns, and durantas.

TIP

Here are some tips on how to make simple, yet elegant, arrangements:

>> **Line flowers or foliage by themselves can make a striking arrangement in a tall, cylindrical vase.** Select a vase or container that is in proportion to the flowers. The vase should be about one-half to one-third the size of the total arrangement.

>> **You can arrange mass flowers by themselves in a low, wide vase or container (see Figure 4-5).** How you want to display the flowers informs your choice of container.

>> **A small arrangement of filler flowers by themselves can add a light, elegant touch to any room.** Many filler flowers are also well suited for drying.

>> **Some flowers can be floated in a bowl for a very simple and elegant effect.** Examples are hibiscus and tuberous begonia flowers. Flowers that are flat or convex on the back are usually the best ones for floating.

>> **Some flowers can work as more than one element.** For example, moth orchid sprays, especially the multifloral types, can be used as line flowers, while large single flowers can be used as mass flowers.

FIGURE 4-5:
Your arrangement doesn't need to be large. This miniature arrangement has only three small flowers for the mass element and three pointed leaves for the line element.

© John Wiley & Sons, Inc.

Supporting houseplant stems in arrangements

Having some way to support the stems of houseplants in an arrangement, so you can position them to face the direction you prefer, is usually a good idea. Here are several methods and materials you can use:

>> For a clear vase, add marbles or rocks.

>> Crossing the top opening of the vase in a tic-tac-toe pattern of florist's tape creates a grid that supports the plant stems.

>> *Frogs* (pincushions on which you impale the houseplant stems) work well in shallow containers.

>> For low containers, florist foam is popular with professional floral arrangers because it's easy to use and retains water well so the flowers last longer.

Making your houseplant arrangement last longer

To make your cut flowers last longer, follow these suggestions:

>> Wait until the flowers are in full bud or just starting to open before cutting them.

>> Before you put houseplant cuttings into a vase, recut their stems at an angle *under* water. Cutting the stems underwater prevents air bubbles from blocking the water entering the stem. To keep them fresh, recut them every couple of days.

>> Condition your houseplant cuttings before arranging them. Place their stems in fresh warm water and let them sit somewhere cool (around 50°F/10°C) overnight.

>> Make sure to remove all leaves that will be submerged under water in the vase. Submerged foliage will rot and pollute the water.

>> If you're using houseplant flowers with short stems in tall arrangements, insert the flower stems into *floral tubes* (water-holding tubes, available at your local florist) and then tape the tubes to a wood stake for more height. Floral tubes give more length and strength to the flower stems.

>> Add a commercial or homemade solution of floral preservative (see the nearby sidebar) to the warm water holding the flowers. Change the water and solution every three to four days.

>> Place the arrangement out of direct sunlight in a cool room. Doing so makes the flowers last longer.

>> Double the life of your houseplant flowers by placing the arrangement in the refrigerator at night or when you're away from home. Cooler temperatures prolong the life of the flowers.

A SUPER-SIMPLE HOMEMADE PRESERVATIVE FOR CUT FLOWERS

TIP

Here's an easy recipe for a solution that helps your cut houseplant flowers last longer: Combine one 12-ounce can of lemon-lime soda (like Sprite or 7UP), an equal amount of water, and 1 teaspoon of household bleach. The sugar in the soft drink serves as food for the flower, the citric acid lowers the water's pH (increases its acidity), and the bleach kills the bacteria in the water that can plug up the water-conducting network in the flower stem.

2

Keeping Your Houseplants Alive and Thriving

IN THIS CHAPTER

» **Evaluating your plants' lighting needs and picking the best lighting option**

» **Providing enough humidity**

» **Giving your houseplants a breath of fresh air**

» **Getting the temperature right**

» **Building a miniature garden for your house in a terrarium**

» **Summering houseplants outdoors**

Chapter **5**

Providing the Right Growing Environment

ouseplants aren't difficult to grow, but you can help them perform their best by ensuring their needs are met. Putting a little effort into modifying your growing environment to help your houseplants feel at home pays off in healthy plants that produce plenty of flowers. Ideally, you'll create a habitat for your houseplants that suits them best. For example, I designed a case to show off my plants when they're at the peak of their beauty (see Figure 5-1). My case is enclosed in glass and has a waterproof bottom tray to catch water draining from the pots, muffin fans on the side to create a gentle airflow, and T5HO fluorescent lights at the top to provide adequate light. (I discuss all these elements throughout this chapter.) It is the centerpiece of our sunroom and always gets a positive response from visiting plant lovers.

In this chapter, I detail houseplants' fundamental light and air requirements and the simplest, most effective ways to provide them, based on more than 50 years of experience growing houseplants.

FIGURE 5-1:
My houseplant
display case.

Photo by Steven A. Frowine

Knowing How Much Light Your Houseplants Need

Opinions vary on how much light houseplants need to grow and flower well. What you need to know is that greenhouse light intensity and color is different from fluorescent and LED light. (LED stands for *light-emitting diode.* See "LEDs: The new kids on the block" later in this chapter for more details on LED lighting.) Greenhouse light intensity and color varies dramatically depending on the time of day, cloud cover, time of year, latitude, and so on. Fluorescent lights and LEDs provide steady, constant illumination. For that reason, the light intensity from fluorescents or LEDs, commonly measured in *footcandles,* can be quite a bit lower than what's recommended for greenhouse growing.

TIP

You can purchase modestly priced accurate light meters to measure footcandles. If you decide to get one, make sure it has a reading scale specifically for fluorescent lights and LEDs.

Fluorescent lights for growing houseplants are usually burned for 12 to 16 hours per day, which is longer than the average natural day length. This longer period is required to accommodate for the lower light intensity of artificial lights compared to the natural light in a greenhouse.

REMEMBER

The real test is how your houseplants perform. If their foliage is too dark green and floppy, their growth habit isn't compact but is *leggy* (leaves are farther apart on the stem of the houseplant and are usually soft and floppy), and they don't bloom on schedule with flowers of good substance and size, then your houseplants aren't receiving enough light. If that's the case, move them closer to the lights or to the center of the tubes, or increase the lighting duration. If the leaves are taking on a yellowish cast, indicating they're getting too much light, place the plants farther away from or on the ends of the tubes or decrease the lighting duration. See the "Clues your houseplants want different lighting" section later in this chapter for more information.

Let There Be Light! Recognizing Natural Light Sources

Light is essential for all green plants, including houseplants. Light, water, and carbon dioxide are the raw materials plants use to produce their food. Providing enough light is frequently the most challenging requirement for indoor gardeners, especially in areas of the country that experience short days and low light during the winter. Fortunately, plenty of species and hybrids of houseplants don't require super high intensity light.

If you're blessed with naturally high intensity light — like the kind found in Hawaii and Florida — you can grow both high- and low-light houseplants. You just need to use greenhouse shading or light-reducing draperies to satisfy those houseplants requiring modest amounts of light.

Houseplants are traditionally categorized by their light requirements — high, medium, and low. Turn to Chapter 2 for an uncomplicated way to determine the intensity of your light source, called the *shadow test.* Most houseplants are in the medium light category, and you can easily grow them under artificial lights or on bright windowsills. In this section, I break down the different places you can grow houseplants, and then I share the signs to look for in your plant to determine whether it's getting the light it needs.

Greenhouses: Your high light source

Although it is possible to grow very high-light-requiring plants using expensive LEDs and High-Intensity Discharge lights (explained later in this chapter) lights, from a practical point of view, houseplants with high light requirements are most successfully grown in bright greenhouses because greenhouses are the most efficient collectors of natural light and because they are exposed on all sides to the full intensity of the sun. The greenhouse option is the most expensive because it requires substantial construction costs and heating bills (especially if you are in a cold climate). One major advantage of a greenhouse is that the size of the plant is limited only by the dimensions of the greenhouse. For example, some palms are just not a good choice for most indoor gardeners because of their sizeable footprint, but they can be right at home in a large home greenhouse.

You don't have to own a greenhouse to grow most of the houseplants in this book.

Windowsills: Not all are created equal

Windowsills are the most readily available and cost-effective source of light. The amount of light windowsill growing can provide is primarily determined by

>> **The roof overhang:** How far the roof extends beyond the wall of the house makes a difference in how much light will reach your plants (see Figure 5-2).

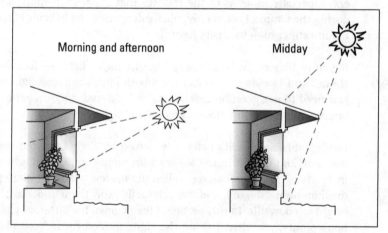

FIGURE 5-2: The extent of the roof overhang has an influence on the amount of light the houseplants receive.

© John Wiley & Sons, Inc.

>> **The size of the windows:** The larger the window, the more light will be available for your plants. Figure 5-3 shows what I mean.

FIGURE 5-3: Bay windows increase the size of the growing area and the amount of light the plant receives because light can penetrate from multiple angles.

© John Wiley & Sons, Inc.

>> **The direction the windows face:** Whether the windows face north, south, east, or west makes a significant difference in the amount and quality of light your houseplants will receive.

- **South-facing window:** A south-facing window gets the brightest sunlight, so it offers the most possibilities. It's an ideal location for houseplants that demand the strongest light. You can place most of your other lower-light-demanding houseplants a few feet back from the window, or you can diffuse the light from the window with a sheer curtain. The southern exposure can be very hot, and therefore damaging, to some plants, especially during summer and in warmer climates. Be aware of this and consider moving your plants to an eastern window, which is generally not as toasty.

REMEMBER

Southern exposure can get hot, especially during the summer.

- **East-facing window:** East-facing windows offer morning sunlight, which is bright but not too hot. During the spring, summer, and fall, this is usually an ideal exposure for most of the houseplants in this book, except those that require extremely high light. During the short, dark days of winter, many of these same houseplants usually prefer a south-facing window.

- **West-facing window:** A west-facing window receives as much light as an east window, but because it gets afternoon light, it's much hotter, which makes it a less-desirable location than the east-facing window. If you need to use a west-facing window, make sure your houseplants don't dry out too much because of the hotter temperature.

- **North-facing window:** A north-facing window simply doesn't provide enough light to sustain healthy growth of houseplants. Use it for low-light plants like ferns.

» **The distance between the plants and the windows:** Light intensity falls off quickly the farther away the plants are from the windows.

» **The age and condition of the glass:** Tinted and reflective glass can dramatically reduce light intensity, so it's usually not recommended for growing houseplants. No matter what kind of glass you have, keep your windows clean, especially during the winter when the light intensity is low, so your houseplants will receive as much light as possible.

» **The time of year:** During the winter, the sun is lower in the sky and the days are shorter. The opposite is true during the summer. As a result, a south-facing window may be fine for certain houseplants during the winter, but you may have to move the plants to an east-facing window during the summer.

SUNROOMS ARE GREAT FOR GROWING HOUSEPLANTS

Many houseplant hobbyists just don't have space for a greenhouse but would like to have an attractive and functional place to grow and show off their houseplants. Sunrooms, which can vary from an adapted greenhouse to a conservatory to merely a room that has large windows, can be a good solution.

The following photo shows my sunroom. It faces east, and the smaller side window faces south and has large, bright windows. I used rustproof stainless steel screws to attach 6-inch composite decking boards to the existing narrow windowsill. The windowsill is now wider to better hold potted plants. Because these boards are waterproof, they won't warp or rot if water leaks onto them from the potted plants. The sunroom is the room my wife, our dogs, and I favor year-round.

© John Wiley & Sons, Inc.

Clues your houseplants want different lighting

TIP

The leaves of plants give you some clue as to their light requirements (see Figure 5-4). Those with very tough, thick, stout, and sometimes narrow leaves frequently are adapted to very high-intensity light. Leaves that are softer, more succulent, and wider are usually a clue that the plant is from a lower-light environment. Orchids are very good examples of this. Compare the very thick, narrower leaves of the cattleyas with the softer wider leaves of moth orchids (phalaenopsis). Also note how thick and narrow the leaves and stems are on some of the succulent plants in very high-light climates.

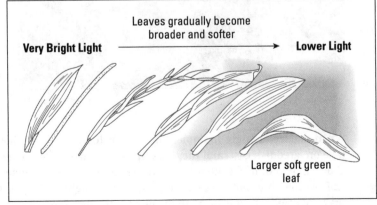

FIGURE 5-4:
The type of leaf indicates a houseplant's light requirements.

© John Wiley & Sons, Inc.

Your houseplants will tell you by their growth habits and leaf color if they're getting adequate, too little, or too much light. When houseplants are getting enough light, you'll notice the following:

>> The mature leaves are usually medium to light green.

>> The new leaves are the same size or larger and the same shape as the mature ones.

>> The foliage is stiff and compact, not floppy.

>> Flowering plants bloom at approximately the same time they did the year before.

One of the most frequent results of inadequate light is soft, dark green foliage with no flowering. Another symptom of inadequate light is *stretching,* which means the distance between the new leaves on the stem is greater than it is for the mature leaves. Also, the leaves are floppy rather than stiff. You can see an example of stretching and floppy leaves and with the lady's slipper orchid in Figure 5-5. With most foliage plants, the new leaves tend to be longer and thinner when given inadequate light.

FIGURE 5-5: When houseplants don't receive enough light, their foliage tends to be soft and floppy rather than firm.

© John Wiley & Sons, Inc.

When houseplants get too much light, their leaves turn a yellow-green color or take on a reddish cast, and they may appear stunted. In extreme cases, the leaves show circular or oval sunburn spots (see Figure 5-6). The sunburn is caused by the leaf overheating, not necessarily by too much light. Although this leaf damage may not cause extreme harm to the plant if the damage is isolated to a small area, it does make the plant unsightly.

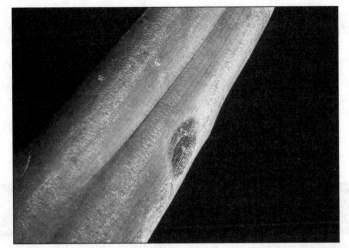

FIGURE 5-6:
A leaf with a round or oval brown spot caused by too much light or sunburn.

© John Wiley & Sons, Inc.

WARNING

If the sunburn occurs on the plant's new growth, which is soft and most exposed to the sun, it can kill that leaf or the entire plant. It's possible to expose some houseplants to higher intensity light than is usually recommended if you increase the ventilation to lower the elevated leaf temperature. Some cut-flower growers like to push their houseplants with the highest intensity light they can take without burning to yield the maximum number of blooms. However, for most hobby growers, I don't recommend this.

Comparing Artificial Light Sources

Artificial light sources make it possible for people without greenhouses or bright windowsills to enjoy growing houseplants in their homes. It's a very practical method of growing for low- to medium-light houseplants.

Wading through the many lighting options available today can be a daunting task, especially for beginners. Table 5-1 lists the most used lighting sources for growing houseplants. This area is constantly evolving, so keep your mind open to new possibilities as they become available. The following sections break down artificial light sources in greater detail.

Fluorescent lights

Today's fluorescent light systems are much different than they were years ago. Current lights are much brighter and more energy-efficient.

CHAPTER 5 **Providing the Right Growing Environment**   73

WHAT IS LIGHT GARDENING?

This phrase can be confusing because all forms of gardening require light (except growing mushrooms). In this book, and in most indoor gardening books, this phrase is frequently used when referring to growing plants under artificial lights — mostly LEDs and fluorescent.

TABLE 5-1   ## Artificial Light Sources

Type	Life Span	Average Temperature the Light Emits	Recommended Distance from Plants	Efficiency	Cost
HID Grow Lights	10,000 hours	600°F (315°C)	6–10 in (15–25 cm)	125 lumens per watt	Around $15 per bulb
HPS Grow Lights	18,000 hours	500°F (260°C)	4–6 in (10–15 cm)	140 lumens per watt	Around $150 per bulb and ballast
LED Grow Lights	50,000 hours	70°F (21°C)	10–16 in (25–40 cm)	25 lumens per watt	Around $200 per square foot panel
T8 Fluorescents	25,000 hours	100°F (37°C)	2–4 in (5–10 cm)	90 lumens per watt	$3–$5 per bulb
T5 Fluorescents	20,000–35,000 hours	95°F (35°C)	2–4 in (5–10 cm)	110 lumens per watt	$5–$10 per bulb

Here I explain in plain English the types of fluorescent bulbs suitable for growing houseplants and recommend which fixtures to use with these bulbs.

TIP

To encourage the most efficient use of energy and to prevent the possibility of exposure to the mercury found in some fluorescent bulbs, some states are starting to ban the sale of all linear fluorescent bulbs (T12s, T8s, and T5s). These regulations are designed to encourage the purchase of more efficient and mercury-free LED units. It is difficult to know when or if other states will follow suit. Check out your state regulations if you buy from a national supplier. If you already have T5 or T8 fluorescent fixtures, you can now buy LED bulbs or tubes that can be retrofitted.

The three Ts: 12, 8, and 5

Fluorescent bulbs (or lamps) are basically available in three types. The T designation refers to the lamp being tubular, and the numbers after the T indicate the diameter of the bulb or lamp expressed in ⅛-inch (3-millimeter) increments. They are as follows:

>> **T12:** These tubes are 12/8 inches (36 mm) in diameter and formerly were the standard 40-watt fluorescent bulb in the United States. Because they're not as energy-efficient as the newer bulbs, they aren't used for growing plants as much as they used to be. In fact, by law, they'll be phased out and replaced by the more energy-efficient T8.

>> **T8:** These high-efficiency 34-watt bulbs are 8/8 inch or 1 inch (24 mm) in diameter. They produce more light per watt, contain less harmful mercury, produce less heat, and are usually powered by instant-start, flicker-free, buzz-free electronic ballasts. Compared to the older lamps, these newer ones burn longer at their full light output.

>> **T5:** These tubes, which are 5/8 inch (15 mm) wide, are the next generation of fluorescent technology, and are presently my favorite of the fluorescent bulbs. T5s were introduced in the 2000s and are very bright, especially the high-output (HO) types. Of course, T5 fixtures and lamps are a bit more expensive than T8s, and T5HO bulbs use more electricity than standard T5s. (A 4-inch T5 uses 28 watts; a 4-inch T5HO uses 54 watts.) The additional light T5HOs emit (2,900 lumens for T5 and 5,000 lumens for T5HO) is worth the additional energy usage.

TIP

Although some people use them, compact spiral fluorescent bulbs aren't usually practical for growing many plants because they produce a narrow circle of light. The standard linear bulbs are the most useful and economical choice. The most common and readily available length is 48 inches (1.2 m). Shorter lamps are more expensive, and because light intensity decreases significantly in the 6 inches (15 centimeters) at the end of the tubes in all fluorescent lamps, they aren't an efficient choice.

Fluorescent fixture setups

Fluorescent fixtures are some of the most accessible and economical lighting systems to buy, and they come in a variety of types and styles. In most cases, the type known as *shop lights* are the most affordable and readily available at hardware or home stores. If you choose these, make sure to get the ones with bright white reflectors, rather than gray, because they'll make your lights more efficient. Mirrored reflectors are even more ideal. Units with this type of reflector are more expensive, but more effective.

TIP

If you have older fixtures in which the reflectors have discolored over time, spray-paint them with glossy or flat white enamel paint. Oil-based paints stand up best to the moisture the light fixtures will be exposed to.

Three-tiered light carts, like the one shown in Figure 5-7, are highly versatile and practical. You can buy units from a plant light specialty store. Most of them are about 2 feet (60 cm) wide by about 4 feet (121 cm) long, so their three shelves provide 24 square feet (2.23 square meters) of growing area. If you grow compact houseplants, this will be enough space to have at least one or more houseplants in bloom year-round. If you collect miniatures, this setup will provide a growing space adequate for your whole collection. The convenience of such a cart can't be beat; you can place it in a heated garage, in a basement, or in a spare bedroom.

FIGURE 5-7: One of my off-the-shelf four-tube units with three tiers.

Although some people have reported success with growing houseplants under two-tube units, I prefer the four-tube units. Because the light from the four tubes overlaps, the result is more than double the light produced by a two-tube unit. The additional light this setup supplies permits the grower to place the plants farther from the lamps (providing easier access for watering and handling).

When houseplants start to produce their tall flower spikes, there usually isn't enough headroom under most fixed-height light units, like the one in Figure 5-7, to accommodate this growing spike. At that point, you can move the houseplants to a windowsill or use a light fixture that can be raised (see Figure 5-8) as the flower spikes develop.

FIGURE 5-8:
An adjustable light fixture like this one is very handy for accommodating developing flower spikes.

High-intensity discharge lights and commercial-grade LED lights

High-intensity discharge (HID) lights — available in high-pressure sodium (HPS) or metal halide (MH) versions — and commercial-grade LED panels are efficient in their light production and especially useful when fluorescent and standard LED lamps can't provide sufficient light or you want a greater working distance between the lights and your plants. (For more on LED lighting, see the next section.) This type of light is also helpful if you have a wide growing area or tall plants that don't fit under standard light fixtures. Figure 5-9 illustrates the growing areas for different HID lights.

HPS and MH lamps can produce quite a bit of heat, so you must not place them too close to the tops of the plants, and you must provide adequate ventilation. You can purchase fans for these units to cool off the bulbs.

TIP

HPS lamps are more energy-efficient than MH bulbs, but the light they emit is orange-yellow and distorts the color of the flowers and foliage. MH lamps produce blue light that's more pleasing to the eye. Some manufacturers now produce lamps that combine the advantages of both.

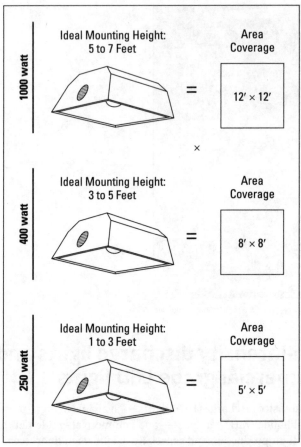

1000 watt
Ideal Mounting Height:
5 to 7 Feet

Area Coverage

= 12' × 12'

×

400 watt
Ideal Mounting Height:
3 to 5 Feet

Area Coverage

= 8' × 8'

250 watt
Ideal Mounting Height:
1 to 3 Feet

Area Coverage

= 5' × 5'

FIGURE 5-9: Approximate growing areas for different wattages of HID lamps.

© John Wiley & Sons, Inc.

LEDs: The new kids on the block

With LEDs (which stands for *light-emitting diodes*), light is produced from individual electronic devices (diodes) instead of from the long tubes of fluorescent fixtures. This newer form of lighting is noted for its energy efficiency and low heat output. All the information about light color still pertains to this light form.

Until fairly recently, the LEDs used in light fixtures didn't emit the right color or intensity of light to grow houseplants, but that's changed. The need for economical light sources for growing hemp and for commercial indoor vegetable growing facilities has driven much of this improved technology.

TIP

Some of the commercial units referred to as *dual band* LEDs put out mostly red and blue light, which can give your plants and flowers a weird unnatural glow. If you want to see natural color on your houseplant foliage and flowers, look for the units that produce full-spectrum light, which appears white. Multicolor white units that blend red, blue, and green diodes also create a natural look for your plants.

LEDs will continue to improve in their light output, and prices will trend downward. It's likely that LEDs will eventually replace most other light forms, primarily because of their energy efficiency.

TIP

Some of the newer LED bulbs can be used in the same fixtures as fluorescent bulbs, so you don't have to buy new fixtures. Just make sure that this is the case with the fixture you now have. (Frequently this is not indicated on the fixture; you may need to ask your supplier.)

Choosing the best lighting option

Determining which lights you should use for your houseplants is one of the most confusing — and sometimes highly debated — topics in light gardening. Distinguishing between science and advertising hype from the various bulb-producing companies isn't easy.

TIP

If you're a beginner light gardener, I recommend starting with a T5 fluorescent light or LED setup. I find them to be the most practical. Later, if you have the need, you can give the HID lamps or LED panels a try.

Table 5-2 compares T5 fluorescents and LEDs to help you decide which one is right for you.

TABLE 5-2 **Comparing T5 Fluorescents and LEDs**

	T5 Fluorescents	LEDs
Light fixture cost	Half of LEDs	Twice as much as T5s
Replacement bulb cost	Half of LEDs	Twice as much as T5s
Lumen output	Varies depending on the unit selected	Varies depending on the unit selected
Energy usage	Twice as much energy as LEDs	Half as much energy as T5s
Light degradation	Degrades about 20 percent after a year or so	Degrades a bit slower
Life of bulbs	About 2½ times shorter than LEDs	About 2½ times longer than T5s
Heat output	Warmer than LEDs	Cooler than T5s

The higher your electric rate, the more you'll pay if you use fluorescents because LEDs are more energy-efficient. If you have only a few fixtures, you may not notice much difference in your electric bill. However, if you have a basement full of light fixtures, the cost difference may be significant.

The truth is that both fluorescents and LEDs work very well. If you already have T5s and want to switch to LEDs, you can buy retrofit LEDs, sometimes referred to as *HO LED bars*, which fit in T5 units. Get the full-spectrum ones if you want the more natural light look.

Knowing Some Tricks for Growing Houseplants Under Lights

Growing your houseplants under lights is very easy, and you can be successful with an artificial light setup, but this method does come with some specific considerations, which I discuss here:

>> Because the light intensity under lamps can be lower than full natural light found in many greenhouses, you can somewhat compensate for the difference by increasing the duration of light your plants receive. On average, lights can be burned 12 to 16 hours per day. Some growers vary the duration of their lighting depending on the natural season — a few hours shorter during the winter and a few hours longer during the summer. I haven't found this to be necessary because most houseplants aren't sensitive to or don't require seasonal light duration changes.

>> The brightest light is under the center of the tubes, although the light may be more uniform under LEDs. Keep this in mind when placing plants with various light requirements under your lamps.

>> The heat from the tubes and ballast may cause a reduction in humidity, which can be an advantage in a cooler location. To conserve heat, wrap three sides of the growing area with polyethylene sheeting.

>> Muffin fans, available at computer-supply stores, are great for creating gentle air circulation that removes excess heat produced by the lights or ballasts. Read more later in this chapter in the "Providing Ventilation: Fresh Air, Please!" section.

>> Eventually, all lights start to lose some of their brightness. When you notice dark bands appearing at the ends of the tubes, it's an indicator that the tubes

are starting to fail, so you may want to replace them as soon as you can. You also can use a light meter (see Chapter 2) placed close to an individual bulb to see if a newer bulb or array of LEDs is brighter than an older one. When your lamps begin to lose their intensity, you'll be using the same amount of electricity to produce less light, so replace the bulbs sooner rather than later.

>> The bulbs or individual LEDs can quickly become coated with light-reducing dust or spray sediment from watering. Clean the bulbs or LEDs by periodically wiping them with a damp soft cloth to remove dust or mineral deposits from water splash.

>> Water and electricity don't mix, so use an outlet protected by a ground fault circuit interrupter (GFCI).

>> In multitiered light gardens, the temperature can vary 5°F from the top shelf to the bottom. Keep that in mind when deciding the best spot to place your plants. Maximum-minimum thermometers (see Chapter 2) placed on the shelves are helpful in determining the temperature differential.

Creating Humidity

Humidity is something you can't see, but you can feel it on a muggy summer day or in a steamy greenhouse. Although cacti and succulents hail from hot, dry climates and prefer this way of living, most houseplants are from the tropics, where high rainfall and humidity prevail. When houseplants get enough humidity, they grow lush, and their leaves have a healthy shine.

WARNING

Insufficient humidity can stunt a houseplant's growth, and in severe cases, it can cause brown tips on leaves. It can also contribute to buds falling off (known as *bud blast*; read more in Chapter 6), leaves wrinkling, and *sheaths* (the tubelike structures that surround the developing flower or leaf buds) drying out, which can result in twisted or malformed flowers or leaves.

During the winter, homes — especially those in cold climates with forced-air heating systems — usually have a relative humidity of about 15 percent. Because that's the average humidity found in most desert areas, you need to raise the humidity to at least 50 percent — a level that will make houseplants happy.

If you're growing your houseplants in a greenhouse, you can regularly hose down the walkways. Alternatively, you can hook up foggers and commercial humidifiers to a *humidistat* (an instrument that reads and regulates humidity) so that the entire operation is automatic.

TIP

Humidity levels that are no problem in a greenhouse will peel the paint, plaster, and wallpaper off the walls of a house. I assume you're probably not going for that look, so you can do the following to get to the desirable humidity range without causing damage to your house:

>> **Put your houseplants in a naturally damp area, like the basement or bathroom.** Your houseplants will appreciate the extra humidity provided by this environment.

>> **Use a room humidifier.** No matter where you put your houseplants, use a room humidifier. I find the best type of humidifier is an *evaporative-pad humidifier* (in which fans blow across a moisture-laden pad that sits in a reservoir of water). An evaporative-pad humidifier is usually better than a mist humidifier because, unlike a mist humidifier, it doesn't leave your houseplants covered with a white film (from the minerals in the water being deposited on the leaves).

WARNING

You may have seen advice to increase the humidity level by growing your plants on top of a waterproof tray filled with pebbles and adding water until it's slightly below the surface of the pebbles. However, I don't recommend this method because the pots, especially heavy clay ones, frequently sink into the pebbles, resulting in the potting material inside them getting soggy. After repeated watering, the pebbles become clogged with algae, turning into a habitat for insects and various disease organisms.

TIP

A better approach is to place sections of egg crate louvers (sold in home-supply stores for diffusing fluorescent lights) in the trays (see Figure 5-10). You can cut this material with a hacksaw to whatever size you need. It's rigid, so it will support the plants above the water, and the water is more exposed to air, so more humidity results. The grating is simple to clean — just remove and spray it with warm water. To prevent algae or disease buildup, you can add a disinfectant like Physan to the water in the trays.

FIGURE 5-10:
An egg crate louver set inside a waterproof tray.

Providing Ventilation: Fresh Air, Please!

In most tropical areas where houseplants live, they're blessed with constant, but gentle, trade winds. Air movement in a growing environment ensures a more uniform air temperature and dramatically reduces disease problems by preventing leaves from staying wet too long. It also evenly distributes the gas (carbon dioxide) plants produce in the dark and use to make their food during daylight hours.

TIP

You don't want to create gale-force winds in your growing area, but you do want to produce enough airflow to cause the leaves of your houseplants to sway slightly in the breeze. I've found that two of the most effective methods for providing such an airflow in both a hobby greenhouse and an indoor growing area are ceiling fans and oscillating fans.

Ceiling fans

Ceiling fans move a huge volume of air at a low velocity in a circular pattern, so they effectively prevent extreme temperature differences, are inexpensive to operate (they use about the same electricity as a 100-watt bulb), are quiet, have variable speeds, and are easy to install. They stand up well to moist conditions, especially if you buy the outdoor type. Another nice feature is that you can adjust the air-circulation pattern on most of them so that they can either push warm air down (the recommended winter setting) or pull cool air up (usually the best summer setting), as shown in Figure 5-11.

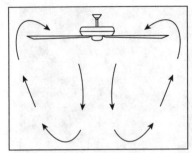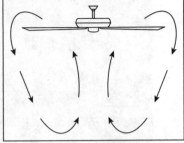

FIGURE 5-11: Ceiling fans can be set to either push warm air down (best for winter) or pull cool air up (best for summer).

Oscillating fans

Oscillating fans are also a good option because they effectively cover large areas with a constantly changing airflow pattern without excessively drying off the plants.

TIP

If you decide to go with oscillating fans, splurge for the better-grade ones. Fans that are very inexpensive have plastic gears that strip easily, so the oscillating feature won't last long.

Muffin fans

You may have small hot or cold spots in your greenhouse, on your windowsill, or in your light cart where just a touch of airflow is needed. This is where small *muffin fans,* sold at electronics or computer-supply stores for cooling computers, are perfect for the job. They're efficient, quiet, and very inexpensive to operate.

Considering Houseplant Temperature Requirements

Most houseplants hail from subtropical-to-tropical climates, so temperatures that are comfortable for you are temperatures they will also enjoy. In general, 60 to 80°F (15 to 26°C) will suit them fine.

REMEMBER

These numbers are guidelines, not absolutes. Most houseplants are quite adaptable to and tolerant of varying temperatures, short of freezing. But for ideal growth, these temperature ranges are good targets.

Too-low temperatures

If houseplants are exposed to temperatures cooler than the recommended ranges, their growth will slow, and in extreme cases, buds may fall off before they open (known as *bud blast*; read more in Chapter 6) and new leaves may shrivel. Also, cooler temperatures can reduce a plant's disease resistance.

WARNING

If you are growing your plants on the windowsill, be aware that during winter, the window glass can get very cold, and you may need to move the plants away from the windows so there is an airspace between the plant leaves and the windowpane.

Too-high temperatures

If it gets too hot, houseplants will show their displeasure by slowing or stopping their growth, having their flower buds wilt before they open, having their leaves and stems shrivel, and, in extreme cases, dying. However, a short bout of higher-than-desired temperatures won't be that harmful if the humidity stays high.

Choosing and Planting a Terrarium

A *terrarium* is a transparent enclosed environment you create for your plants, and there's something magical about these small self-contained gardens. It's extremely easy to make your own miniature plant world. The container you choose doesn't need to be fancy. It can be any type of clear glass or plastic container like a mason jar, clear pasta sauce jars, various bottles, brandy sniffers, fish bowls, or aquariums. If you want to make a design statement, look for some of the miniature glass houses available at home stores.

TIP

I prefer terrariums to be clear glass rather than plastic because plastic scratches easily when you clean it, and it can discolor over time.

Some terrariums are covered or have a sealed top, while others are open. Plants that enjoy high humidity do best in covered terrariums; the advantage of such a terrarium is that it seldom needs watering because moisture is recycled. In fact, one of the reasons many folks fail with closed terrariums is that they overwater, and the plants rot.

An important consideration is selecting plants that won't quickly outgrow their mini environment. Some of the many plants that fit well in closed terrariums are acoruses, small begonias, small ferns, peperomias, pileas, fittonias, calatheas, selaginellas, marantas, *Ficus pumila*, and cryptanthuses. Check out other smaller growing plants described in Chapter 12, including some of the carnivorous plants.

Open-topped terrariums are perfect for plants that don't require much humidity. See Chapter 10 for some smaller growing cacti and succulents that are ideal candidates for open-topped terrariums.

The construction of a terrarium is quite simple:

1. **Place a 1-inch layer of gravel or pebbles on the bottom of the container to absorb excess water.**

2. **Cover the gravel with about ½ inch of activated carbon or charcoal (available at aquarium or pet stores).**

3. **Spread 1 or 2 inches of potting material on top of the activated carbon.**

    I prefer commercial mixes over garden soil because they drain better and don't harbor insects and diseases.

4. **Add your plants.**

5. **(Optional) Add a thin layer of green moss on top of the potting mix after planting.**

    Some people use moss to make the surface of the potting material more attractive.

There aren't many rules of design except that taller plants should be placed at the back of a terrarium that will be viewed from the front or in the center of a terrarium that will be viewed from all sides. Figure 5-12 shows one example.

Plants from arid climates that prefer drier air and soil (like cacti and succulents) do better in a terrarium with an open top or side, like an aquarium or globe. Frequently, the potting mix in a cacti and succulent terrarium is topped with a layer of sand or fine gravel to make the planting look more desert-like. See Figure 5-13.

FIGURE 5-12:
Simple closed
terrarium.

Potting Mix

Activated Charcoal

Pea Gravel

© John Wiley & Sons, Inc.

FIGURE 5-13:
Cacti and
succulent
terrarium.

Konstantins Pobilojs/Shutterstock

Giving Your Houseplants
a Summer Vacation

Almost every geographical area has a period during the summer when the outside temperature and humidity are tropical. When this time arrives, your houseplants will thank you for an outside vacation. They will thrive outdoors as they enjoy the moist, warm air and natural rainfall. At the same time, you can use these plants to make your deck or patio into a tropical retreat.

For the light gardener, summering plants outdoors means a welcome relief from high electric bills; and for the greenhouse and windowsill grower, it provides an opportunity to clean up the growing area. Besides providing an opportunity to clean up your indoor growing area, having a space outdoors allows you to apply pest controls, if necessary, without making your house smell.

Most houseplants aren't in bloom during the summer, so they aren't at their best visually, and they respond very favorably to a summer vacation outdoors. The natural temperature differential between day and night, especially in the early fall, is highly effective in setting flower buds for the upcoming late-fall and winter blooming. Most houseplants are tropical in nature and should be moved indoors when the evening outdoor temperatures get down to 60°F (15°C).

If you decide to move your plants outside for the summer, keep a few things in mind:

>> Be sure you don't place your plants in a spot that's much brighter than their inside environment or they may burn.

>> Be sure to keep up the watering because they'll likely dry out faster outdoors than they did in their inside home.

>> While they're in this ideal growing environment, they'll appreciate regular fertilization to support their inevitable growth spurt.

Growing plants in a shade house

If you live in an area where you never experience freezing weather, you can enjoy growing your houseplants outdoors year-round. Although some houseplants can withstand and even prefer sunlight and can be grown directly in the ground, most of the houseplants in this book prefer at least some shade and are usually grown in pots or on slabs of bark or wood. Hence, building an outdoor structure that has some type of benching and provides a diffused light of about 50 percent shade is a good idea.

A *shade house* is a structure to which wood slats (or *lath*) or shading fabric (usually a knitted polyethylene fabric) is attached to reduce the light intensity to a level that's favorable for houseplants. The goal for growing houseplants outdoors is usually 50 to 60 percent shade. You achieve this shade level with various spacings of wood lath or with different densities of shading fabric. Figures 5-14 and 5-15 show what my shade house looks like.

FIGURE 5-14:
My shade house is an 8-foot (2.4-m) square simply constructed using wood lath and 4-x-4-inch (10-x-10-cm) pressure-treated wood posts.

© John Wiley & Sons, Inc.

I installed a watering system with multiple small sprayers or misters controlled by a timer with a manual override. I grow the plants on stepped-wire frame benches that ensure even lighting and easy watering. If you don't want to install a watering system in your shade house, make sure you have a water faucet close to the structure so you can water your plants by hand. A nearby faucet is also helpful in a dry, hot climate that demands a humidification system. (Read more about humidification earlier in this chapter in the "Creating Humidity: Most Houseplants Adore Moist Air" section.)

I covered the roof of my shade house with 6 mil (0.006-inch-thick) heavy-duty clear plastic, which is stretched over a peaked wooden frame. I used to leave the roof open so my plants received natural rainfall, but I found that it sometimes rained when I didn't want it to (at night, when it was too cool, or when it was already wet). I find the covered roof gives me the control to water when my plants need it.

FIGURE 5-15:
Inside the shade house, plants are arranged on stepped-wire benches to allow easy watering and good air and water drainage.

Summering houseplants in a portable greenhouse

I've also summered houseplants in a portable greenhouse on the deck (see Figure 5-16). A *portable greenhouse* is a greenhouse made of lightweight materials that can be easily moved. It's rarely heated and usually only used in mild weather to shelter houseplants during the summer. If you use such a structure, be sure to put it in a place that receives shade during the heat of the day or use a commercial shading fabric to cut down the light intensity. Also, be mindful of the daytime temperatures inside your structure. These units require good systems of ventilation; otherwise, temperatures inside them can skyrocket when it's sunny.

FIGURE 5-16:
An outdoor portable greenhouse can be an ideal place to put your houseplants in the summer.

Letting your plants hang around

Houseplants that have higher light requirements, like some orchids and most of the other flowering plants, grow wonderfully dangling from pot hangers clipped to the pot (see Figure 5-17) and then suspended from a pole or other support. Just make sure the light intensity of the growing area matches the needs of your houseplants.

FIGURE 5-17: Summer your houseplants outdoors by using pot hangers to hang them from a freestanding support or a suspended rod against the garage.

© John Wiley & Sons, Inc.

KEEPING THINGS IN BALANCE

When it comes to your houseplants' growing conditions, it's a matter of keeping everything in balance. Here are some tips to keep in mind:

- If the air temperature is cool, houseplants need less water and light.
- If the humidity is high, houseplants need more air circulation.
- If the light is very bright or the temperature is high, the humidity needs to be high.
- When houseplants are not actively growing, reduce or stop fertilizing.
- If the temperature is high, houseplants will require more frequent watering.

IN THIS CHAPTER

» **Mastering the art of watering**

» **Knowing when and how to water**

» **Recognizing symptoms of over- and underwatering**

» **Helping your plant recover from over- or underwatering**

» **Selecting and using houseplant fertilizers**

Chapter **6**

Watering and Fertilizing Your Plants

Probably more houseplants are killed by improper watering — usually by overwatering — than by any other practice. Understanding how to properly water your plants is one of the more challenging aspects of growing houseplants. In this chapter, I explain some simple but very effective methods that will turn you into a watering pro.

The fertilizing game can also be very confusing — so many different types and formulations! In this chapter, I guide you through the maze of fertilizer terms to get to the important information so you can choose the fertilizer that helps you grow healthy houseplants with the best blooms.

Water, Water Everywhere: Understanding the Art of Watering Houseplants

When I give talks about houseplants, one of the first questions my audience asks is "How often should I water my houseplants?" I really wish this question had an easy answer, but it doesn't because so many variables are involved in watering. In the following sections, I cover some of the factors that affect how often you should water.

The type of houseplant

Some houseplants, like cacti, succulents, and some orchids, like to dry out between waterings. Others, like most foliage and flowering plants, prefer not to dry out completely. Bog plants, like most carnivorous plants (Venus flytraps and most of the pitcher plants), are accustomed to soil or other growing media that's constantly wet. The difference in their watering needs has a lot to do with where houseplants grow naturally. If a houseplant's native habitat is an area where it doesn't get natural rainfall on a regular basis, it won't need watering as often as houseplants that grow in areas of frequent rainfall.

The type of pot

You can grow houseplants in plastic or clay pots. The potting material dries out much more slowly in plastic pots than it does in clay pots. The following details can help you more accurately judge whether your plants are due for water:

>> **Plastic pots:** The potting material dries out from the top down, so even though the potting material may be dry on top, it may be damp 1 inch (2.5 centimeters) below the surface.

>> **Clay pots:** The potting material dries out more uniformly. Clay pots are *porous* — they wick moisture away from the potting mix — so they allow water to evaporate through their walls.

>> **Ceramic pots:** These pots are usually ornamental and more expensive than the other two types. Plants in them are watered similar to plastic pots because ceramic pots are not porous and dry out from the top down.

TIP

The bottom line: If you're using a plastic pot, you'll want to water less often than if you're using a clay pot.

All types of pots will grow houseplants; they merely have different watering requirements. For houseplants that don't like to be dry (like most foliage plants and terrestrial orchids), I prefer to use plastic pots or ceramic pots. For those that need to dry out more between waterings (like most cacti and succulents and some orchids), you may find clay pots to be a better choice.

If a houseplant performs better in a plastic pot but you like the look of a nonplastic container (clay, ceramic, an old boot, whatever), nest the plastic pot in your preferred, slightly bigger container.

In Part 3, I provide an overview of numerous houseplants to choose from that are available throughout the United States.

The type and age of the potting material

Potting materials vary dramatically in terms of the amount of water they retain. For instance, *sphagnum moss,* a highly water-absorbent plant harvested from bogs to be used as a potting material, and coconut husk chips usually stay wet much longer than bark, which isn't as water-retentive.

If you're using a potting material that absorbs a lot of water, you'll want to water less often than if you use a potting material that doesn't absorb the water. To decide whether the potting material is absorbent, soak some of it in water for a few hours. Then remove the material and squeeze it. If it's absorbent, it will release the water under pressure, like a sponge.

It's also important to note potting material requires frequent watering for the first few weeks, until it gets properly wetted. As it gets older, it retains water longer.

The roominess of the pot

The potting material of an overgrown houseplant (sometimes referred to as a houseplant that is *pot-bound*) dries out much more quickly than the potting media of a plant that has plenty of space in the pot. When pot space is limited, there's less potting material to hold onto the water, so the overgrown plant quickly uses it up.

In general, most houseplants need to be repotted every one to two years. In Chapter 7, I give you the complete scoop on repotting houseplants.

The humidity, temperature, and ventilation of the growing environment

Are you growing your houseplants in high humidity or low? Houseplants and potting materials in low humidity dry out more quickly because the drier air rapidly absorbs the moisture from both the plant and the potting material.

Air temperature and ventilation are also factors. Warmer temperatures increase water evaporation because warmer air absorbs more moisture, and the plants are growing more quickly. Consequently, they require more water. If you're growing houseplants in a cooler temperature, you won't need to water as often.

The more ventilation your houseplants get — especially if the air is vented to the outside, or if the air is hot and dry, as in most centrally heated homes during the winter — the quicker the water in the potting material evaporates. Gentle air movement is ideal. It keeps the air fresh without excessively drying out the plants or potting material.

The growing stage

Most houseplants go through a rest period (that is, they're *dormant*) in the winter, when it's generally cooler and there's less light. During this period, they don't need to be watered as frequently as they do when they're actively growing. When they start active growth in the spring and summer, more frequent watering is called for.

Quenching Your Houseplants' Thirst

After you've considered factors such as the type of houseplant, potting material, and growing environment (see the preceding section), you need to decide when and how much to water. These sections take you through one of the simplest ways to determine when to water your houseplants and explain some tips to make watering easier.

Using the pot-weighting method

I find the pot-weighting method of deciding when to water is one of the easiest. In this method, you're relying on feel instead of precise weights. Follow these simple steps:

1. **Thoroughly water the houseplant in its pot.**

2. **Pick up the pot and estimate its approximate weight.**

   Now you know how heavy it is when it's saturated with water.

3. **Wait a day or so and "weigh" it again.**

   You'll feel the difference in the weight as the potting material becomes drier.

4. **Repeat Step 3 each day until you judge, by looking at the surface of the potting material and sticking your finger into the top 1 inch (2.5 cm) or so to see if it's damp, that it's time to water.**

   Keep in mind whether this type of houseplant prefers to be on the damp or dry side.

REMEMBER

5. **Note what this dry weight is.**

   Now the houseplant is ready to be watered thoroughly.

This entire process may sound tedious, but you'll be amazed at how quickly you catch on. And when you do, you'll always know the right time to water. Just lift the pot, note its weight, and you'll have your answer.

Knowing some tips and tricks for watering your houseplants

If you're still not quite sure about watering, keep the following watering tips in mind:

- » **Grow houseplants of the same type and size in the same potting media and pot type in the same area.** This strategy will make watering them easier because they'll have very similar moisture requirements.

- » **Water with warm water.** Very cold water can cause root and bud shock, which sets back the plant and slows its growth.

- » **Always use a water breaker.** A *water breaker* is a water diffuser that you attach to the end of your hose to soften the flow of water. A few houseplants like being watered with a sprinkling can that has a long spout equipped with a *rose* (a water diffuser with many small holes attached to the end of the spout). These devices allow thorough watering without washing away the potting material.

  A huge selection of watering wands is available. I really like the ones with multiple settings on the head that allow you to drench or mist without changing attachments. Regulating the flow of water is much easier with wands equipped with finger triggers than it is with those that have an on-and-off valve. (See Chapter 3 for more information on tools and supplies.)

>> **Never let the water breaker or end of the hose touch the ground or floor.** This commandment was given to me by my first horticulture professor, D. C. Kiplinger, who preached that floors and soil are where diseases and insects hang out, and a hose can be an all-too-effective way of spreading them.

>> **When you water, water thoroughly.** The water should pour from the bottom of the pot. This method of watering ensures that the potting material is saturated and flushes out any excessive fertilizer salts.

>> **Never let the pots sit in water for more than an hour.** If your houseplant pots have saucers, make sure to keep them free of water. Excess standing water will prematurely rot the potting media and the plant's roots and will be a source of accumulating fertilizer salts and *pathogens* (disease-causing organisms like bacteria, fungi, or viruses).

>> **Water your houseplants early in the day or afternoon.** That way, the foliage will have plenty of time to dry off before nightfall. Wet foliage in the evening is an invitation for disease.

WARNING

Don't water your houseplants with water that has passed through a water-softening unit. Such water may contain high amounts of sodium, which can be harmful to houseplants.

Over- or Underwatering: Roots Tell the Story

Over- and underwatered houseplants show many of the same symptoms because the effect of both practices is the same: damaged or destroyed root systems, which result in the houseplant becoming dehydrated. The signs of dehydration include

>> Pleated leaves on houseplants like miltonia orchids (see Figure 6-1)

>> Excessively shriveled *pseudobulbs* (thickened, swollen stems) of some houseplants, like cattleya orchids

>> Droopy, soft, and puckered leaves on most all houseplants.

>> Yellow and wilted bottom leaves on philodendron and most all other houseplants

>> Soft or discolored leaves on succulents (and plants may drop the affected foliage)

>> *Bud blast* (buds falling off instead of opening) on all houseplants

FIGURE 6-1:
The pleated or
puckered leaf of
this houseplant is
a sign that the
plant is
dehydrated.

© John Wiley & Sons, Inc.

BLASTED BUD BLAST!

Nothing is more disappointing than having the buds on your houseplants shrivel up right before they open! This is referred to as *bud blast,* and it occurs when a houseplant undergoes several types of stress. Here are some of the specific causes of this exasperating situation:

- Low humidity
- Hot air from a furnace or cool, dry air from an air conditioner directly blowing on the houseplant
- Over- or underwatering
- Poor root development
- Temperatures that are too high or too low
- Water collecting in the buds or bud sheaths
- Dramatic change in the plants' environment, like bringing them inside after they've been outside
- Natural gas leaks in the house
- Ethylene gas from ripened fruit
- Light that's too bright on the developing flower buds
- Pollution, such as smog

Of course, before you do anything to correct watering problems, you have to first decide if improper watering is an issue. To better evaluate whether over- or underwatering has caused these symptoms, you must remove the houseplant from its pot. Many beginner growers are reluctant to do this, but if you're careful, removing the houseplant from its pot won't disturb most houseplants to any degree, and it's an absolutely necessary procedure to see what's going on with the root system.

To figure out if you've under- or overwatered your houseplant, follow these steps:

1. **Turn the houseplant, in its pot, upside down.**

2. **Gently rap a hard object (like the handle of a gardening tool) against the pot to loosen the potting material.**

   Cup your hand over the surface of the pot to catch the loosened potting material as it falls out. Doing this over a workbench or a table covered with clean newspaper to hold the potting material is a nice, neat approach.

3. **If the potting material doesn't loosen easily, use a thin-bladed knife to circle the inside of the pot to separate the potting material from the wall of the pot.**

   TIP

   In some situations, the potting material may be so packed into the pot that it won't come out easily. If that's the case, you may have to cut the pot if it's plastic or break it if it's made of clay or a ceramic material.

4. **When the houseplant is removed from the pot, check out the potting material and the roots.**

   Is the potting mix soggy? Does it have a bad (rotting) smell? Are the plant's roots dark and mushy? These are all signs of overwatering.

   If the roots are dry and shriveled, not stiff and plump, and have no or few growing root tips, the houseplant probably hasn't gotten enough water. The potting material may be too coarse, making poor contact with the roots; otherwise, you simply haven't watered the houseplant often enough.

5. **If the roots look okay or only slightly damaged, repot the houseplant in fresh potting material.**

   See Chapter 7 for more details on potting houseplants.

If you find that the roots are badly damaged, read the following section for more information.

Houseplant ER: Rescuing and Resuscitating a Dehydrated Houseplant

The approach you take to remedy root damage depends on how dire the situation is.

TIP

If the houseplant still has some healthy, firm roots, cut off all the soft, mushy roots with a sterile tool, like a single-edged razor, and repot the houseplant in new potting material. Go light on the watering for a few weeks to encourage new root development. Using a spray bottle, mist the houseplant a few times a day to prevent the leaves from drying out.

TIP

If the roots are almost all gone, emergency measures are called for and recovery is not guaranteed. This is what I recommend:

1. **Cut off all the dead or damaged roots.**

2. **Drench the roots with a liquid rooting hormone like Dip 'n Grow.**

3. **Let the liquid hormone dry on the roots for about an hour, and then repot the houseplant in fresh potting material that has been dampened.**

4. **Don't water for a day.**

5. **Water once, and then put the potted houseplant in an enclosed terrarium (like a high-top propagator) or an empty aquarium, with damp sphagnum moss or pebbles on the bottom to add humidity.**

   A *high-top propagator* is a clear plastic box with vents at the top and a tray below to hold potting material.

6. **Close the top of the terrarium and put it in a location with diffused light.**

   In a greenhouse, pick a shady spot with no direct sunlight. Under fluorescent lights, put the terrarium at the end of the tubes, where there's less illumination. If the terrarium is in the cool part of your greenhouse or growing area, put the entire terrarium on water-resistant soil or seedling heating mats, available at most garden centers. Get one that has a built-in thermostat set for about 70°F (21°C) to provide bottom heat to stimulate rooting.

7. **If you're concerned about disease, spray the houseplant leaves with a disinfectant solution.**

   A good disinfectant is Physan, a commonly used hospital disinfectant available online, from mail-order houseplant-supply companies, or at garden centers.

As with all pesticides, be sure to read the directions carefully. If you use a disinfectant or any other chemical control incorrectly, you can damage the plant.

In this environment of 100 percent humidity, the leaves won't dehydrate, so there will be no stress on the houseplant while it re-roots itself. Water the potting material only when it gets dry, keep the gravel or moss in the bottom of the terrarium damp, and leave the houseplant enclosed until new root growth is very clear. This may take a few months.

This method has no guarantees, but by following this procedure, I have sometimes managed to save houseplants that were in the hopeless category. Many times, though, a dehydrated houseplant is just too far gone to be saved, so you may be better off throwing it away and getting a new one to take its place.

Figure 6-2 shows my houseplant rescue, the place where I put houseplants that have suffered a loss of roots. It's like a miniature greenhouse with high humidity, which encourages dehydrated houseplants to form new roots.

FIGURE 6-2:
My houseplant rescue, where I put houseplants that have suffered a loss of roots.

© John Wiley & Sons, Inc.

Realizing Fertilizers Are Plant Boosters — Not Magic Potions

Many people place too much faith in fertilizer. They think fertilizer is some type of elixir that will save the day. Actually, if a houseplant is in poor health, fertilizer is rarely the answer.

WARNING

In fact, if the roots are damaged (a common problem), applying fertilizer will make the problem worse. If the roots aren't functioning well, they can't absorb the fertilizer, and if the fertilizer isn't used by the houseplant, it can accumulate in the potting material. This buildup of fertilizer salts can further dehydrate and damage the remaining roots.

TIP

Fertilizers are most useful as a boost to help an already healthy houseplant grow better.

REMEMBER

Many people mistakenly think of fertilizer as food — which it isn't. Plants produce their own food from sunlight, carbon dioxide, and water. That's the miracle called *photosynthesis.* By fertilizing, you're merely providing extra minerals to the potting soil/growing media for your houseplants to use to make photosynthesis more efficient.

The number and variety of fertilizers on the market can make your head spin! You'll hear a lot of mumbo jumbo about why one fertilizer is better than another. Fortunately, the choice isn't nearly as complicated as some manufacturers seem to make it.

Knowing what to look for in houseplant fertilizers

From my experience (and from listening to other veteran houseplant growers), I've come to some conclusions about fertilizers. The following suggestions apply to most houseplant-growing situations:

>> **Look at the label and choose a fertilizer that contains *nitrate nitrogen* or *ammoniacal nitrogen,* not *urea.*** Although all forms of nitrogen can be used by plants, research shows that the nitrate and ammoniacal forms, not urea, are most beneficial and available to houseplants. These chemical terms may sound like Greek to you, but you don't really need to know any more than to look for these types of nitrogen in your fertilizer. The label tells you what you need to know.

>> **Pick a fertilizer with 20 percent or less nitrogen.** The nitrogen percentage is the first number listed on the label. High amounts of nitrogen — much more than 20 percent — aren't necessary to grow the best houseplants no matter what medium they're grown in. The houseplant can use only so much of any nutrient, and as a result, the excess merely ends up as a pollutant.

>> **Don't worry about the amount of phosphorus in the fertilizer.** Horticulturists previously thought that a high-phosphorus fertilizer was necessary for better blooming, but that's no longer the case. Most of the houseplant fertilizers on the market contain sufficient phosphorus for growth and flowering.

>> **Make sure the fertilizer contains supplemental elements.** In most cases, a fertilizer with supplementary calcium (up to 15 percent) and magnesium (up to 8 percent) is a real plus (basically a 2-to-1 ratio). That's especially true if your water source doesn't already contain calcium.

For most water sources, adding *trace elements* (chemicals in very small amounts), including sodium, manganese, copper, zinc, boron, iron, and molybdenum, has been found to be beneficial to houseplant growth. Don't worry about the exact amounts; just check the fertilizer container or label to see if they appear in small amounts.

Any fertilizer that meets these requirements will do. To find out if your chosen fertilizer passes muster, carefully look at its container. By law, the manufacturer must list the chemicals included in the fertilizer. Figure 6-3 shows an example of a label so you can see what to look for.

WATCH OUT FOR FERTILIZER BURN

When too much fertilizer has been applied, if fertilizer has been applied when the potting media is dry, or if the houseplant's roots are hypersensitive to the salts in the fertilizer, the roots can become dehydrated by the fertilizer's moisture-robbing salts, resulting in *fertilizer burn*. This damage shows up as brown or black root tips or leaf tips. It looks as though the root tips or leaves have been burned (thus, the name). To prevent it, don't apply more fertilizer than is recommended and fertilize only when the potting material is damp.

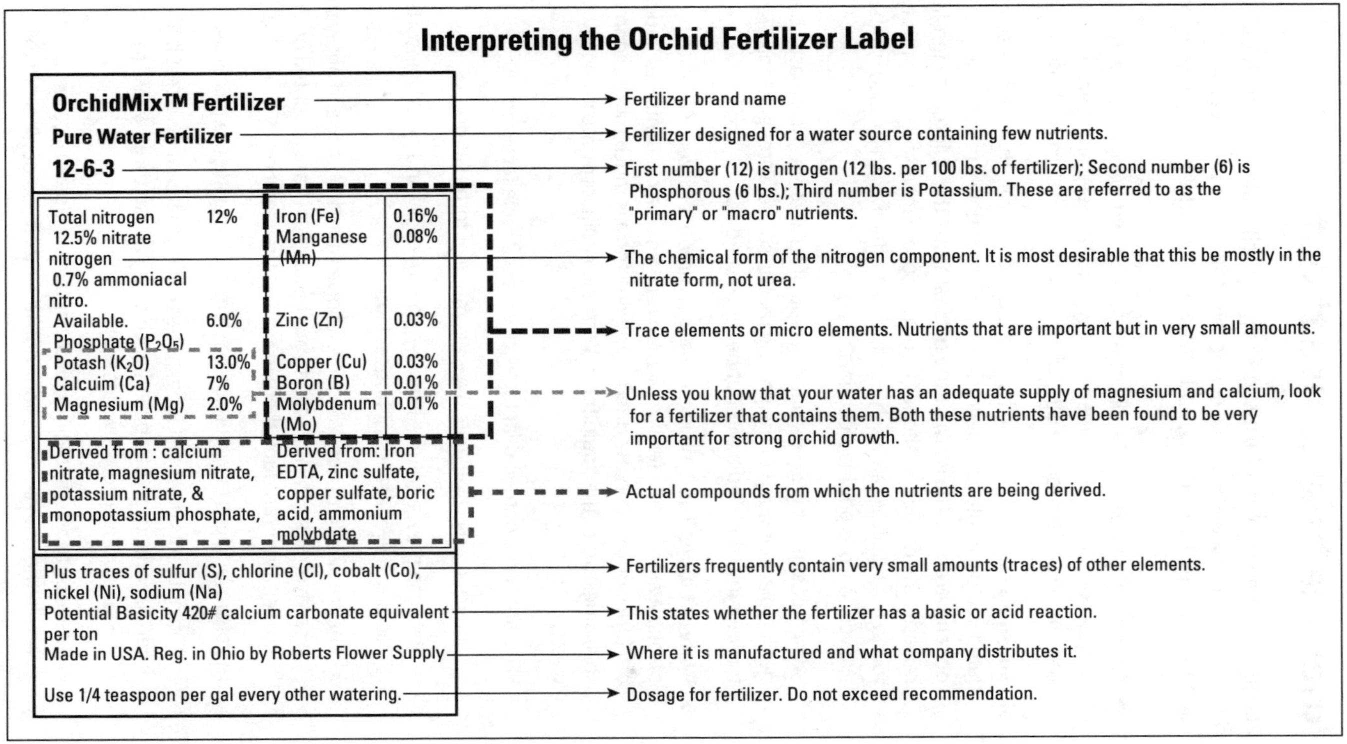

Interpreting the Orchid Fertilizer Label

OrchidMix™ Fertilizer → Fertilizer brand name

Pure Water Fertilizer → Fertilizer designed for a water source containing few nutrients.

12-6-3 → First number (12) is nitrogen (12 lbs. per 100 lbs. of fertilizer); Second number (6) is Phosphorous (6 lbs.); Third number is Potassium. These are referred to as the "primary" or "macro" nutrients.

Total nitrogen 12%
12.5% nitrate nitrogen
0.7% ammoniacal nitro. → The chemical form of the nitrogen component. It is most desirable that this be mostly in the nitrate form, not urea.

Available. Phosphate (P₂O₅) 6.0%
Potash (K₂O) 13.0%
Calcuim (Ca) 7%
Magnesium (Mg) 2.0% → Unless you know that your water has an adequate supply of magnesium and calcium, look for a fertilizer that contains them. Both these nutrients have been found to be very important for strong orchid growth.

Iron (Fe)	0.16%
Manganese (Mn)	0.08%
Zinc (Zn)	0.03%
Copper (Cu)	0.03%
Boron (B)	0.01%
Molybdenum (Mo)	0.01%

→ Trace elements or micro elements. Nutrients that are important but in very small amounts.

Derived from: Iron EDTA, zinc sulfate, copper sulfate, boric acid, ammonium molybdate → Actual compounds from which the nutrients are being derived.

Derived from : calcium nitrate, magnesium nitrate, potassium nitrate, & monopotassium phosphate,

Plus traces of sulfur (S), chlorine (Cl), cobalt (Co), nickel (Ni), sodium (Na) → Fertilizers frequently contain very small amounts (traces) of other elements.

Potential Basicity 420# calcium carbonate equivalent per ton → This states whether the fertilizer has a basic or acid reaction.

Made in USA. Reg. in Ohio by Roberts Flower Supply → Where it is manufactured and what company distributes it.

Use 1/4 teaspoon per gal every other watering. → Dosage for fertilizer. Do not exceed recommendation.

© John Wiley & Sons, Inc.

FIGURE 6-3: The label on a houseplant fertilizer reveals what the product contains. Read it closely.

Identifying types of fertilizers and knowing how to use them

Fertilizers come in many forms: *granule* (which looks like small pieces of gravel), *slow-release*, and *water-soluble* being the most commonly available. The following list describes the three types, and Table 6-1 lists the pros and cons of each:

>> **Granule:** Most granule fertilizers are best suited for agricultural or lawn application. I don't recommend this type for houseplants because it releases too much fertilizer too quickly, which can result in damaged houseplant roots.

>> **Slow-release:** Slow-release fertilizers are chemicals that have been encapsulated in a perforated biodegradable shell that slowly releases nutrients based on temperature. The warmer the temperature, the quicker the fertilizer releases the nutrients. Although some houseplant growers use this type, I've found the fertilizer can wash out and isn't effective when used with some of the very porous potting materials.

TIP

Some houseplant growers put this type of fertilizer in small plastic baskets or netting placed on top of the potting media, so the water goes through the fertilizer into the media without being washed out.

>> **Water-soluble:** This type is the most common fertilizer used with houseplants. Water-soluble fertilizers are packaged as a concentrated liquid or in dry form. Buying it in the dried crystalline form is much more economical than splashing out for the liquid form. With the liquid form you're mostly paying for water.

TIP

Here are some of the advantages of water-soluble fertilizers:

● They're readily available in a wide range of formulations.

● Because they're soluble in water, they're easily and quickly absorbed by roots and even leaves of houseplants.

● They're simple to use. You just dissolve them in water and apply them with a sprayer or sprinkling can. If your houseplants are mounted on slabs or in baskets, you can dunk them in the fertilizer solution.

The disadvantages of water-soluble fertilizers include the following:

● The nutrients don't last long in the potting material. As a result, the fertilizer needs to be applied once every two to three weeks (or constantly if you're using a very low dosage).

● These fertilizers, in their original containers, are very concentrated. As a result, they can damage your houseplants if you don't dilute them correctly.

TABLE 6-1

The Pros and Cons of Different Fertilizers and How to Use Them

Type of Fertilizer	Advantages	Disadvantages	How It's Applied
Granule	Readily available Easy to use Inexpensive	Short-term (lasts a few to several weeks) Can easily burn houseplant roots Often doesn't include valuable trace elements	In dry form On top of or incorporated into the potting material
Slow-release	Easy to use Lasts a long time (three to nine months, depending on the formulation)	Can sometimes burn sensitive houseplant roots In coarse potting material, can be washed out when watered Relatively expensive	In dry form On top of or incorporated into the potting medium
Water-soluble	Readily available in a wide range of formulations Easy to apply Nutrients are instantly available for plants	Must be applied often — every few weeks when plants are actively growing	Diluted in water and applied by watering can or sprayer

The application rate or dosage of all fertilizers depends on the concentrations used. The safest procedure is to always check the fertilizer container for the manufacturer's recommended application rate. Never apply more than recommended or plant damage can result.

TIP

Here are some pointers to help you know when it's time to fertilize your houseplants:

>> **Fertilizing often at a more diluted rate is better than fertilizing less often at a higher concentration.** Some houseplant growers, including me, find that feeding their houseplants with a diluted amount of fertilizer every time they water works great. It's the most natural way (as opposed to the feast-or-famine routine of fertilizing at a higher concentration every two to three weeks). If you want to fertilize each time you water, with most houseplant fertilizer formulations use about ¼ teaspoon (1.2 cubic centimeters) of the dry crystalline fertilizer per gallon of water.

WARNING

>> **Never apply more fertilizer than the manufacturer recommends.** When in doubt, apply less, not more, fertilizer. Remember that fertilizers are a form of salt, and salts were some of the earliest weedkillers, so they'll damage houseplants at high concentrations.

>> **Drench the potting material, several times in a row, every few weeks or so with fresh water that has no nutrients.** This process, called *leaching*, washes out any excess fertilizer salts.

>> **Look at the houseplant's leaves and flowers.** Very dark green leaves that are succulent and floppy can be a sign of overfertilizing. If houseplants are overfertilized, they also produce poor-quality flowers.

>> **When your houseplants are actively growing, fertilize them.** When they aren't, don't.

>> **If your houseplants are diseased and in poor condition, stop fertilizing.** Houseplants make use of fertilizer only when they're healthy and actively growing. For easy ways of applying fertilizers, check out fertilizer injectors in Chapter 3.

PREVENTING FERTILIZER DEPOSITS ON POTS

As water evaporates from the potting material, it leaves behind any solid minerals or salts that were dissolved in the water, including fertilizer salts. These salts can accumulate on the edges of your pots. When you notice this salt crusting, remove it with a damp cloth. If you don't, the leaves of your houseplants can be burned when they touch the fertilizer deposits.

Because clay pots are porous, they tend to accumulate more salt deposits on their edges than plastic pots do. One way to prevent this is to dip the tops of clay pots into about ½ inch (1.27 cm) of melted *paraffin* (wax used to make candles) before potting your houseplants in them.

Chapter **7**

Getting the Skinny on Containers, Potting Mixes, and Repotting

Most houseplants are essentially container plants. Raising houseplants in containers is quite possibly one of the most satisfying and fun types of gardening. It's so easy — all you do is supply the potting mix and water and fertilize your plants as needed. You can move pots around to capture more sun, create a group display, or, during warm weather, decorate front steps, a back patio, or an outdoor tabletop. You can even use some of your potted houseplants to inject color or interest in your in-ground displays when the weather is mild. With a variety of containers, some attractive and colorful houseplants, and a dash of creativity, you can really boost your home and garden's interest and appeal.

In this chapter, I walk you through how to select containers that will suit you *and* your plants. I also help you decide which potting mix is best for your plants — whether you make it yourself or buy ready-made mix. Repotting or transplanting your plants when they need more growing space can be an intimidating experience, so I share steps to take to make this process painless and simple.

Exploring Different Kinds of Containers

You can grow houseplants in containers of all kinds. Hunting for pots and other potential containers can be a lot of fun. Sometimes, you may get so excited that you put the cart before the horse — in other words, you choose the pot first and the houseplant second. Of course, selecting a pot before purchasing a plant has the advantage of letting you picture and plan the look you want.

Before you impulsively start collecting all sorts of pots, remember three key practical concerns when picking out a container:

>> **Drainage:** Most potted houseplants don't like to sit in soggy potting material, so ensuring there's a way for the water to drain is critical. Turn over every pot or potential container to see whether it has drainage holes. If a container doesn't have an "escape hatch" for water, perhaps you can add a hole with an awl or high-speed electric drill/masonry bit.

You *can* grow houseplants in pots without drainage holes, but doing so requires a lot of care to make sure the plant's roots aren't sitting in water. *Note:* If you don't want water getting onto the display surface, you want to include a waterproof saucer. Plastic and ceramic platters are best; terra cotta platters can leak. Lots of pots are sold as pot-and-saucer sets.

TIP

To decrease the possibility of cracking or breaking a clay pot when you're drilling one or more drainage holes, tape over the area to be drilled with masking or duct tape and then drill through the tape.

TIP

Don't risk breaking an expensive or unique pot by trying to make a drainage hole. Instead, use the container as a *cachepot,* a decorative pot that hides another container: Fill the bottom 2 inches of the pot with pea gravel, and then put the plant into a smaller plastic pot that fits into the ornamental one. This is called *nesting.*

>> **Color:** A neutral hue (white, tan, brown, or a muted green) lets the houseplant be the star. On the other hand, a brightly patterned container adds drama and excitement to an otherwise ordinary plant display. You can also try to match a color on the container to a flower or foliage color. Done well, this effect can be quite fabulous.

>> **Longevity:** Inexpensive pots tend to be less durable and break, crack, or fade when left for a long time in the sun and weather if you've put them outdoors during mild temperatures in the summer. Thicker, heavier pots, which may be more expensive, are worth the investment.

TIP

Match the size of the plant with the size of the container. Bigger plants are better off in bigger pots, but a small plant can look extra tiny in a large container.

As you choose pots and other containers, keep a couple things in mind:

» **Make sure the pot complements the plant.** You have a huge choice of container sizes, styles, colors, and materials, so think carefully about how you pair plants with pots.

» **Group different pot sizes and shapes.** Start with one big pot and then surround it with smaller pots of varying shapes and sizes. It helps to stick to one material, like clay or wood, and one style, like rustic or modern. Your display can get busy looking if you mix too many kinds of pots. See Figure 7-1.

FIGURE 7-1:
You can create your own jungle with a collection of small and large houseplants grouped together.

Fusionstudio/Shutterstock

The following sections provide a rundown of container materials, shapes, features, and so on.

Examining standard container materials

What a container is made of is actually very important, and it's something you should be aware of when searching for the perfect container. For example, you want a container that

» Is nontoxic to houseplants

» Doesn't overheat quickly when exposed to the sun

» Is durable enough to serve and support its contents and look good on display

Here are the container material options you're likely to encounter:

>> **Plastic:** Lots of containers are made of plastic, from flimsy to substantial. It's an extremely practical, inexpensive, and versatile material. However, it doesn't breathe well, so it tends to hold in moisture, which may or may not be a problem for your chosen plants.

If you go with plastic, have fun — don't limit yourself to the plain white or green plastic pots you see everywhere. With a little searching, you can find many other colors and patterns. Some of the better faux terra cotta plastic pots are really quite attractive and are a great lightweight alternative to pottery or real terra cotta. If you opt for self-watering plastic containers, make sure they have an overflow, so your plants won't be overwatered. See Chapter 6 for more information on self-watering pots.

REMEMBER

One very beneficial feature of plastic pots is their lighter weight, especially compared to terra cotta or ceramic pots. This is especially helpful for large houseplants that must be moved periodically.

>> **Terra cotta:** Technically, terra cotta is unglazed pottery. It's a garden classic that looks handsome in many settings, and it's generally quite affordable. Drawbacks? Well, it wicks moisture away from plant root systems, and over time, it tends to develop cracks. It can also become encrusted with mineral deposits from water and fertilizer and promote the growth of algae. Plants that really like to dry out, like cacti and succulents, are very happy in terra cotta containers.

>> **Glazed pottery:** With glazed earthenware pots, you get to enjoy the heftier weight of clay but with more color options — and perhaps more elegance. These containers are durable. They tend to draw the moisture out of potting material slower than terra cotta pots do.

>> **Wood:** Containers made of wood, especially softwoods like pine and fir, sop up moisture from potting material and eventually rot or fall apart, yet there's no denying the wonderful rustic look they give your plants. The solution may be to nest a plastic pot inside a wooden container. Otherwise, you may get more use out of something constructed from rot-resistant woods such as cedar or teak.

>> **Metal:** You can press metal containers into houseplant-holding service. Remember the need for a drainage hole and beware of displaying a metal container in full sun, which causes it and its contents to really heat up. Some possibilities include old olive-oil containers, buckets, and cast-iron kettles. Rust can be an issue with some metal containers. Containers made of stainless steel and galvanized steel will hold up longer. To be on the safe side, always

thoroughly clean out these containers to remove any food or other residue from them. I always run them through the dishwater.

>> **Fiberglass and resin:** These containers are durable and very attractive. Some of the better ones look strikingly like stone, but they're not as heavy. The best ones are a bit pricey.

Getting creative with containers

Unusual containers and everyday items recycled as containers can be a lot of fun and add unexpected beauty or whimsy to your houseplant displays. If the item isn't entirely suitable (maybe it's an odd shape or not able to provide good drainage), simply nest a plastic pot inside it and let your growing plant hide the actual container from view over time. Check out these options:

>> **Hanging baskets:** Some possibilities include plastic, clay, wood, and coconut-*coir* (fiber) or moss-lined wire rigs. With a hanging basket (see Figure 7-2), always make sure that you've accounted for the weight when the houseplant is freshly watered. Also ensure that it's adequately supported by wires, chain, string, rope, or what have you because a full hanging basket can be quite heavy.

>> **Wall containers:** A wall garden is a clever and often quite charming way to display plants. You fasten wall containers to a vertical surface (or a trellis against a wall), preferably at eye level so you can readily appreciate your plants.

Many containers intended for this use have one flat side so they fit flush against the wall (these containers are sometimes called *half pots*); though this feature isn't a requirement, it does look better and allow the houseplants within to grow upright. Obviously, the supporting wire, brackets, or hooks have to be equal to the job, and that means holding the weight of a *filled* container. Although you can rig something yourself, well-stocked garden-supply stores often have a nice selection of wall containers, which come with whatever support is necessary.

>> **Old shoes and boots, tea kettles, wicker baskets, cookie tins, and more:** You can recycle all sorts of wacky and whimsical objects to hold and display potted houseplants — just use your imagination! Browse garage sales, thrift shops, junk piles, or even your own garage, basement, or attic. Any vessel of water-resistant material can be a candidate. Avoid containers that at one time held toxic chemicals, as well as those constructed of wood products that contained harmful preservatives.

FIGURE 7-2:
My *Begonia boliviensis* 'Santa Barbara' works perfectly in this coir-lined hanging basket.

Growing houseplants hydroponically in self-watering containers

Self-watering pots have made it easy to grow houseplants *hydroponically*, or without any soil at all. The most frequently used media is *lightweight expanded clay aggregate*, or *LECA* (small clay pellets or balls). I have tried growing some of my moth orchids in this media and have been very pleased with the results.

I've also found hydroponic growing is a great solution for houseplants that prefer to be kept uniformly damp but not wet — African violets and their relatives and most small foliage plants are examples.

The principles of these pots are quite simple. One pot holds the potting material and fits inside a larger outside pot that serves as a water reservoir. A rope or wick threads through the bottom of the inner pot, and the ends of the wick dip into the water of the larger pot's reservoir (see Figure 7-3). The water travels via the wick into the potting mixture of the top pot. There is a large range of these pots available at various retail outlets.

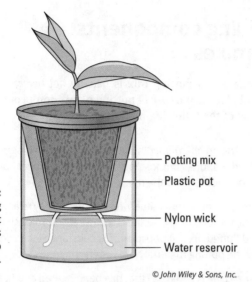

FIGURE 7-3:
A self-watering
pot is excellent
for houseplants
that prefer not to
dry out.

Potting mix
Plastic pot
Nylon wick
Water reservoir

© John Wiley & Sons, Inc.

Getting the Right Potting Mix

Because a container-grown houseplant is confined to its space, its roots can only find nourishment and stability in whatever potting material you provide. So potting mix isn't the place to cut corners, and it's worth the effort to provide a welcoming environment for your houseplants. The following sections give you info on choosing potting material or making your own.

Comparing potting mix to soil

TIP

You may be surprised to find out that most of the materials used to pot houseplants don't contain soil. Why? Because garden soil varies so much in quality. It can be heavy red clay (not great for most houseplants because it has poor drainage), high-quality garden loam (rare and hard to find), or compost (which is heavy but can be a good component of a potting mix). Soil by itself, even the good stuff, usually doesn't drain sufficiently for most houseplants, so combining even the best compost or soil with peat moss, HydraFiber, coir, perlite, finely ground and composted bark, or vermiculite is almost always called for.

Another drawback to soil is that it may contain weed seeds, insect eggs, or disease organisms, unwelcome guests you may not discover until it's too late.

Understanding components of potting mixes

Material sold as container or potting mix is usually *not* heavy and dense. Most commercial mixes sold for the purpose of potting plants don't contain soil. Rather, they're a combination of the following materials:

» **Organic matter:** The *organic matter* in potting mix is typically some or all of the following: dried manure, compost, peat moss, HydraFiber®, and finely ground bark. It adds nutrients to the mix.

» **Perlite:** *Perlite* appears as crunchy little white pebbles (they're actually smaller than most pebbles); interestingly, perlite is a natural volcanic ash that's been superheated and fluffed up, like popcorn. This substance increases the flow of air while helping the potting material hold water.

» **Vermiculite:** *Vermiculite* is a mineral that has been heated and fluffed up, though its form is flat and flaky. It increases airflow, retains moisture, and helps make minerals accessible to your plants.

» **Coarse sand:** The sand in potting mixes isn't beach sand, which is too salty, or river sand, which is too fine and smooth. Coarse sand, which is usually crushed quartz, sandstone, or granite, helps with drainage.

» **Moisture-retaining or water-storing gels:** When they encounter water, these gels swell and then slowly release the water back into the potting mix over time. See the nearby sidebar for more details about these materials.

» **Composted bark:** This is usually finely ground pine bark that has been composted.

» **Fertilizer beads:** These fertilizer sources usually look like tiny yellow or brownish round pellets or ball bearings and contain a fertilizer that releases gradually over a few months.

RETAINING WATER WITH POLYMER GELS

Moisture-retaining soil polymer gels are a good idea if your pots dry out really fast. If you go on vacation or are simply not the sort of person to water diligently, these gels naturally absorb moisture when you water the plant, swell up with it, and then gradually release it to the roots for use between waterings. They come in crystal form and should be mixed into the soil prior to planting. Follow package instructions; even a little too much makes your soil mixture erupt into a sticky mess when you first water it.

>> **Coir:** You can use *coir,* or shredded coconut husks, as a substitute for peat moss. Be sure to wash it well before you use it because it can contain root-damaging salts.

>> **Charcoal:** Manufacturers include a bit of charcoal in potting mix mainly to absorb odors and gases from the natural decomposition process of the other ingredients.

Most potted houseplants are perfectly happy with a general, all-purpose potting mix. You may want to buy a more specialized one if you're growing something with special needs — for instance, potted cacti and succulents prefer a higher sand or perlite content.

PEAT MOSS: YAY OR NAY?

For years peat moss has been a standard potting mix component, but sometimes it gets bad press. Here are a few of the pros and cons of this material.

Pros:

- It is very effective at retaining moisture in the potting material.
- It mixes well with any of the other materials commonly added to potting mixes.
- It is sterile, so it is free of disease organisms, weed seeds, and insects.
- It prevents the potting material from compacting.

Cons:

- Peat moss is not a completely renewable resource, and the harvesting of it releases methane and carbon dioxide that can contribute to global warming.
- It has become quite expensive these days and is more difficult to find from garden suppliers.
- It can be difficult to rewet after it has dried out.

An alternative to peat moss is HydraFiber, which is fine-textured processed pine wood and bark. It's great as a potting mix component for houseplants that appreciate consistent moisture. You can purchase it at garden centers and home stores and find it in some premade potting mixes.

Of course, if you're aware of a certain houseplant's special requirements, nothing's wrong with buying regular potting soil and then mixing in whatever else the plant needs — sand, shredded bark, peat moss, HydraFiber, coir, moisture-retaining gels, and so on.

TIP

You may see *sterile* potting mix touted on bags and bins. That label means the mix has been heat-treated to kill possible pests, diseases, and weed seeds. That's a good thing!

If you want to be sure that the mix you're using is free of insects and diseases, you can sterilize it by microwaving it in a microwave-safe container for 2 to 3 minutes on the High setting. Lightly cover to prevent any spatter.

REMEMBER

You get what you pay for. Cheap potting mixes seem to have poorly shredded bark or lack perlite or vermiculite. You can't always rip open a bag in the store and shove your hand in it to check it out (though some places have a display of samples to help you choose). So read the bag with care — not the claims about how terrific the contents are, but the list of ingredients and their various percentages.

Figuring out which potting materials are best

You may have been thinking while you read the preceding section, "How the heck am I supposed to choose a potting material when none of them are perfect?" Don't worry. The individual potting materials are rarely used by themselves — they're usually formulated into mixtures so the final product will retain water, drain well, and last a reasonable amount of time. Every houseplant grower has their favorite potting mix formulation — kind of like how every baker has their favorite apple pie recipe.

TIP

The combination of potting materials that works best for your houseplants depends on various factors. Answer the following questions to get an idea of what you need:

>> **How often do you water?** If you tend to be heavy-handed with the sprinkling can or hose, use materials that drain well and decompose slowly, such as medium fir bark, pine bark, or coarse perlite,

>> **What type of houseplants are you growing?** Most houseplants that naturally grow on or in soil or organic matter prefer to be kept slightly damp all the time, whereas those that live in trees, like bromeliads or air plants, or

those that grow on rocks or in sandy areas, like cacti and succulents, want to dry out thoroughly between waterings. When you browse catalog listings or search online for information about your plants, look for the recommended growing conditions or ask the grower you're buying from.

>> **How mature are your plants?** Large plants usually do best in coarse potting materials, and small plants do better in fine potting materials. (See the next section for information on mixing potting material to suit your plants.)

>> **How big are the roots of your plants?** In general, small roots grow better in fine, water-retentive materials like combinations of HydraFiber, peat moss, coir, vermiculite, compost, and fine perlite. Large roots perform best in coarse materials like coarse perlite, chunky perlite, and bark chips.

Whipping up your own mix

You can create your own potting mix, but remember that it's not really about saving money because you have to purchase individual ingredients separately and then mix them. It's certainly not a matter of saving time, either. What it is, my friend, is a matter of control. When you make your own mix, you can ensure every bit of it is of good and consistent quality. Best of all, you can customize. If the store-bought mix seems too heavy, you can easily lighten it by stirring in some more perlite or finely ground bark. The most commonly available bark is composted hardwood, fir, or pine bark — all are fine to use.

Here are some recipes to follow when stirring up a batch of your own mix:

>> **A standard mix, suitable for most common houseplants:** One part high-grade compost (packaged or your own), one part coir, peat moss, HydraFiber. and one part perlite or coarse sand

>> **A light mix, for plants that like good drainage, like cacti and succulents:** Two parts coir, peat moss, or HydraFiber, one part coarse sand, and one part perlite

>> **A heavy mix, for plants that like their potting material more moisture-retentive:** One part peat moss or HydraFiber, two parts fine bark or composted bark, and one part sand or perlite

>> **Large houseplant mix:** One part sterilized high-quality topsoil, one part peat moss or, two parts fine bark, and one part sand or perlite

Repotting Houseplants without Fear

For some, the idea of repotting or transplanting your houseplants is intimidating. However, you should have no fear because the process is simple and straightforward. I have laid out the steps in this section. Don't worry if everything does not go exactly as planned. Plants are very forgiving.

To properly plant a container, follow these steps:

1. **Choose a container wider and a little deeper than the pot you're taking the houseplant from (see Figure 7-4).**

FIGURE 7-4:
A cross-section of a container, ready for planting.

2. **Knock the plant out of its current pot by putting your hand over the surface of the pot to retain the soil and protect the plant as you hold the pot upside down and tap its rim on a hard surface or thump the bottom of the pot with your fist.**

TIP

Squeezing the side of a plastic pot also helps. If the plant still won't come out of the pot, break or cut the container. Don't try to pull it out by grabbing the top of the plant.

3. **If the roots are not tightly bound in the pot, you can run a butter knife around the inside of the pot to release the plant. If the roots are firmly wound around the bottom and sides of the pot, pry them loose with your fingers or cut through them shallowly (vertically) with a sharp knife.**

4. **Put enough potting mix in the bottom of the pot to bring the *crown* of the plant (the spot where the roots join the stem, or, if you can't see the roots, the top of the root ball) about even with the top of the pot.**

5. **Fill the potting mix in and around the root ball, making sure you press it firmly, to eliminate any air pockets.**

6. **Water the plant deeply with a slow stream of water until the water flows freely from drainage holes at the bottom of the pot.**

    If the potting mix around the root ball settles, fill in the depression with more potting material.

7. **To make the planted container look neater and to prevent the potting material from washing out when you water it cover the top of potting material with a layer of fine-texture mulch or sheet moss.**

    This will keep the potting material moist and cool, allowing the plant to become established.

TIP

Many people use pebbles in their containers, which aren't necessary, especially with today's well-drained potting materials and containers that have sufficient drainage holes in the bottom.

Playing the Matching Game — the Right Plants for the Right Pots

So you're ready to start choosing plants. Almost any sort of houseplant can adapt to life in any type of container. For instance, you can try a small foliage plant in a small ceramic pot; or you can grow a wide array of specimen-size foliage plants like dracaenas, scheffleras, dieffenbachias or flowering plants like hibiscus in a big planter box or tub. (Don't know what any of those houseplants are? Don't worry! I describe them all in Part 3.)

REMEMBER

A container display looks best and serves its residents best when plants and pots are in proportion to one another. You don't want a little plant to get lost in a big pot. Another factor to consider is that you may tend to overwater a plant in an oversized pot because all that extra potting material won't dry out enough between waterings. If in doubt, it's better to err on the smaller size container-wise.

At the other end of the size spectrum, it's not practical or attractive to allow a large plant to teeter or look top-heavy in a too-small pot. Plus, the roots need to fit without being crammed in the container. So make a match. (Consider the plant's potential mature size, not the size of the youngster you first install.)

Think about what you want your display to do for you. Then read on for some advice on how to pull it off.

Up-close-and-personal displays

If you like to display potted plants where you're nose to nose with them almost daily, choose houseplants with interesting details. I'm talking plants with pretty or very colorful blooms, fragrant flowers or foliage, unusually shaped or colored leaves, or edible parts.

TIP

If you're placing a container indoors on a wooden floor or any surface that is not waterproof (or on the deck if you are summering out some of your houseplants), add pieces of molded baked clay or pot feet underneath the container to allow it to drain and permit the surface underneath the container to dry and prevent rotting or discoloration of the surface of the flooring. Figure 7-5 shows how potted feet can provide drainage for the container and protection for the surface on which it's placed.

FIGURE 7-5:
Pot feet provide drainage and protection for the surface below the pot.

Brandon Blinkenberg/Shutterstock

Tucked-in attention-grabbers

For pots that you strategically position to draw interest to their part of the room, you want lush, dramatic leaves, big flowers, and attention-grabbing colors — anything that causes you and your visitors to trot over for a closer look. Avoid houseplants with fine or wispy textured leaves and stems, plants with small or fleeting flowers, and ones with dark colors (which recede into the shadows).

Containers of mixed company

No rule says a container should hold only a single houseplant, so feel free to tuck in several types, in effect making a mini container garden (see the nearby sidebar). Remember, when planting, don't crowd — the plants will fill in and grow upward and outward, and you want the show to last a while and not require constant editing. (In other words, you want to avoid a lot of pruning, trimming, and even the necessity of taking out an entire plant that's too crowded.) Here are a few guidelines to get you started:

>> Combine plants of similar light and moisture needs.

>> Include both foliage and flowering plants.

>> Combine herbs like thyme that don't have significant flowers with other plants that have showier flowers like some of the flowering begonias.

>> Include plants of different forms: spiky or strappy-leaved, rounded or mounded, and low and trailing. This sort of variety works well in your indoor garden and translates easily to container compositions, just on a smaller scale.

>> Position taller plants in the middle (or to the back if you plan to display the container against a wall so people can't view the plants from behind); put shorter plants at the taller plants' feet.

>> Place plants with trailing or cascading stems at the very edge so they can get where they want to go unimpeded.

Whether you mix different plants in one pot or decide to plant single-plant pots and fiddle with multi-pot displays, here are a few more ideas that lead to good-looking results:

>> **Use foliage color and texture.** Flowers eventually go out of bloom, but if you mix in some foliage plants, like various dracaenas, philodendrons, yuccas, crotons, and ferns. the display still looks good.

>> **Move the best plants forward.** When a pot is really looking good, move it up front where people can see it.

>> **Rotate your containers.** Plants naturally lean toward the sun, and pot displays can start to look one-sided if you do nothing. During peak growing, turn each pot a quarter-turn every few days or at least once a week, and your displays will look nicely balanced.

Mixing colors, foliage, or flowers in a containerized display is an art, and when done well, it makes a wonderful impression — something you're proud of and delighted with. Remember, the color can come from foliage as well as flowers, and colorful foliage often delivers a longer-lasting show. Here are some color combinations you can try:

>> **Bold primary colors:** Mix one or two plants each of blue, yellow, and red. Look for colors of similar strength or intensity.

>> **Compatible combos:** Colors that fall between the primary colors (called *secondary colors*) tend to be harmonious companions. Try yellow-orange with violet-blue or red-orange with blue-green.

>> **Pastel hues:** Stick to selections of softer hues (pink, pale yellow, soft blue, light purple, cream rather than white, and so on). Complement your flowering plants with gentler-hued foliage plants such as those with gray, silver, or sage-green leaves.

>> **Single-color shows:** Combine several different plants that share the same flower or foliage color. Sure, you may end up with slight variations in tone, but you actually want that; varying the shade of your chosen color makes a more diverse and interesting display. Firm matches or all the same plant can end up looking like a dense color blob.

>> **Attractive opposites:** Contrasting colors always look fabulous together, particularly if they're of similar strength or intensity. Try blue with orange or purple with yellow.

>> **Color boosts:** Favor one hue, say, purple, and then tuck in a similar hue for subtle contrast, such as a blue companion. Try an all-red show with a dash of orange or yellow, or an all-pink display with a jolt of red, and so on — you get the idea!

>> **An all-foliage display:** Green is a color, too! If you're putting a pot in a shady spot in your indoor garden, consider filling it with a variety of leafy plants of different forms and slightly different shades of green. Many of the foliage plants, like some of the tradescantias, display brilliant leaf colors. This setup makes for great texture and complexity.

REMEMBER

Houseplant admirers grow plenty of plants mainly for their colorful or patterned leaves. Examples include cannas, caladiums, coleus, ferns, and bromeliads, just to name a few.

Chapter **8**

Multiplying Your Favorite Houseplants

What can be more fun than producing more of the plants you love for free? Well, almost free. Horticultural folks refer to multiplying your own plants as *plant propagation.* Because this subject can be quite involved, you can find entire books devoted to it. In this chapter, I focus only on what you need to know as a houseplant grower.

Cloning Your Plants through Vegetative Reproduction

Vegetative reproduction (also known as *vegetative propagation, vegetative multiplication,* or *vegetative cloning*) is any form of asexual plant reproduction in which a new plant grows from a fragment of the parent plant. Unlike sexual reproduction (see the "Growing Plants from Seeds: Sexual Reproduction" section later in this chapter), no transference of male and female genetic material occurs. As a result, this form of reproduction or multiplying enables you to produce more plants exactly like the parent. No change in the genetic makeup of the new plants happens.

In fact, you may have already done vegetative reproduction by, for example, putting a stem from a favorite houseplant in water, waiting for it to develop some roots, and then potting it.

Cutting and rooting stems

Rooting stem cuttings (see Figure 8-1) is the most used method to propagate most houseplants. Make sure you have these supplies handy before getting started:

» A clean pot (a 4" pot will do)

» Soilless potting mix

» A sharp blade (knife or single edged razor blade)

» A plastic bag that will fit the diameter of the pot

» Sticks or bamboo stakes (chopsticks work great!) to prop up the plastic bag

» Rubber band to secure the bag to the pot.

Here are the steps to take for rooting stem cuttings:

1. **Get a clean, preferably new pot (because a new one is sterile) or soak a used pot for few hours in a 1:10 solution of chlorine bleach to water to sterilize it.**

    Rinse the pot thoroughly after soaking to remove the chlorine residue.

2. **Obtain some soilless potting mix, available at any garden center, sterilize it, and fill the pot to within an inch or so of the rim.**

    Soilless potting mix works much better than garden soil because it drains well. It is best to dampen the mix in the package before you use it. When you place the dampened mix in the rooting container, it should not need to be watered again until the cutting is rooted.

WARNING

    Although most of the commercial mixes say they're sterile, I don't take their word for it. Many times, this material has been stored outdoors and exposed to the elements.

TIP

    To sterilize it, heat the dampened potting material by cooking it in an oven for 30 minutes until it reaches 180°F, or microwave it on High for 2 to 3 minutes. This kills all the disease organisms, weed seeds, insects, and their eggs.

3. **Use a sterile sharp blade to cut off a healthy piece of the plant's stem (about 3 to 4 inches [7.5 to 10 centimeters]) with two or three leaves attached (see Figure 8-1A).**

I prefer using a new single-edged straight razor blade rather than a knife because I know it's extremely sharp and sterile.

4. **Dip the cut end of the cutting in a powder or liquid rooting hormone. This is optional but in many situations it will result in faster and more vigorous rooting.**

I prefer the liquid form because the cut surface absorbs it better.

5. **Slightly tamp down the surface of the potting material in the pot and then use a pencil, *dibble* (a small gardening tool with a pointed end), or chopstick to make a hole in the medium about the size of the diameter of the stem cutting.**

6. **Place the cutting in the hole and press the potting mix firmly around the stem.**

You want to make sure the stem stands on its own.

7. **Place three or four 12" vertical bamboo sticks into the potting material around the inside rim of the pot, as shown in Figure 8-1B. They should extend about 8" above the potting mix in the pot, depending on the depth of the pot into which the stakes are placed. The size of the stake can vary to accommodate the size of the cutting.**

The bamboo sticks will support the plastic bag you place over the pot in Step 8.

8. **Secure a clear plastic bag over the outside rim of the pot with a rubber band.**

This bag serves as a miniature greenhouse for the cutting and provides the high humidity it needs to become rooted. In most cases, if the potting mix is damp when the pot is covered with the plastic bag, the cutting doesn't need to be watered again until the roots form because the moisture is recirculated inside the bag.

Don't allow the bag to touch the leaves of the cutting because dampness on the inside of the bag can cause diseases to form on the leaves.

9. **Place the bagged pot in an area with a temperature of 65 to 75°F (18 to 23°C) where there's bright light but no direct sunlight.**

Direct sunlight will cook the plant inside the bag.

10. **Wait.**

The time it takes for the roots to form varies greatly depending on the type of cutting. If they're soft green stems, like you'd find on geraniums, begonias, coleus, and most smaller foliage plants, they may be rooted in four to six weeks or even sooner. If the stems are brown and woody, like those on cuttings of larger growing tropical shrubs, like hibiscus and small growing trees like rubber plants and dracaenas., it can take two to three weeks longer.

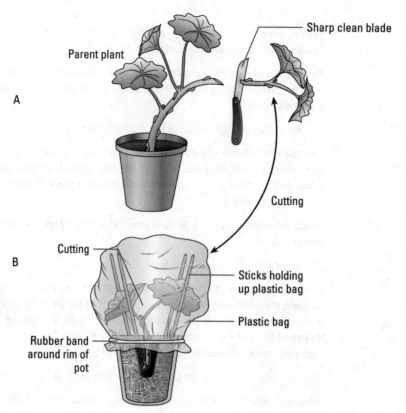

Parent plant

A

Sharp clean blade

Cutting

B

Cutting

Sticks holding
up plastic bag

Plastic bag

Rubber band
around rim of
pot

FIGURE 8-1:
Cut with a sterile
blade (A) and add
sticks to support
the plastic
bag (B).

11. When sufficient time for roots to form has passed, remove the plastic bag and gently tug on the cutting.

12. If you feel resistance when you slightly tug on the cutting that indicates that the cutting is firmly rooted, you can continue to grow it on in this pot or, if necessary, move it to a larger pot. Then water it well.

Alternatively, if the roots aren't well established, moisten the potting material if needed, cover the pot with the plastic bag, put the pot back where it was, and wait a little longer.

Reproducing with leaf cuttings

Leaf cuttings are a slight variation from stem cuttings. African violets and other plants with succulent leaves can be propagated by removing healthy leaves from the center of the plant and either placing them in potting mix, as shown in Figure 8-2, or suspending the leaf stem in water.

FIGURE 8-2:
African violets can be propagated from a leaf cutting started in a pot of perlite and peat moss.

Pegasene/Shutterstock

Houseplants with large leaves that have prominent veins, like rex begonias, can be propagated by laying the leaf on a bed of moist sterile potting media in a plastic container and cutting some of the main veins with a sterile sharp knife or razor blade (see Figure 8-3). Weigh the cut areas down with pebbles to be sure that the cuts actually touch the potting media. Cover the container with a clear plastic lid or plastic wrap. In several weeks, you'll see baby plants sprouting from the cuts. Don't be too eager to transplant these babies. Wait until they are a couple inches (about 5 cm) tall and have a well-developed root system before you transplant them into their own container.

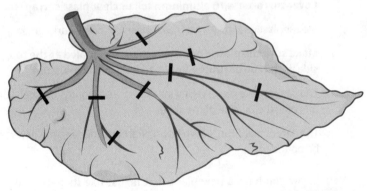

FIGURE 8-3:
One way to multiply houseplants like begonias is to cut the main veins of the leaves, prompting new plants to sprout from the veins.

© John Wiley & Sons, Inc.

Propagating by air layering

Air layering is a very useful form of propagation for large houseplants with thick stems like dracaenas and dieffenbachias. The idea is that you can produce a plant on top of a plant. It seems strange, but it really works.

Air layering involves propagating a plant by cutting partway into a stem or branch and packing the area with moist media, commonly sphagnum moss. Then you cover the moss-packed area with a waterproof sheath to hold in the moisture and stimulate root formation. When the stem or branch forms roots, you can remove the covering to expose an independent plant.

To air layer, pick a sturdy limb or stem on your houseplant that's about pencil diameter and stick to the following steps:

1. **Girdle the stem with a sterile sharp knife or single-edged razor blade.**

   Girdling means removing a band of bark about 1 to 2 inches wide all the way around the stem, as shown in Figure 8-4A. This encourages root formation at the open area.

2. **Wrap the girdled stem with a handful of long-fibered sphagnum moss (available at most garden stores or online) that has been dampened (as in Figure 8-4B).**

   Make sure to squeeze any excess water from the moss. You want it damp, but not wet.

3. **Cover this area with aluminum foil or clear plastic wrap (see Figure 8-4C).**

   A clear plastic sandwich bag that's been cut open works great.

TIP

4. **Make sure the plastic or other covering is sealed at the top, bottom, and side with tape or rubber bands to hold in the moisture.**

   You can remove the covering in two or three months or when you see roots touching the outside of the sheet.

   The parent plant can stay in its original container and the new rooted plant can be potted up.

Voila! Now you have a new plant that is just like its parent. Water the new plant in well.

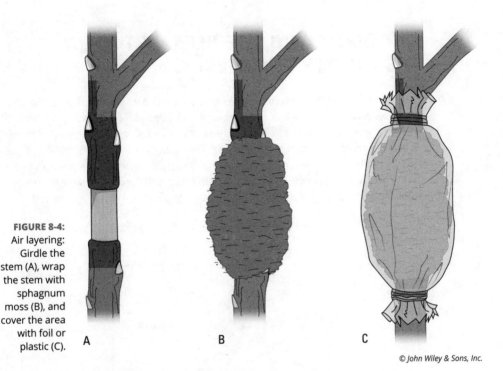

FIGURE 8-4:
Air layering:
Girdle the
stem (A), wrap
the stem with
sphagnum
moss (B), and
cover the area
with foil or
plastic (C).

A   B   C

Growing Plants from Seeds: Sexual Reproduction

Most folks don't grow their houseplants from seeds. They usually buy mature plants. However, if you want to grow a particular plant that you can't find as a mature plant and you see its seeds in a catalog, at a garden store, or online, or if you want to grow a wide variety of a certain plant (like some of the succulents or cacti) and you can buy a seed packet of mixed varieties, you may be up for this adventure. It's the most economical way to start a plant collection, and it's fun! You can also try reproducing some of the palms and many gesneriads and begonias from seeds.

As you can see from Figure 8-5, seeds are little packages of life that contain all the critical parts they need to grow:

>> A seed coat to protect the seed from drying out

>> A food source (called the *endosperm*) to get the plant started when it sprouts

>> A live embryo — the spark of life — from which leaves, stems, and roots grow

THE BIRDS AND THE BEES (ACTUALLY, IT'S MOSTLY THE BEES)

When pollen is transferred from one flower to another (that's where the bees come in), the process is called *pollination*. It begins when a bee deposits pollen grains from the *stamen* (the male part of the flower) on the *stigma* (the sticky tip) of the *pistil* (the female part of the flower). The pollen grains grow down through the *style* (the cylinder connecting the pistil to the flower's ovary). When a growing pollen tube reaches and is united with an *ovule,* or egg, in the ovary, fertilization occurs, and the ovule develops into a seed. This whole process is referred to as *sexual reproduction.* Whew! I was sweating explaining all this sexual stuff.

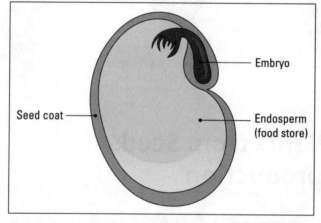

Embryo

Seed coat

Endosperm
(food store)

FIGURE 8-5:
The basic
components of
most seeds.

© John Wiley & Sons, Inc.

Recognizing the different kinds of seeds

When buying seeds, you need to be aware of the broad categories of seeds and their characteristics. Here are the most common forms and types of seeds that you find at garden stores, in seed catalogs, and online:

>> **Open pollinated seeds:** These seeds come from varieties that are genetically true to type, so their seeds produce a plant similar to the parent. Heirloom varieties produce open pollinated seeds, but not all open pollinated seeds produce heirlooms. Most houseplant seeds fall in this category.

>> **F_1 hybrid seeds:** Also referred to as *hybrid* seeds, F_1, or *first generation,* seeds are produced from specific parents with known characteristics resulting in offspring that will be highly predictable. F_1 seeds are popular for growing

veggies such as tomatoes because they usually are resistant to various diseases. With flowers, especially annuals, hybrids often have larger flowers and disease resistance.

» **GMO seeds:** GMO stands for *genetically modified organism,* and it refers to any organism with genetic material that has been altered using genetic engineering techniques. This subject is controversial, and I don't discuss it here because these seeds aren't available to the houseplant grower. They're seeds of major food crops used by some large commercial farms.

» **Organic seeds:** These seeds have been produced with no synthetic fertilizers or pesticides.

» **Conventional seeds:** These are most of the seeds that are produced and sold to the indoor gardener.

» **Treated seeds:** Some seeds are treated with a fungicide to prevent disease problems. A company selling seeds with this treatment must specify so on the seed packet. In most situations, fungicide-treated seeds aren't necessary or recommended for home gardeners. If you're an organic gardener who rejects chemicals, you don't want treated seeds.

» **Pelleted seeds:** Some seeds are extremely small and dustlike. (There are *one million* begonia seeds per ounce!) Hence, these tiny seeds are *pelleted,* or coated with an inert material to make them easier to sow.

Knowing the benefits of sowing seeds

Growing your own plants from seed is fun and rewarding, and it can be a practical choice. Here, I outline some of the key reasons to try growing your own plants from seed:

» **To produce large quantities of a variety:** Plants look better when they're planted in masses or sweeps, but doing so can get expensive. Growing them from seed is an economical way to produce many plants of the same type.

» **To produce plants that you can't get at your local garden center:** For example, I often can't find many gesneriads and begonias at any garden center. So, I buy the seeds of these varieties and grow them myself.

TIP

Many plant societies like The Gesneriad Society, begonia societies, and carnivorous plant societies offer seeds of unusual or rare varieties and hybrids to their members. See the appendix for a list of some of these societies.

» **To enjoy the chance to discover something new:** With many mixed seed selections, you never know exactly what you'll get. You may produce a new variety of a plant you've never tried before.

>> **To have fun:** Sowing your own seeds is fun. It also gives you bragging rights. You can say with pride, "I grew these plants from seed!" Then your fellow plant lovers may respect your skills even more.

Buying seeds: What to keep in mind

Success with growing houseplants from seed depends on many factors. Here, I outline some of the most important:

>> **Buy from a reputable company.** You can find plenty of dependable seed companies out there. Talk with people in your online plant forums or in-person friends, members of plant societies, and trusted houseplant growers to find out their favorite seed sources. Cheap outdated seeds are no bargain because they may not grow or may have low germination rates, so you'll have to spend more money buying more seeds.

>> **Check the seed packet for the date of packaging, germination percentage, and sell-by date.** The *germination rate* (the percentage of the seed that's expected to sprout) is sometimes also on the packet. This information may not be available if the seeds are from a plant society or specialty seed provider.

>> **Preserve the freshness of the seeds by storing them in a cool, dry place.** Some seeds stay viable longer than others. I like to store my opened seed packets in a sealed jar in which I place a drying agent like a small packet of evaporated dried milk or silica gel (available at craft stores). Put the sealed jar in the refrigerator until you need to sow more of these seeds. Most seeds can be stored for years using this method.

SAVING YOUR OWN SEEDS

Saving the seeds from your own plants is fun, and can be especially worthwhile if the seed is rare, expensive, or not readily available.

- Harvest seeds when they mature. Mature seeds are usually brown and dry. If they're green and not mature, they likely won't sprout.

- Select seeds from your most healthy and vigorous plants. Notice which flowers and leaves are larger and have better color. You want these plants to be your seed bearers.

- If the seeds are in a dried pod, tear open the pod to remove the individual seeds.

- If the seeds are inside a fleshly fruit, remove any pulp and soak the seeds in water overnight. You have to do this for seeds from the fleshy fruits of some cacti. You want to soak off any remaining bits of pulp because it can interfere with germination.

- Store the seeds in a cool, dry place. When storing seeds in a sealed container, add a drying agent like silica gel or evaporated dry milk.

- Label the container that holds the seeds. Include the name of the variety, when it was harvested, and from where.

- Figure out which seeds will likely store well and the best way to store them. From trial and error, you can find out which seeds store well and which should be planted right away. In general, it's best to store your seeds in paper packets. Seeds stored in sealed foil packets may be prone to drying out and won't last as long once the seed packet has been opened.

Testing seeds

If you harvest your own seeds or run across a packet of storebought seeds you've had for a while, you can try one of the following testing techniques to see if they're still viable.

Floating technique

If you pour your seeds into a container of water and they float, more than likely they're poor germinators. However, if your seeds sink to the bottom of the container, they should still be viable. This technique isn't 100 percent reliable, but it's a quick way of checking older seeds to see which ones are likely viable before planting them. Keep in mind that some seeds float regardless of their viability.

Wet towel technique

Major seed companies use the simple wet towel technique to check seed viability and predict germination rates. You can do this test yourself by following these easy steps:

1. **Wet a paper towel.**

2. **Sprinkle a sample of your seeds on the towel.**

3. **Roll up the paper towel, place it in a plastic bag, seal it and label it with the plant name so you don't forget which seed you sowed.**

4. **Place the bag in a dimly lit area where the temperature is 70 to 75°F (21 to 24°C).**

   Don't place it in direct sunlight.

5. **Check it every few days to see if the seeds have sprouted as in Figure 8-6.**

FIGURE 8-6:
The wet towel
technique.

TIP

Some seeds have hard seed coats that benefit from a technique called *scarification*. This mechanical technique involves weakening, opening, or otherwise penetrating the coat of a seed to encourage germination by allowing water to enter the seed. A simple way to accomplish this is to scrape the back of the seed on sandpaper until you see that the seed coat has been penetrated. The seed coat is usually darker than the rest of the seed. This technique is most useful on larger seeds with hard seed coats. At this point you can plant the seed directly or use the presprouting techniques explained above.

Getting better results from sowing seed

Adequate light, soil moisture, correct germination temperatures, and sterile or pasteurized potting mixes are important considerations in seed starting. Here are some suggestions for maximizing the potential of your seeds:

REMEMBER

>> **Make sure you have adequate artificial or natural light.** This factor is critical because some seeds need to be exposed to light to germinate well. Check the seed packet or seed supplier for specific information. For seedlings that need strong light to grow into sturdy plants, I suggest you choose a bright

south-facing window or sufficient fluorescent or LED lights, and then place the seedlings close to (usually a few inches from) the light source. Refer to Chapter 5 for more discussion about using growing lights.

>> **Check the seed packet or look online to find recommended germination temperatures for the seeds you're sowing.** Many seeds germinate at around 70°F (21°C). If your growing area is much cooler than the recommended temperature, germination can take longer, and in some cases, the germination rate will be low. If the growing area isn't at the recommended temperature for ideal germination, I suggest using seed starting mats (available at most horticultural suppliers). Make sure the heating mat is waterproof and designed for horticultural use, not for achy muscles.

>> **Use sterile or pasteurized seed starting potting mix.** Young seedlings are extremely vulnerable to diseases and insects, so using sterile or pasteurized potting mix is essential to protect them against these problems.

TIP

If you want to pasteurize you own seedling mix, place it in a metal container, put the container in the oven, and heat it until the mix reaches 180°F (82°C). Use a meat thermometer to measure the temperature, and then leave it in the oven for 30 minutes after it has reached this temperature. This baked potting mix smells like raisin bran, though my wife doesn't agree with my perception of its scent.

You can also pasteurize your potting mix using a microwave oven. Place it in a microwave-safe container and cook it on High for 2 minutes.

>> **Consider starting larger seeds like some of the tropical shrubs annuals in pots that they will be grown in.**

>> **Use flats for starting smaller seeds.** *Flats* are usually rectangular containers with small holes in the bottom for drainage. Clear plastic berry clamshells (see Figure 8-7), egg cartons, or vegetable containers are great to reuse for seed starting — and they're free!

>> **Initially water your seeds from the bottom by placing the seed container in about an inch (2.5 cm) of warm water for 15 minutes or so.** The potting material will gradually absorb the water, and the seeds won't be washed out, which can happen if the container is watered from the top. After the potting material has absorbed the water, let it drain, and place the container in a warm, dry place. Check the potting material periodically to make sure that it stays moist. If you're using a clear plastic clamshell, close the lid; for a container without a lid, use clear plastic wrap to hold in the moisture until the seeds germinate.

TIP

If you have extremely fine seeds, like begonia and gesneriad seeds, you can ease the process by mixing the seeds into a tablespoon or so of fine white sand before you sow them. Doing so can help you distribute the seeds more evenly.

FIGURE 8-7:
Use a plastic
container
to plant
smaller seeds.

Photo by Steven A. Frowine

Also check out seed starting kits offered in various seed catalogs, at garden centers, and online; they can make this job easier.

Thinning seedlings

You can easily sow too many seeds in a given space, especially if the seeds are very small. As a result, you end up with crowded seedlings battling each other for nutrients and light. If this scenario continues, all the plants will suffer. You need to step in and save the day by thinning.

TIP

To do so, use scissors to snip off any weak or unwanted seedlings at the surface level of the potting material. Don't try to pull them up because doing so can damage the plants next to the ones you remove.

Even though thinning can be an excruciating task, it's an important one. Not removing crowded and weak seedlings can lead to disease and poor growth of the stronger ones because of too much competition for water, light, and nutrients. You can refer to the seed packet for the correct spacing information.

Hardening off seedlings

After the young plants have grown in an enclosed container with very high humidity, constant soil moisture, and generally high temperatures for germination, they need to be weaned off this environment to get adjusted to their new growing space with average room humidity, more erratic levels of soil moisture, and usually lower room temperatures. This process, called *hardening off*, prepares them for their new environment.

The shock of introducing seedlings to a new setting too quickly can kill them. Follow these steps when hardening off your seedlings:

1. **Slowly reduce the frequency of watering so the plants dry out a little more than before.**

2. **Gradually lower the temperature where they're being grown until it's close to the new environment to which you'll introduce them.**

3. **Keep them in their original containers with the lid or plastic cover removed.**

4. **Watch the seedlings for several days to check how they're doing.**

5. **Gradually move them to a location with more light.**

    After a week or two, if they're still doing well, you can transplant them into larger pots (see the next section).

Transplanting seedlings

Transplanting your seedlings is a delicate procedure. Before you decide to uproot them, wait until the seedlings have at least one set of *true leaves* (developed foliage leaves; see Figure 8-8). Keep the following points in mind as you transplant your seedlings:

» **Whatever you do, don't pull the seedlings out of the potting material.** Gently pry them out with a spoon.

» **Use care when you separate them so you damage as few roots as possible.** If the roots of the seedlings are intertwined, gently tease them apart by hand or with a small fork.

» **Keep as much potting material on the roots as you can.** This will prevent excessive damage to the small roots encased in the potting material.

» **When you handle the seedlings, be careful not to squeeze the stems too hard or you'll damage them.** Handling seedlings by the leaves is usually a safer bet.

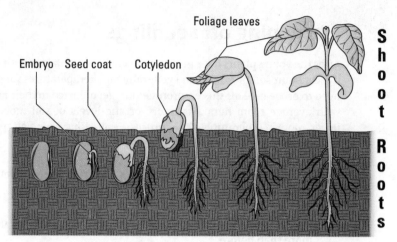

Foliage leaves

Embryo Seed coat Cotyledon

Shoots Roots

FIGURE 8-8:
How seedlings
develop.

© John Wiley & Sons, Inc.

>> **Make a generous hole for the seedling roots with a pencil or dibble (see Chapter 3 for more information on dibbles) so the roots won't get too scrunched when they're transplanted.** Firm press the potting material around the seedling roots.

>> **Carefully water the seedlings.** Be sure to push the seedlings upright if the watering knocks them over.

TIP

Make sure you water the seedlings well as you transplant them. Carefully monitor their watering needs because until their roots get established, they're vulnerable to drying out. After about a week, when they look strong, you can fertilize them with any all-purpose water-soluble fertilizer to give them a boost.

Chapter **9**

Keeping Your Houseplants Pest- and Disease-Free

Although houseplants are relatively pest- and disease-free plants, if you have them long enough, you'll eventually have to deal with an invasion of some bug or disease. Fortunately, there aren't many pests or diseases to contend with, and they aren't that difficult to identify. In this chapter, I stress the safest and most effective ways to control the most common pest and disease problems.

REMEMBER

Whether you're dealing with pests or diseases, always start with the least toxic solution for the issue. The more poisonous options should be your last line of defense because when you and your plants are indoors in your living space, you are more exposed to the vapors of these pesticides than you would be if these materials were applied outdoors. If you're careful and inspect your houseplants on a regular basis and detect problems before they progress too far, you'll rarely have to resort to highly poisonous solutions.

Preventing Problems before They Start

TIP

You can prevent most insect and disease problems with good plant sanitation. Here are some steps you can take to head off problems before they get out of hand:

>> **Always sterilize your cutting tools.** See the nearby sidebar, "How to sterilize your tools," for more information.

>> **Regularly inspect the tips of new growth, developing buds, the fronts and backs of flowers, and the undersides of leaves and where the leaves attach to the stems.** This is where most bugs hang out. Diseases tend to show up on the tops of the leaves and in the center of the plant where new growth emerges.

>> **Provide the best growing conditions possible.** When houseplants are under stress, they're more susceptible to diseases and insect infestations.

>> **When repotting, always use new or cleaned and sterilized pots.** All types of disease organisms and harmful salts can accumulate on older pots. See the nearby sidebar for information on sterilizing pots.

>> **Buy plants that are clean and healthy.** Beware of bargain or leftover plants — many have serious problems. Unless they're in excellent condition, stay away from them. Check out Chapter 2 for information on finding healthy plants to purchase.

>> **Don't allow weeds to infest your pots of houseplants.** They can harbor insects and diseases.

>> **Keep the floor or ground in your growing area free of weeds, dead leaves, and dead flowers.** Diseases and insects can hang out here.

HOW TO STERILIZE YOUR TOOLS

I use the following two methods of sterilization:

● **Chemical sterilization:** Soak your tools in a dilute household bleach solution — one part bleach to 10 parts water — for a few minutes before you use them. Most chemicals used to sterilize tools or pots, including bleach, are highly corrosive, so after you've sterilized your tools, be sure to thoroughly rinse them with clean water to prevent the metal from rusting. Make sure that you freshen your cleaning solution regularly because the chlorine in the bleach will evaporate and become ineffective after a day or so.

- **Heat sterilization:** This is a very fast and clean way to sterilize tools. You can use a compact propane torch, but I've found the most convenient option is a small butane hand torch (see Chapter 3) like the ones sold to caramelize the topping on crème brûlée. With these torches, you merely flame the cutting edges of the tool until they turn red. Let the tool cool, and it's ready to use. This method won't cause any damage to your tools.

TIP

Always isolate new houseplants from your other plants for four to six weeks. During this time, scrutinize them for any signs of insects or diseases.

Besting the Bugs

The most important aspect of pest control is vigilance. People often say, "I don't know where these bugs came from! All of a sudden my houseplant was infested with them!" Well, I'm here to tell you that isn't the way it happens. Even though most insects do reproduce faster than rabbits, infestations don't happen overnight.

REMEMBER

Things can get out of hand quickly, though, if you don't make a point of closely inspecting your houseplants regularly. Keep on the lookout because detecting pests when they're few in number makes getting rid of them much easier. And by the time you've seen one pest, it's highly likely this unwanted creature has already laid eggs, and more critters will show up soon.

TIP

Many of the pests I describe in this chapter, like mites and thrips, are very tiny, so they're difficult to see with the naked eye. Buy yourself a 10x hand lens to make examining your houseplants for bugs much easier.

In the following sections, I discuss common pests you may encounter and share ways to prevent them from harming your houseplants.

Identifying common houseplant pests

When you first notice pests, you need to identify them promptly and properly so you can be sure to apply the most effective control.

TIP

In many cases, especially if many pests are present, you'll have to apply control measures at least three times with treatments every seven to ten days,. This is because these creatures have probably laid eggs that are resistant to the control measure and will hatch later. By repeating the control several times, you'll kill these next generations of pests after they emerge from their eggs.

TIP

HOUSEPLANT EUTHANASIA: THROWING OUT YOUR SICK PLANTS

Sometimes the best solution to a pest problem is to dispose of a sickly houseplant. If you've tried the preventive and curative measures I outline in this chapter and the houseplant still doesn't seem to be recovering, or if the infestation is beyond control, getting rid of the plant is the best solution. When a plant becomes too weakened by infection or a bad infestation of insects, it isn't likely to recover. It can be hard to give up hope of recovery, but the infested plant can spread its problem to your healthy houseplants. So, bite the bullet and bury the sick plant in your trash can! Don't compost an ailing plant or its potting mix because it can be a carrier of diseases or insects. If you want to reuse the pot, sterilize it with a chlorine bleach solution, as explained in the "How to sterilize your tools" sidebar earlier in this chapter.

Aphids

Aphids are probably the most common insect pests of them all. They come in many colors — including green, red, pink, black, and yellow — and they're usually found on succulent new growth, including flower buds (see Figure 9-1). They feed with syringe-like mouth parts and are particularly damaging to buds, causing the flowers to be deformed when they open. Aphids are also very effective carriers of disease, especially viruses.

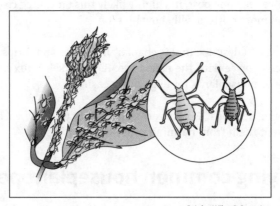

FIGURE 9-1:
Aphids are usually found in clusters on flower buds and young shoots and leaves.

© John Wiley & Sons, Inc.

TIP

If you see sticky, clear droplets anywhere on your plant, look for aphids. This material, called *honeydew,* is aphid waste. Other piercing/sucking insects, such as scale, can also excrete this sticky substance. This substance can serve as a food source for black mold, which can cover affected leaves. Black mold is unsightly and can block the leaves from light, so sponge it off it with warm sudsy water when you find it on a plant's leaves.

Mealybugs

Their name pretty much describes what these insects look like: mealy or cottony masses (see Figure 9-2). They're found in similar areas on houseplants as aphids — growing tips, buds, and flower stems. Mealybugs are one of the most common and destructive insects for many houseplants. One type in particular is found on the roots.

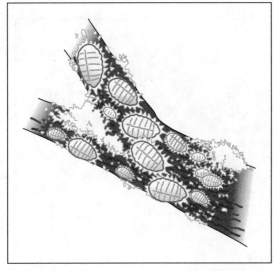

FIGURE 9-2:
Mealybugs look like white cottony masses that are frequently misdiagnosed as a fungus.

© *John Wiley & Sons, Inc.*

Because these bugs are a fuzzy mass, they're frequently misdiagnosed as a fungus. You usually need multiple insecticide treatments to get rid of this bothersome pest. Any houseplant grower who says they've never dealt with this pest is either not observant or very lucky.

Mealybugs are very persistent and require constant vigilance to eliminate.

Thrips

Thrips can be very destructive, especially to flower buds, maturing flowers, and young leaves. They're miniscule and look something like long, light-colored gnats. They're very difficult to see with the naked eye, but their damage is easier to detect — it shows up as light streaks on the flowers or *stippling* (spots or speckles) on the leaves. Thrips usually deform the flower buds and are carriers of some diseases, such as viruses that can be especially damaging to gesneriads.

Scale

Scale are another creature that comes in various forms, but most have a shell that serves as a type of armor for the soft insect body (see Figure 9-3). You must penetrate this shell with a chemical or rub it off before you can kill the insect. Scale are frequently found on the undersides of leaves near the middle vein or on the edges of leaves. They also commonly hang out on flower stems. It's very difficult to totally eliminate this insect, but with persistence, you can effectively control it.

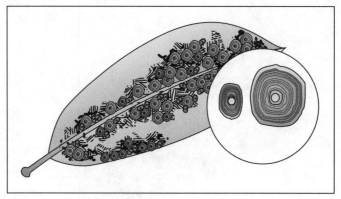

FIGURE 9-3:
Scale is a very common pest on houseplants.

© John Wiley & Sons, Inc.

Spider mites

These critters are spiders (see Figure 9-4) that are often found on houseplants when growing conditions are hot and dry. They can be green or red, but no matter their color, they're very difficult to see because they're so small. That's why a magnifying glass is handy to confirm their presence. In extreme infestations, you'll see fine webbing on the leaves. Before the infestation gets this bad, the foliage takes on a stippling effect, which is a result of the spider mites' feeding. Most insecticides are not effective in controlling mites.

Slugs and snails

Snails and slugs (see Figure 9-5) head most people's list as one of the most revolting of all houseplant pests. They can do extensive damage to young houseplant roots and stems and developing and maturing flowers. They usually come out at night, so if you suspect you have them, use a flashlight to search your plants for these culprits in the evening. Also, look on the bottom of your pots — this is another favorite hiding place. They love cool, damp spots. When they travel across dry surfaces, they leave a telltale slime trail.

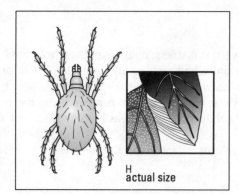

FIGURE 9-4: Spider mites are small, hard-to-see pests that can be very destructive.

H
actual size

© John Wiley & Sons, Inc.

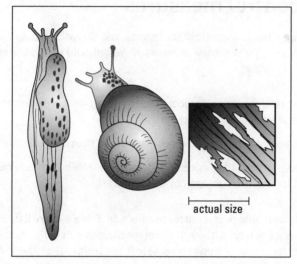

FIGURE 9-5: Snails and slugs eat holes in flowers and leaves at night.

actual size

© John Wiley & Sons, Inc.

Cockroaches

Another very unpopular beast, cockroaches also feed at night and enjoy munching on flowers and flower buds. You don't need an illustration to identify this one!

Bees and other pollinating insects

These aren't harmful creatures — they don't cause any physical damage to house-plants, but if they land on flowers and pollinate them, the flowers will soon collapse. So, if you want your flowers to last as long as possible, keep pollinating insects out of your growing area.

Mice

More than once, to my great distress, upon inspecting my plants in the morning, I discovered that a creature had nibbled off the young leaves or flower buds of some of my prized beauties right before they opened! Oh, how frustrating! Mice are frequently the culprits, which is easy to confirm if you notice the presence of their tiny droppings. Luckily, mice can be easily controlled.

See Table 9-1 later in this chapter for the best ways to rid yourself of all these pests.

Finding safe and effective pest-control measures

Many of the chemical controls for insects and diseases can damage the plants to which they're applied if they're misused. You should err on the side of caution by doing the following:

>> Always read the pesticide label to see if houseplants are listed as a plant the chemical should *not* be used with.

>> When applying the pesticide, never use more than the recommended dosage.

>> Make sure the potting material is damp. A moisture-stressed houseplant is much more easily damaged by pesticides.

The readily available pest-control methods in Table 9-1 are listed in their approximate order of safety. Although other pesticides exist, I'm keeping it simple by giving you the most effective and safest controls. All of these materials can be found at home stores, garden centers, or online. No matter which type of pest you have, always start with the first line of defense before moving on to something more aggressive. Some of the least toxic solutions must be applied more frequently because they kill on contact and aren't *residual* (meaning they don't stick around after they're applied). Most don't smell bad — an important feature for plants growing indoors. Some, like Orange Guard, also serve as *repellents* (which means they'll kill the pests currently on the plant and repel future pests).

WARNING

Don't spray aerosol insect controls, such as those designed for killing ants, roaches, and wasps, on your houseplants. These poisons are intended to be used to kill insects outdoors and in the kitchen, but if sprayed directly on your houseplant, they can cause serious damage because the propellant contains chemicals that are toxic to plants.

TABLE 9-1

Common Houseplant Pests and Their Controls

Pest	First Line of Defense	Second Line of Defense	Comments
Aphids	Wash off with warm water.	Insecticidal soap, Neem Orange Guard (orange oil) All Seasons Horticultural Oil Isopropyl alcohol applied with a cotton swab	If aphids are on the houseplant's flower buds, try repeatedly washing them off with warm water. Using any chemical may damage the delicate developing buds or flowers.
Mealybugs	Physically remove as many of them as possible with a soft toothbrush. You can also use a cotton swab drenched with isopropyl alcohol. Alcohol will kill the insects by dehydrating them on contact but this control must be applied repeatedly until no more of these pests show up.	Insecticidal soap All Seasons Horticultural Oil Neem	For houseplants with mealybugs on their roots, remove the houseplant from the pot, soak the roots in an insecticidal soap solution for a few hours, and then repot in a clean new pot with new potting material.
Mice	Live traps	Old-fashioned snap traps (peanut butter is an effective bait).	I don't recommend using poison baits because they can harm your pets. Also, the dead mice frequently end up in the walls of your house, and the smell takes weeks to go away.
Roaches	Orange Guard	Roach aerosol sprays — use on the floor, not on plants.	Orange Guard both repels and kills roaches. And it smells good!
Scale	With a cotton swab drenched with isopropyl alcohol, wipe across the armored shell of this insect. Make sure you penetrate the shell. Orange Guard	Insecticidal soap Neem All Seasons Horticultural Oil	This pest is difficult to eliminate. Apply controls repeatedly to get rid of it. Before I spray, I usually try to rub off the armored shells of the scale with my fingers or a soft toothbrush, and then I wash the leaf with mild soapy water and spray with my chosen control.

(continued)

TABLE 9-1 *(continued)*

Pest	First Line of Defense	Second Line of Defense	Comments
Snails and slugs	The yeast in beer is a strong attractant to snails and slugs. Put out a shallow platter of old beer (about ½ inch deep) and wait for these creatures to belly up to the bar at nightfall. The next day, you'll find them drowned in the brew. Put out pieces of lettuce in the evening to attract slugs and snails. In the morning, you can remove the lettuce, with the feeding pests attached, and discard it.	Sluggo and other iron phosphate–based baits	If you use bait, be sure to choose one that has low toxicity to pets, such as Sluggo.
Spider mites	Wash off with a strong stream of warm water.	Insecticidal soap All Seasons Horticultural Oil Orthene	To prevent mite infestations, keep your houseplant properly watered and in a growing area that isn't too hot or too dry.
Thrips	Neem All Season's Horticultural Oil Insecticidal soap	Conserve (spinosad) Pyrethrin	Conserve and Neem can be combined to be more effective.

TIP

Ready-to-use insecticides are convenient, but if you check the label, you'll see you're paying mostly for water and very little of the active ingredients. It's much more economical to buy the pesticide in a concentrated form, dilute it with water, and then use a quart-size hand sprayer to apply it.

WARNING

All horticultural oils aren't the same. Don't use dormant oils — they're meant to be used on dormant plants like fruit trees and will greatly harm houseplants. Use the ones called *all-season* or *superior* oils. They're much thinner and more refined and are meant to be used when the plants are actively growing.

Applying pest-control treatments

It's important that you use the correct methods of applying pest control because it may make the difference between success and failure. Here are a few guidelines:

>> Before you spray, remove or dislodge the pests with a soft bristle toothbrush. Many insects have protective layers that are difficult for the spray material to penetrate, so breaking up or removing this material greatly improves the effectiveness of the spray.

>> Wash off the leaves with warm, slightly sudsy water. This will physically remove many of the pests, their eggs, and the protective material surrounding them.

>> Spray both the top and bottom of the leaves as well as the juncture where the leaves attach to the stem.

>> Do not spray when the plants are in full sunlight. Move them to a shady place before applying a spray.

>> Do not apply pest control when the soil is very dry.

>> Do not spray at a higher concentration than recommended on the pesticide container.

>> Spray in an area that has good ventilation and is not in the way of people or pets. You can return the sprayed plant to its original growing area after the pesticide has dried.

Identifying Fungal and Bacterial Infections

Houseplants are tough, and if you grow them in the correct environmental conditions and take the preventive measures I mention earlier in this chapter, they'll rarely suffer from fatal diseases. Still, being aware of what can happen when things go wrong is a good idea.

Diseases are somewhat trickier than bugs to deal with because you really can't see them. You just see the damage they leave behind — such as rotten plant centers or spots on the leaves.

WARNING

The damage that most fungal and bacterial diseases leave behind shows up as circular or oblong spots on the foliage or flowers (see Figure 9-6). Sometimes diseases also cause the center growing point, called the *crown*, to turn black or rot, which may lead to the death of the plant. When this happens, the crown has been killed by the infection, and the pattern of spots or rot is one of the ways you can identify the disease. Although it is always best to correctly diagnose the disease problem you are facing, this is sometimes difficult to do. Fortunately, most of the controls I mention in this chapter are effective against a broad range of diseases.

WARNING

Houseplant growers dread viruses because there's no practical cure for them. The most obvious symptom of a viral infection is streaking or color breaks in the flowers. Fortunately, viral infections aren't common, especially if you buy high-quality plants and follow the prevention methods outlined earlier in this chapter. If you suspect a problem, home tests are available to determine whether your plant is infected by a virus. If the test proves positive, the best course of action is to discard the plant so the disease doesn't infect your other plants.

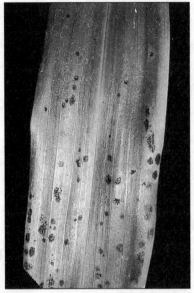

FIGURE 9-6:
Leaf spots like these are usually caused by fungal organisms.

© John Wiley & Sons, Inc.

Noticing when your houseplant has a virus

Detecting virus symptoms such as stunted growth, mosaic patterns in leaves, or abnormal streaking in the flowers are difficult. Fortunately, you can buy test kits online, but because commercial growers are extremely careful these days with their sanitation to insure that their plants are virus-free, it is seldom necessary to test for virus yourself.

TIP

To keep your houseplants healthy, refer to the section "Preventing Problems Before They Start," earlier in this chapter. This information pertains as much to houseplant diseases as it does to pests, but I have a few other pointers that relate specifically to preventing disease:

>> **Water your houseplants during the day so the moisture will evaporate from the leaves before nightfall.** Cool, damp leaves and water left in the crowns of the plants in the evening are an invitation to disease.

>> **Make sure your houseplants have enough airflow.** This reduces the time moisture stays on the leaves and removes stagnant air from the growing environment. See Chapter 5 for more information on this topic.

>> **Sterilize your cutting tools each time you use them on another plant.** Tools that have cut diseased plant tissue can carry the disease to a healthy plant. See the "How to sterilize your tools" sidebar earlier in this chapter for more information.

After you detect a diseased plant, do the following as soon as possible:

>> **Remove diseased leaves with a sharp sterile knife or scissors.** See the sidebar "When surgery is required," later in this chapter.

>> **When you find a disease problem, treat it right away.** Putting off treatment can cost your houseplant its life.

Handling a sick plant

As soon as you discover that your houseplant is sick, I recommend you stick to these steps:

1. **If the plant is badly diseased, discard it.**

   You probably won't be able to save it, and it may infect your healthy plants.

2. **If you find dark brown spots that look like disease and they're close to the end of the leaf, remove this section of the leaf.**

   See the sidebar "When surgery is required."

3. **As a general sanitation practice, after you've performed surgery or if your houseplant has a diseased spot that can't be removed surgically, spray the leaves with a mild fungicide/bactericide and hope for the best.**

   Physan 20, Phyton 27, Natriphene, or RD-20 (also called SA-20) are all mild fungicides/bactericides that work for this purpose. These materials are available at some garden stores and on-line.

TIP

   Some folks have found that dabbing ground cinnamon on the cut is effective to prevent the spread of disease.

4. **Reevaluate the area where you're growing the houseplant to be sure it's getting enough air circulation, and you're doing all you can to follow the recommended disease-prevention measures.**

WARNING

All chemical pesticides are poisons that have some toxicity to humans. Read the precautions on the pesticide label and follow them carefully.

Wear rubber gloves when mixing and spraying these pesticides, but remember that not all gloves are equal. Choose chemical-resistant gloves, and avoid lined gloves because they can absorb pesticides. Waterproof nitrile, butyl, and PVC gloves that extend up the forearm are good choices.

WHEN SURGERY IS REQUIRED

Performing surgery to cut out an infection is the simplest and most effective method of stopping the spread of disease. A single-edge razor blade is ideal for the job because it's extremely sharp and sterile and can be disposed of after the operation. Using a sharp blade is important so that you damage as little as possible of the healthy tissue in the process.

Remove all the damaged or diseased tissue by cutting the leaf off about ½ inch to 1 inch into healthy tissue that shows no signs of the disease. Be careful not to cut into the diseased tissue and then into healthy tissue, or you'll spread the disease.

Some people dress the edge of the cut with a natural fungicidal material like sulfur or cinnamon.

3
The Best of the Houseplants

IN THIS CHAPTER

» **Understanding the basics of succulent growth and care**

» **Discovering the best houseplant succulents**

» **Creating attractive succulent wreaths and tabletop gardens**

» **Identifying cacti suitable for indoors and windowsills**

» **Examining cold-hardy selections for outdoor displays**

Chapter **10**

Succulents and Cacti: Easy-Care Plants

I f you're concerned that you don't have a green thumb, or if you simply want to experience success with container-grown plants right off the bat, succulents and cacti are your new best friends. They're easy and low care.

As you may know, plants in pots dry out quickly. Clay pots wick moisture away from the plant's root system. Water may move through the potting material quickly and leave potted plants clamoring for more. The situation can be stressful for both plants and owners — but *not for these plants!*

Succulents and cacti are, as a rule, hassle-free. As with all members of the plant world, some are more easygoing and others are more challenging, but all are durable and resilient. This chapter suggests the best choices for getting started with plants of manageable size that are a cinch to grow, colorful, and attractive. I can't help mentioning a few unique plants that require more attention, but I make it clear that they take extra work, and I detail their special needs. Trust me, once you start down this road, you're going to be encouraged and, in time, delighted with your displays.

While succulents and cacti aren't no-care plants, their care tends to be straightforward and easy. Throughout this chapter, I explain what to do, caution you about what not to do, and suggest a couple of fun projects associated with these tough but pretty plants. Finally, I tell you how to display potted succulents and cacti outdoors — climate and season permitting, of course.

REMEMBER

If your potted succulents and cacti are happy, they'll live a long time — several years or even several decades. However, when flowers develop on some plants, which may only happen after many years in your care, the plant may die back but leave behind *pups* — your next generation of this beautiful plant.

Caring for Houseplant Succulents and Cacti

A *succulent* is a plant that stores moisture in its fleshy leaves (or stems) to survive periods of drought. All cacti are succulents, but not all succulents are cacti.

These plants (or their parents/ancestors) evolved where rainfall is scarce, so their water-holding leaves, and often their stems (if they have any), developed to get them through the dry times.

In this section, I give you basic information about potting, watering, and providing light for your succulents and cacti. For complete success, be sure to heed my advice. Taking care of this special category of plants is different (and I daresay easier!) than caring for other houseplants.

Potting

Grow these plants in clay rather than plastic pots because plastic holds in too much moisture. My favorite pot material is terra cotta because the look goes so well with many cacti and succulents.

Keep the following things in mind:

>> The optimum growing medium is half sterile potting soil and half succulent and cactus mix. (Just read the bags to find the right stuff!) Succulent and

cactus mix contains sand, which ensures good drainage, and it's what they're used to in their native habitat.

>> If you have any doubts about the mix your succulents or cacti came home in, take the time to repot them as I've suggested in the first bullet.

>> Drainage holes in containers are a *must*. Standing water or too much moisture around succulent and cacti roots leads to rot and plant death.

TIP

When combining several plants in one large container, always put the ones with the biggest root balls in first.

Watering

To summarize, less is best when it comes to watering succulents and cacti. Here are some general guidelines:

>> Always check first. Push your finger into the potting mix up to your first knuckle. If the potting media doesn't feel moist and your finger comes out dry, you may water. If bits of potting mix or sand cling to your finger, hold off.

>> When you water, don't wet the foliage. Wet the potting mix.

>> Easy does it. Let your plants dry out completely between waterings. "Soak and dry, soak and dry" should be your mantra.

>> Water a bit more (every two to four weeks) when your plants are growing and pull back to less watering during their slow time. In most cases, this simply translates to more water in summer and less in winter.

>> Overwatering leads to poor growth and rot. Err on the side of caution (or, let's be honest, neglect) with these plants!

>> *Never* let a potted cactus or succulent sit in a saucer of water. If there's any excess, dump it out.

>> Wrinkled or puckered leaves are a sign that a plant *needs* water.

>> Definitely don't mist pot-grown succulents and cacti. Some are sensitive to water droplets, and misting may cause rot.

WARNING

You're overwatering your succulent or cacti houseplant if it becomes droopy and less stable in its pot. Look closely at the point where the plant enters the potting mix — if it's dark, brown, or mushy, that's an indicator that rot is setting in. Again, it's always better to err on the side of too little water!

Lighting

Succulents and cacti are adapted to plenty of sunshine, but you need to know the following things about their light needs:

>> It's a good idea to gradually acclimate new plants to the light in your home, even if they're touted as loving full sun. At first, give them just a couple of hours per day, slowly extending their exposure over a week or two. Alternatively, start them off in a place with morning sun, which tends to be less intense than afternoon light.

>> After the initial adjustment period, most of these plants need a permanent spot with lots of light. (I note exceptions in the plant lists in this chapter.) Up to six hours a day of indirect sunlight in south- or east-facing windows or just a few inches from LED or florescent lights is ideal for most succulents and cacti.

>> If their growth stretches toward the light or looks spindly over time, you'll need to move them to a brighter spot.

>> Protect potted succulents and cacti from blazing sunlight when you move them outdoors for the summer. Provide a little shelter or shade from about noon to 2:00 p.m.

TIP

If you find it hard to meet your succulent or cacti's light needs simply by where you place them, explore providing supplemental or artificial light. Consult Chapter 5 for details and tips about lighting.

WARNING

Sunburn alert! You're probably thinking, *Sunburn on succulents and cacti, really?* Yes, plants that get scorched by too-hot or too-direct light may develop tiny brown spots or areas of discoloration on their foliage, especially along the edges. (Watch for this especially when you first bring plants home, as they may have begun their life in a sheltered greenhouse or shade house.) These spots aren't symptoms of a plant pest; they're sunburn — literally, little blisters.

Move an affected plant out of direct, hot sunlight to a shadier spot, and it will recover. Protect plants from direct, hot light, particularly if you move their pots so they can spend summer outdoors.

Other maintenance tips

Here are a few pointers to help you be successful in growing succulents and cacti.

>> **Keep them warm.** Don't expose your potted succulents and cacti to cold or freezing temperatures, which can cause them to falter or die.

WHAT'S THAT WAXY COATING FOUND ON MANY SUCCULENTS?

Termed *epicuticular wax* or *farina*, the coating on succulents is a white or gray-blue film or bloom, and it's perfectly natural. Sometimes, it looks powdery. It may coat not only leaves but also stems, including flowering stalks. Farina helps succulents in two ways: by sealing in water to keep the plant, well, succulent and by warding off sunburn.

The coating may be thicker on succulents growing in bright sunlight. It can be brushed or rubbed off, accidentally or on purpose, and it will not be renewed. So, handle it with care. (Leaves will be fine if they lose some coating, though they won't look as nice. New leaves will come along later, with a good coating, to replace them — no worries!)

» **Rotate the pots.** Give the pots a quarter-turn every week or two for balanced growth. That way the plants won't grow lopsided and will look better.

» **Feed sparingly.** Bear in mind that succulents and cacti in nature like to grow in lean, nutrient-poor soil, so fertilizing is generally not required. If you do choose to nudge their growth or flowering with a little plant food, deliver it only when they're actively growing (usually spring and summer), and don't overdo it. Use a little diluted general-purpose plant food or perhaps a long-term slow-release one, and see how they respond.

» **Check periodically for bugs.** Pests usually appear only if you bought an afflicted plant or the plant is unhappy with its growing conditions. (More details in Chapter 9.)

Meeting the Succulents

Scads of succulents are available to gardeners, for indoor or outdoor use (or both). Indeed, there are so many choices, you may feel bewildered or overwhelmed. To help you navigate them, I suggest you focus on the following qualities:

» **Look for plants that have colorful foliage.** This way, you don't have to wait for them to look good; they will be beautiful right away. Flowers, when they appear, are a bonus.

» **Seek out plants of manageable size.** How do you know? Check the tag, read the plant description (in a catalog, website, or reference book), and believe the mature-size dimensions provided. That said, many of these plants are slow growers — there's little chance of your displays being overwhelmed by unmanageable or rapid growth.

The rest of this section is a curated list of succulents meant to get you started. I can vouch that all these plants not only meet the above criteria but aren't hard to find or grow.

TIP

Be conservative at the outset of this gardening adventure. Buy and display a few, experience success and delight, and then add to your collection over time.

Figure 10-1 shows a sampling of succulents you may find at your garden store. This photo is also in the color insert.

FIGURE 10-1:
Succulents are found in a huge array of colors and shapes.

Jason Finn/Shutterstock.com

Genus: *Adromischus*

These small, stubby plants are related to the more familiar jade plants (*Crassula*). Their thick leaves are flat and generally oval in shape, and they come in different shades — often with a pattern or speckles. Native to South Africa, they are sun lovers, and you'll want to give them a bright spot to prevent the colors from fading. Flower spikes may appear in autumn, rising above the foliage and lasting for several weeks. These plants are very easy to grow. And yes, if you acquire several, you may refer to them as *adromischi!*

>> *Adromischus cristatus* (**ravioli plant**): What fun — thick, roughly triangular foliage with distinctive wavy edges. The leaves have a felt-like texture, thanks to a light coating of moisture-conserving hairs. The plant forms a loose *rosette* (a circle or spiral of leaves), which allows you to appreciate them individually.

>> *Adromischus filicaulis:* Stout, fleshy little fingers of foliage in a dense, crowded form. They're generally bright green with red to gray mottling toward the tips.

>> *Adromischus herrei:* An unusual-looking plant indeed, with stout, cylindrical leaves that are textured and ridged. Their color runs the gamut from purple to red-brown to green.

WARNING

Be advised that all plant parts are poisonous, so these succulents aren't a good choice for any spot where curious children or pets may play or nibble.

Genus: *Aeonium*

This succulent, which is popular in mild climates as an outdoor landscaping plant, includes many good smaller–size choices appropriate for container growth and appreciation. They are easygoing and totally nontoxic.

Aeoniums come in two forms: low rosettes, sometimes practically flat in the pot, and a branching variety that has rosettes held aloft on curving stems. In either case, the leaves are waxy, and the plants are quite durable. Indeed, neglect or intermittent watering seems to improve their foliage color — primarily reds, rusts, and greens.

Note that these plants shed lower (older) leaves as they grow. Just remove and discard them to keep your display attractive.

Most aeoniums grow in winter and spring and slow down in summer. The following are some varieties you can look for:

>> *Aeonium arboreum* '**Atropurpureum**' **or** '**Black Rose**': A tree-form cultivar that reaches up to 3 feet in height and shows off handsome maroon leaves. The color is best when the plant is placed in bright light.

>> *Aeonium arboreum* '**Zwartkop**': Another fairly large tree-form cultivar. The foliage is such a dark burgundy that it seems nearly black. It's very dramatic.

>> *Aeonium* '**Garnet**': This hybrid is hard to miss or misidentify thanks to its beautiful leaves; the tips of each one look dipped in rich red.

>> **Aeonium haworthii 'Kiwi' or 'Tricolor':** This smaller one has leaves rimmed in red or dark pink if the plant gets lots of light.

>> **Aeonium tabuliforme:** This one is distinguished by a flat, dense saucer of leaves. The leaves are so dense, you can't see underneath them. The foliage tends to be light green.

Genus: *Agave*

While some agaves are substantial succulents best grown outdoors in sunny, arid settings, others make excellent potted plants. Display them indoors in a bright, dry spot or in similar conditions outdoors on a patio, deck, or balcony. (If your climate has cold winters, plan to shift them indoors to nonfreezing temperatures until warm days return; remember to water them less in fall and winter.) Some agave leaves have spines, whereas others don't — this may be a consideration when choosing which plants to grow. You don't have to worry about them being poisonous or otherwise objectionable.

Agave roots tend to spread outward, not so much downward, as they grow. Therefore, you want to pot them in a container that's wider than it is deep. Here are a few to consider adding to your indoor garden:

>> **Agave americana 'Marginata':** In the ground, this two-tone beauty can grow to be as tall as a person and at least as wide, but in a large pot, it will be smaller and tidier in appearance. It grows very slowly, so select the pot and the location with care. Don't bury the neck of the plant but let it rise a bit above the potting mix (otherwise, the roots may rot).

>> **Agave victoriae-reginae (Queen Victoria agave):** A compact and elegant choice, with white-rimmed dark green leaves and no spines. Slow growing, ultimately reaching 1 foot (0.3 meter) tall and somewhat wider.

   This is one of my favorites. I think of it as the aristocrat of agaves. (See Figure 10-2 and the color insert.)

>> **Agave vilmoriniana (octopus agave):** When this plant reaches its mature size of about 3 to 4 feet (0.9 to 1.3 m), its arching and twisting leaves certainly earn the common name. Leaf margins are sharp, so place it where people can admire it without brushing against the plant. This one appreciates a little less light in the afternoon.

FIGURE 10-2:
Agave victoriae-reginae is an elegant succulent.

Genus: *Aloe*

You probably know the type of aloe cooks like to keep on their kitchen windowsill so it's handy for treating burns, but the genus contains a variety of houseplant-worthy choices. All have fleshy leaves that manage to stay fresh-looking even when you neglect to water them for a few weeks. They tend to form stemless rosettes that look good in a pot. Once mature, aloes often form *pups* (mini plants) that you can separate from the parent and repot so the main plant doesn't get crowded. It's a convenient way to expand your collection or give some away as gifts.

Consider getting a few different aloes — they're easy and rewarding!

>> *Aloe (Aristaloe) aristata* **(lace aloe):** This small, handsome aloe — the leaves get only about 3 to 4 inches (7.6 to 10.1 centimeters) long — features white dots or warts.

>> *Aloe* **'Black Gem':** This hybrid has a rosette of thick, fleshy triangular leaves. Its leaves are green in low light but turn bronzy-purple in bright light. It produces orange-red flowers in the spring if given strong light. It's slow growing and very compact — about 6 to 8 inches (15 to 20 cm) tall at maturity. See Figure 10-3.

>> *Aloe mitriformis (perfoliata)* **(thorny aloe):** This is another smaller-size option — less than 5 inches (12.7 cm) tall when mature. The leaf edges are toothed (hence the common name), but they're more decorative than daunting.

» *Aloe vera* (**common aloe**): Justly popular, this handsome, carefree plant fills its pot with fleshy, light green leaves, faintly marked or dotted in white (see Figure 10-4). Snap off one if you happen to accidentally burn yourself while cooking and immediately swab the spot; the sap is very soothing. This plant grows to about 1 to 2 feet (0.3 to 0.6 m) tall, depending on the pot size.

FIGURE 10-3: The leaves of this aloe can turn purple or bronze when exposed to strong light.

Photo by Steven A. Frowine

FIGURE 10-4: Many cooks keep *Aloe vera* on hand because it's frequently used to treat minor burns.

Photo by Steven A. Frowine

Genus: *Anacampseros*

These cute little undemanding succulents hail from South Africa, which means they like hot and dry conditions. They'll win your heart with their beautiful colored foliage. They stay small but may trail or spill over the side of a pot.

>> *Anacampseros rufescens:* Like a pudgy little bouquet, this mat-forming succulent features green leaves with purplish undersides for an appealing two-tone effect — the color is richer when the plant is placed in more light. The mature size is up to 2 feet (0.6 m) tall and wide, but it grows slowly, and you can keep it from getting too large by potting it in a smaller container.

>> *Anacampseros telephiastrum:* This variety is a tidy little clump of fleshy leaves that sometimes sends out short but crowded stems and short silvery hairs. Foliage varies in color; expect shades of green and brown (flowers, if they appear, are pink). Mature size is 6 inches (15 cm) tall and wide. 'Sunset' has pink-hued leaves.

Genus: *Bryophyllum*

These branching succulent plants, which hail primarily from South Africa and Madagascar, are related to jade plants and kalanchoes. Mature leaves can send forth little plantlets.

Bryophyllum pinnatum (Kalanchoe pinnata) (miracle leaf, leaf of life, patharcatta) is a tropical plant valued for its medicinal uses (treatment of kidney problems and urinary disorders, but don't try this at home — preparation and application are tricky). This plant has stems and leaf rims that range from purple to red (see Figure 10-5. Mature size can be over 3 feet (1 m) tall and wide.

Genus: *Ceropegia*

Because the growth habit of this plant is trailing or vining, it's a fine choice for a hanging basket in a sunny window or a pot on a tall shelf. Trouble-free and easygoing.

Ceropegia woodii (Ceropegia linearis ssp. woodii) (string of hearts, rosary vine) is a trailing vine that looks delicate, but it's not; it's a tough, durable succulent. It tolerates periods of no water and doesn't require extra humidity. The tiny heart-shaped leaves are dark green blotched with white; their undersides are purple. In bright light, they take on a coppery sheen. The leaves are attached in pairs, and there are a lot of slender stems between sets that will hang down as much as 2 feet (0.6 m).

FIGURE 10-5:
Baby plants
sprout from the
edges of the
leaves of this
unusual plant.

Genus: *Cotyledon*

Silvery-blue or silvery-green spoon-shaped foliage distinguishes this durable and good-looking genus. Because the plants are naturally shrubby, use larger pots so your plants can reach mature size. They generate spikes of colorful, drooping, bell-like flowers that rise above the foliage.

From *Cotyledon orbiculata* (pig's ear), you can expect handsome plants with egg-shaped, often smooth, wavy-edged leaves in beautiful shades of light green, sage green, or blue-green, sometimes rimmed in contrasting red. Flowers can be orange, orange-red, or yellow. A plant in a pot can grow to 1 to 3 feet (0.3 to 0.9 m) high and wide. A cultivar called 'Higginsae' ('Prince of Paradise') has powdery gray leaves.

Genus: *Crassula*

The fleshy, moisture-storing leaves of these plants are quite substantial and drought-resistant (hence the name — *crassus* in Latin means *thick*). The stems are thick, too. That should clue you — don't overwater these plants! There are many, but here I describe the two most popular ones and one that is less common:

>> *Crassula argentea* **(jade plant, money tree):** This tree-type crassula is a happy jade plant that can grow to be downright magnificent. The leaves are indeed a jade green color and generally oval (or coin-shaped). A spot in bright light causes two good effects: The leaves get reddish rims, and frothy clusters of little white to pale pink flowers form. Size varies from 1 to 5 feet (0.3 to 1.5 m) high and wide. See Figure 10-6.

>> *Crassula mesembryanthemoides:* From South Africa, this is a shrubby-looking succulent with green tear-shaped leaves that are covered with hairs (see Figure 10-7). It grows about 12 inches (30 cm) tall and has clusters of pink tubular flowers in the spring.

>> *Crassul rupestris* (**Rosary Vine, Buttons on a String.**): This is still a crassula, but it's quite different in appearance, with stemless, dark green leaves that crowd along the main stems. Young plants grow upright, but over time the stems start to twist downward, giving the mature plant a sprawling or vine-like look. This plant can grow 1 foot (0.3 m) high and wide.

FIGURE 10-6:
The jade plant may be the most popular and widely grown houseplant.

Olga Miltsova/Shutterstock

FIGURE 10-7:
This crassula is a shrubby succulent with hairy leaves.

Photo by Steven A. Frowine

MAKING A SUCCULENT WREATH

Making a succulent wreath like the one shown in the photo is a gratifying project! The result is beautiful and durable, whether you display it in your own home, give it as a fabulous gift, or sell or donate it at a craft fair.

© sumikophoto/Shutterstock

First, gather your supplies:

- 9-inch ready-to-plant sphagnum moss wreath form
- Green 24-gauge florist's wire
- U-shaped floral pins
- Approximately 100 succulent cuttings
- Something to poke holes in the moss (chopstick, pencil, or screwdriver)

When you have everything you need, follow these steps to assemble the wreath:

1. Lay the wreath form flat on a good work surface.
2. Create hanging loops with the florist's wire at north, south, east, and west intervals on the back of the wreath form. This gives you options when it's time to hang or rotate it.

3. Poke holes in the moss and insert the cuttings, crowded close together so the moss is hidden from view. Handle the cuttings gently so you don't break them or bruise their leaves. Secure them with floral pins (you can poke them through the stems but not the leaves).

   Note: Do not insert plants in the back of the wreath — only the top and the sides.

4. Leave the wreath flat until the cuttings root into the moss. This usually takes about two weeks.

Once your creation is completed, give this living wreath the same growing conditions as you would all your other succulents.

Genus: *Echeveria*

These charming plants originated in the Mexican desert, so right away you know they want lots of sun and warmth but low humidity. Those conditions are easy to find on a bright windowsill in your home! A potting mix with good drainage is important. This is my favorite genus of succulents. The symmetry and variety of colors of the leaves are astonishing.

Echeverias form ball–shaped or dense rosettes; some are branched and hold the rosettes aloft. Both kinds are fun to show off in containers.

» *Echeveria elegans* **Mexican snowball):** The most popular and recognizable plant in this genus features a loose ball-like rosette (see Figure 10-8). The fleshy leaves are silvery-green to silvery-blue, and the plants can grow up to 6 to 8 inches (15.2 to 20.3 cm) tall and up to 12 inches (30.5 cm) wide. If flower stalks appear, the blooms are pink or yellow.

» *Echeveria* **cultivars and hybrids:** There's a rainbow of choices in this genus. Most nurseries don't get into the exact parentage and just sell them by common name. Here's a sampling of what you may find in the 4- to 8-inch (10.1- to 20.3-cm) range, all wonderful for growing in containers:

   • 'Black Prince': Maroon to garnet foliage

   • 'Cassyz Winter': Soft pink outer leaves, lime green center

   • 'Ebony': Green leaves with fiery red tips

   • 'Imbricata': Powder blue foliage

   • 'Mira': Blue-green leaves with red tips

     I love the colors in 'Mira' (see Figure 10-9 and the color insert). It gets about 3 to 5 inches (7.6 to 12 cm) in diameter.

- 'Tippy': Soft green leaves with ruby red tips

- 'Topsy Turvy': Inward-curling leaves and orange and yellow flowers in the fall (See Figure 10-10.)

FIGURE 10-8: Mexican snowball echeveria is simple but elegant.

Photo by Steven A. Frowine

FIGURE 10-9: *Echeveria* 'Mira' displays perfect symmetry, which is typical of this group of succulents.

Photo by Steven A. Frowine

FIGURE 10-10: 'Topsy Turvy' displays unique scooped leaves.

Photo by Steven A. Frowine

Genus: *Euphorbia*

This is a large and wide-ranging genus, including garden perennials, holiday poinsettias, and even plants that are considered weeds. But it also includes quite a few fine succulent houseplants, all of which are no trouble to grow and will prosper in a pot. Some almost look like cacti (complete with spines), whereas others have fleshy leaves and interesting forms.

WARNING

Be aware that all euphorbias contain compounds — often in their milky sap — that some people are allergic to. It can cause an irritating skin rash. The plants are also toxic for cats and dogs.

The following are some euphorbias you're likely to find where you shop for plants:

» *Euphorbia lactea* **'Cristata' (crested euphorbia):** The straight species, *Euphorbia lacteal* (shown in Figure 10-11), is honestly not a particularly unusual plant, but 'Cristata' is another story. It's actually two different species grafted together: A mutated form of *Euphorbia lactea* that's wavy and fanlike is grafted on top of another species, *Euphorbia neriifolia,* which is a column-shaped euphorbia that serves as the base of the plant. The result is almost surreal.

» *Euphorbia millii* **(crown of thorns):** Yes, it's thorny, but you'll forgive its prickly nature when you behold its red, pink, orange, yellow, or white flowers (technically, *bracts,* or modified leaves, which maintain their color show practically year-round (see Figure 10-12 and the color insert). This is a slow-growing plant; it may only be 2 feet (0.6 m) tall in a pot. The newer hybrids are a far cry from the species in terms of producing much larger flowers in a huge range of colors. It's called *lucky plant* in Thailand, so many homes there have at least one plant at the entrance.

>> ***Euphorbia obesa* (baseball euphorbia, Turkish temple):** The round, ball-shaped stem, complete with seamlike ridges, is a fun, intriguing sight. Over time, it becomes more cylindrical. At maturity, plants are 8 inches (20.3 cm) tall and 4 inches (10.1 cm) wide.

FIGURE 10-11: The crested euphorbia seems otherworldly.

Photo by Steven A. Frowine

FIGURE 10-12: New color forms of crown of thorns are constantly being introduced.

Photo by Steven A. Frowine

>> *Euphorbia tirucalli* **(pencil cactus):** The flowers of this succulent from Africa are nothing special; the pencil-shaped branches are what make it a curiosity (see Figure 10-13). The stems are usually green but can turn orange or yellow in certain conditions. Although this plant can get up to 10 inches (25.4 cm) tall, it usually remains much shorter as a houseplant. The sap of this plant, like some of the other euphorbias, can be irritating to the skin.

FIGURE 10-13: This peculiar succulent doesn't have any significant leaves or flowers.

Photo by Steven A. Frowine

Genus: *Faucaria*

These succulents are unique for having clumps of stemless leaves, blessedly soft spines, and proportionally large flowers embedded in the foliage instead of being carried aloft on stalks. They grow mostly in the spring and fall, slowing down in the heat of summer and the cold of winter. They're little, often no more than about 3 inches (7.6 cm) in diameter.

>> *Faucaria felina* **(tiger jaws):** A robust sight thanks to its chunky leaves, this plant really does resemble open jaws — although the spines are soft. Late-fall flowers with slender bright yellow or orange petals are plush and can measure 2 inches (5 cm) across.

>> *Faucaria tigrina* **(tiger jaws):** This form is very similar to the preceding species, but this one forms clumps with triangular leaves that have more spots (see Figure 10-14).

Photo by Steven A. Frowine

Genus: *Gasteria*

At first glance, you may think these plants are aloes because of their long, succulent green leaves. But they are rougher-textured and may have interesting markings. Also — perhaps good news! — they tolerate low light well, so they're a fine choice for interior displays. Tough and drought-tolerant, gasterias are perfectly safe for a home with children or pets.

WARNING

Be careful when watering your gasteria (occasionally) that no moisture gets on the leaves or, if you put your plant outside for the summer, that no rainfall or sprinkler drops land on the leaves. They're sensitive to this, and surface water will lead to rot.

The *Gasteria carinata* var. *verrucosa* (ox tongue) is an undemanding, low-light succulent that forms a rosette of thick leaves arranged in two rows. They're covered in short, white bumps or warts that resemble taste buds. Figure 10-15 shows an example of a "warty" gasteria.

Genus: *Graptopetalum*

Silver-leaved and branching, plants in this genus are fairly low growing. So, you get a treelike form in a smaller plant — very nice for container gardening. One in particular is a standout: widely available and easy to grow.

Graptopetalum paraguayense (ghost plant, mother-of-pearl plant) has gray-green leaves gathered in mini rosettes. They gain a lovely pink hue in more sun and are blue-gray in partial shade. If you keep it in the same spot year-round, you may be treated to all these colors as the seasons change. The stems become pendant over time, spilling down over the edge of the pot or hanging basket. Dainty, starry yellow flowers appear in spring. Trailing stems can get as long as 3 feet (0.9 m).

Photo by Steven A. Frowine

FIGURE 10-15:
The little bumps on the leaves give this gasteria its common name.

Genus: *Graptosedum*

If the name sounds a bit odd, it's because this genus is a manufactured one. It's the happy result of crossing *Graptopetalum paraguayense* (see the preceding profile) and *Sedum adolphi* (described later in this chapter). The stout, tough leaves are contributed by the first parent, and the wonderful colors by the second. It's sometimes sold as California sunset plant.

These are small, rosette-forming beauties that are no trouble to care for. They may flower in spring, but honestly, the foliage is the show. Once established, plants will make lots of pups that are easy to separate off and repot.

Here are the stars of the genus:

>> *Graptosedum* **'Darley Sunshine':** Never a dull moment! The foliage is light to mint green, but it gains a pretty pink blush in more sun. Cooler fall and winter weather make the leaves go more purple. It grows 8 inches (20.3 cm) tall.

>> *Graptosedum* **'Vera Higgins' (also called 'Alpenglow' or 'Bronze'):** What a beauty! The small, pretty rosettes in hues of rose to red-bronze develop the best color in bright light. As it grows, it trails over the edge of the container. It gets only 6 inches (15.2 cm) tall.

Genus: *Graptoveria*

Here's another happy cross between two good succulents. Again, ghost plant, *Graptopetalum paraguayense*, is a parent; the other parent is usually *Echeveria gibbiflora* or a closely related echeveria. From the first parent comes durable foliage and from the second, spoon–shaped leaves on short–stemmed rosettes.

There are lots of these. The following selections offer a range of colors. If you don't readily find these exact selections, you'll surely find ones that appeal.

» 'Debbie'/'Debbi' is a rosy pink plant that may develop beautiful warm orange tones as well.

» 'Fred Ives' has soft green foliage blushed pink.

» 'Moonglow' sports thicker-than-usual ivory-green foliage.

» 'Platinum' features elegant silvery leaves.

Genus: *Haworthia*

Meet the handsome haworthias, which resemble aloes but with fleshy, interesting foliage. This native of South Africa is naturally small. They grow densely, forming compact stemless rosettes that look dramatic in containers. Classification and naming are complex, but don't fret — just choose a size you want with leaf markings you find appealing.

As for growing conditions, they like it warm and bright and thrive in indoor settings. Keep them on the dry side during their winter rest period because they naturally use less water when there is less warmth and light.

» *Haworthia (Haworthiopsis) attenuata* **(zebra haworthia):** Aptly named, its white-dotted dark green leaves are arranged in stripes. The plant grows 4 to 12 inches (10.1 to 30.5 cm) tall and twice as wide.

» *Haworthia bolusii:* This one is an attention-grabber! It forms small rosettes (and, in time, pups) that are light green and feature long, wavy, translucent white bristles — the effect is weblike. It grows to 3 to 4 inches (7.6 to 10.1 cm) in diameter.

» *Haworthia margaritifera (Tulista pumila)* **(pearl plant):** The rosette on this one is ball-shaped with tentacle-like leaves speckled white (see Figure 10-16), and it grows to around 5 inches (12.7 cm) across.

MAKING A SUCCULENT TABLETOP GARDEN

This project turns out so well that displaying it for your own pleasure may not be enough. You may want to throw a dinner or tea party and use it as a centerpiece. Alternatively, you can give away or sell your homemade tabletop garden.

(continued)

(continued)

Gather these supplies:

- A broad, shallow container, at least 3 inches (7.6 cm) deep
- Heavy-duty plastic (such as a contractor-grade trash bag)
- Succulent potting mix
- Crushed rock or moss for a finished look after plants are in place
- A variety of rooted succulents in various colors, some large, some small, some trailing; perhaps a few small cuttings
- Scissors
- Chopstick
- Paintbrush

To assemble your tabletop garden, follow these steps:

1. Cut the heavy-duty plastic to size and use it to line the container.
2. Slightly moisten the potting mix and press it firmly into the container. The mix should be an inch or so shy of the rim around the edges and a bit mounded in the middle.
3. Plant your largest plants in the center, followed by the smaller ones at their feet, all the way to the rim.

   Tip: Face the smaller plants outward at an angle on the garden "slopes" and tuck trailing plants along the edges to hide the container's edge from view.
4. Use the chopstick to press the plants and cuttings into place. You can also use it to tuck the liner out of view anywhere it remains visible.
5. Sprinkle crushed rock or tuck in moss to hide the potting mix and give the project a finished look.
6. Use the paintbrush to lightly dust potting mix off the leaves and tidy up all over. Voilà!

Grow your newly created tabletop garden in the same conditions as you would your other succulents.

Succulents come in a huge range of colors, shapes, and sizes.

Parodia leninghausii (lemon ball cactus, golden ball cactus) gets its name from its golden spines, but it also has yellow flowers when it blooms.

Agave victoria-reginae (Queen Victoria agave) is one of the most elegant and popular agaves.

Echeverias (like this *Echeveria* 'Mira') present their leaves in a whorled rosette in various shades of green, silver, and red.

Echinocactus grusonii (golden barrel cactus) grows in a perfectly spherical form.

Euphorbia millii (crown of thorns) is a newer hybrid that has expanded the color range and flower size of this colorful succulent family.

Disocactus ackermannii (red orchid cactus) will surprise you with its gorgeous scarlet flowers.

The cream and gold on the leaves of the *Calathea* 'Golden Gem' really catch the light.

Peperomia caperata (watermelon peperomia) has a leaf pattern reminiscent of a favorite picnic treat.

Phalaenopsis Ruey Lih Beauty is a great example of a moth orchid. They come in all colors, bloom for months, and are inexpensive.

Vinicolor slipper orchids are easy to grow and stay in bloom for weeks.

This cattleya hybrid, *Rhyncholaeliocattleya* Goldenzelle 'Lemon Chiffon' AM/AOS, is a gorgeous soft lemon yellow that highlights the advances in breeding.

Pilea cadierei
(aluminum plant) is
very popular because
it's so easy to grow.

Adiatum raddianum
(maidenhair fern) is one
of the most graceful and
elegant houseplants.

Calathea roseopicta
(rose painted calathea)
has brilliant foliage.

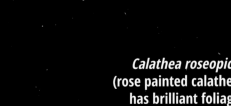

Maranta leuconeura 'Tricolor' (herringbone plant) is a good example of the intricate patterns in the leaves of marantas.

Neoregelia carolinae 'Tricolor' (blushing bromeliad) is a standout because of its green-and-white foliage and red center.

Dieffenbachia is a classic undemanding houseplant.

Dracaena marginata 'Tricolor' (Madagascar dragon tree) is a favorite of many houseplant enthusiasts, but it isn't really a tree.

Fatsia japonica (Japanese aralia) is a somewhat hard-to-find foliage plant, but it's worth the search.

Stromanthe sanguinea 'Triostar' has variegated foliage that shines.

Nepenthes alata (pitcher plant) is a tropical plant that forms a bug-eating pitcher at the tips of its leaves.

This easy-to-grow pothos, *Epipremnum* 'N'Joy', is sought after for its lovely green and white variegations on its heart-shaped leaves.

Plectranthus ciliatus is a golden variegated form of *Plectranthus*.

The green and golden forms of pothos are both bone-tough, so *Scindapsus aureus* (golden pothos) is a popular houseplant.

Tradescantia fluminensis 'Variegata' (Spiderwort) is an excellent houseplant for a hanging basket.

Although most bromeliads are primarily grown for their outstanding foliage, some also have striking flower spikes.

Crossandra infundibuliformis (firecracker plants) sports attractive glossy green foliage and bright orange flowers.

The flowers of *Senecio confusus* (Mexican flame vine) look like they are on fire.

Acalypha hispida (chenille plant) has chenille-like reddish streamer flowers

Abutilon hybrida has a misleading common name, flowering maple, because it isn't related to the maple, although its leaf shape is similar.

Euphorbia pulcherrima (poinsettia) comes in many variations of red, red and white, speckled, pink, and white.

Kalanchoe blossfieldiana (florist kalanchoe) has truly brilliant flowers.

Striking foliage and a brilliant yellow flowers are hallmarks of *Aphelandra squarrosa* (zebra plant).

Justica (Jacobinia) carnea (Brazilian plume) is crowned with an abundance of bright pink tubular flowers.

Anthurium andreanum (flamingo flower) Although there are many types of anthuriums, this is one most people are familiar with.

Today's African violet varieties come in just about every imaginable flower color. *Saintpaulia* 'Cajun Blueberry Hill' is a vibrant blue.

Sinningia speciosa (florist gloxinia) has bell-shaped single or double flowers.

This *Kohleria* hybrid is a lesser-known houseplant you should give a try because it is almost constantly in bloom.

Streptocarpus are available in an amazing array of flower colors and are definitely one of the most spectacular flowering plants out there! This one is *Streptocarpus* 'Neil's Samson'.

Begonia corallina (angelwing begonia) gets its name from the shape of its leaves.

Begonia 'Elatior' is typically covered with masses of flowers.

The long, wiry weeping stems of *Cissus discolor* (begonia vine) make it a perfect houseplant for a hanging pot.

Hoya pubicalyx (wax plant) flowers beautifully when it gets sufficient light, and it also has a heavenly fragrance.

Brugmansia (angel's trumpet) has unique, elegant dangling flowers.

This speckled yellow beauty is from the *Canna* genus, which is known for its various flower colors.

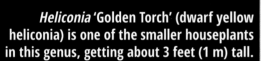

Heliconia 'Golden Torch' (dwarf yellow heliconia) is one of the smaller houseplants in this genus, getting about 3 feet (1 m) tall.

Plumeria like this one (Plumeria rubra, also known as frangipani) are sweetly scented and often are used in Hawaiian leis.

Genus: *Kalanchoe*

This is a popular, easy-to-care-for group of plants distinguished by waxy, durable leaves that are flatter than most succulent leaves. The leaves are scalloped around the edges, and they're sometimes adorned with a band of color (red, reddish-brown). Calandiva is a hybrid of kalanchoe with rose-like flowers instead of flower clusters.

The plants in this diverse group are widely available. Here are a couple of dependable choices:

» ***Kalanchoe blossfeldiana* (florist kalanchoe):** This is the most popular and widespread type, valued for its bright, long-lasting clusters of flowers in red, orange, magenta, coral, pink, yellow, cream, or white. Individually, the flowers are small, but they're carried in clusters on stalks above the succulent leaves to provide a good show (see Figure 10-17 and the color insert). If your plant isn't in flower when you get it, you can induce it to bloom by placing the plant in a dark place — like a closet — for about 14 hours a day for about 10 days. (in other words, creating fall-like conditions). In a month or so, you will be rewarded with flowers. Potted plants reach 12 to 18 inches (30.5 to 45.7 cm) tall, and half that or more in width.

» ***Kalanchoe luciae* (flapjack plant, paddle plant):** It's easy to see how this plant got its common name, with its crowd of distinctive paddle-shaped leaves (see Figure 10-18). They're jade green and gain reddish hues and rims in cooler temperatures, helping them pop. This plant grows 8 to 12 inches (20.3 to 30.5 cm) wide.

» ***Kalanchoe tomentosa* (panda plant):** When you compare the panda plant in Figure 10-19 to the paddle plant in Figure 10-18, you can see how different kalanchoes can look from each other. The silvery, fuzzy leaves give this plant a velvety texture. The leaves are edged in a contrasting brown. This undemanding, resilient plant grows about 18 inches (45 cm) tall.

Genus: *Lithops*

I can't think of an easier, lower-maintenance succulent houseplant than these cute, intriguing lithops, or living stones. This plant gives fresh meaning to the idea of pet rocks, eh? They're adapted to tolerate lots of light and high heat. New leaves develop each year — something you'll enjoy observing if you're attentive.

FIGURE 10-17: There is no plant with a wider range of dazzling, brilliantly colored flowers than this kalanchoe.

Photo by Steven A. Frowine

FIGURE 10-18: As the leaf pads grow larger, they resemble pancakes.

Photo by Steven A. Frowine

Not only are lithops tiny — typically an inch or so (2.5 cm) in diameter — but they grow very slowly. Look closely, and you can see that they have a pair of leaves with a small space separating them; little holes may be visible on the surface of the leaves. On mature and thriving plants, showy yellow or white flowers may appear in the leaf gap in fall or winter.

TIP

Watering can be tricky. Apply a little bit only when the plants are actively growing (in the cooler months). Wrinkling on the tops means the plant needs water. Over-watering leads to mushiness, root rot, and death.

Photo by Steven A. Frowine

There are several dozen species and more than a hundred varieties. They all look quite similar, though, with subtle variations in plant color and markings. Rather than send you off searching for certain lithops, I suggest you simply try whichever ones you can find or fill a container with an assortment. Enjoy!

Figure 10-20 shows you a sampling of these interesting plants.

SIM ONE/Shutterstock

Genus: *Pachyphytum*

Stalks full of clusters of chubby leaves distinguish this genus. The foliage is often mauve, revealing the plant's close relationship to *Echeveria*. When the stalks grow longer/taller, the plants look like funky little trees.

Lots of sun, well–drained potting mix, and a light hand with watering are all they ask. They cannot tolerate cold weather at all, so keep their pot indoors unless your climate is quite warm.

>> *Pachyphytum bracteosum:* Dense gathering of plump leaves, usually waxy blue-green, though the color darkens to lavender-blue the hotter and drier the growing conditions get. Mature height is around 6 to 12 inches (15.2 to 30.5 cm).

>> *Pachyphytum hookeri:* This Mexican native is found in rocky, dry areas. Its gray-green leaves grow in rosettes (see Figure 10-21), which are covered with a white powdery material and can be tipped in red if the plant is in a very bright spot. It can reach 6 inches (15.2 cm) wide and up to 20 inches (15.8 cm) tall, but it's slow growing and seldom reaches this height indoors.

>> *Pachyphytum oviferum* **(moonstones, moonstone plant, sugar almond plant):** The leaves on this plant are so round and chubby, they resemble almonds or tiny eggs. They're lavender to purple with a silvery-white bloom. Mature height is about 6 inches (15.2 cm).

FIGURE 10-21: The pachyphytums look like echeverias but have fleshier leaves.

Photo by Steven A. Frowine

Genus: *Pachyveria*

Here we have hybrid plants that combine the best of both parents, with *Pachyphytum*'s thick–leaved rosettes and *Echeveria*'s always–desirable color variations. These are durable sun–lovers, and they stay a manageable size for container display.

>> *Pachyveria* **'Blue Giant':** As stubby leaves in rosette-forming succulents go, these are slender and not tightly packed. The color is gorgeous — rich purple infused with blue. This one grows about 8 inches (20.3 cm) wide.

>> *Pachyveria* **'Claire':** The powdery blue-green leaves are densely packed in a rosette, and the margins can develop burgundy coloration. Summer flowers, if they appear, are yellow. It matures to 8 inches (20.3 cm) in diameter.

>> *Pachyveria* **'Haageana (*haagai*) Tolimanensis':** This hybrid (with a name that doesn't pass muster as far as proper naming formats go) is relatively common in the trade. It has blue-green leaves (see Figure 10-22) with a stem that can get up to 1 foot (0.3 m) tall.

Like all the plants in this group, the leaves are brittle and can break off easily if roughly handled.

WARNING

>> *Pachyveria glauca* **'Little Jewel':** For this petite beauty with red-tipped silvery-blue leaves, more sun leads to maroon coloration. The form is star-shaped, and it may produce orange flowers in winter. Approximately 6 inches (15.2 cm) in diameter.

FIGURE 10-22:
This attractive and popular pachyveria sports fleshy leaves and orange to red bell-shaped flowers.

Photo by Steven A. Frowine

Genus: *Pleiospilos*

Nope, these aren't lithops, though they certainly look similar and are indeed closely related. Like the living stones they resemble, these are unpretentious little plants that surprise and delight with their showy flowers. The difference is their flowers are bigger and neon orange — wowza! Also, pleiospilos are at their peak in spring and summer, whereas lithops ramp up in fall and winter (consult the entry earlier in this chapter).

Pleiospilos nelii 'Split Rock' (mimicry plant) is more egglike than stonelike, to be honest. At first, it has two gray-green leaves with a cleft down the middle. New leaves develop at right angles. There are no guarantees you'll get flowers, but if orange blooms develop and burst forth, they are quite showy and said to smell like coconuts. The plant grows to approximately 4 to 5 inches (10.1 to 12.7 cm) in diameter.

Genus: *Portulacaria*

Native to South Africa and commonly called elephant bush, this plant has a tidy, treelike growth habit, small, succulent, glossy green leaves, and red stems. Its appearance is reminiscent of the jade plant *(Crassula argentea)*, described earlier in this chapter. It prefers good light, well-drained soil, and watering only when actively growing (it rests in winter).

TIP

Yes, elephants like to eat it, as do goats and other wild animals. So do people — the tart flavor of the small leaves enhances soups and salads. It also has some medicinal uses. Evidently, it uses carbon dioxide more efficiently than other plants, making it popular as an air-purifying indoor plant.

When you grow *Portulacaria afra* as a houseplant, place it in plentiful but indirect light in a draft-free room. In a pot, the plant tends to stay in the 3-foot (0.9-m) range. Cultivars, including variegated ones, exist. See Figure 10-23 for an example of the variegated form of this species.

Genus: *Sedum*

These perky little succulents, also known as stonecrops, are deservedly popular as groundcover in mild climates, but as a rule, they aren't frost-hardy. Happily, many also make excellent houseplants.

FIGURE 10-23:
Elephant bush
matures into a
plant resembling
a bonsai.

Photo by Steven A. Frowine

Some are rosettes, some are mat–formers, and many are trailing. You may combine several in a pot, planter box, or hanging basket for an interesting display. Whatever you decide, rest assured they're easy to grow, varied, and beautiful. Here's a representative sampling, but believe me, there are many to choose from:

>> *Sedum adolphi* **(golden sedum):** This species has light green to warm-hued orange foliage (see Figure 10-24); summer sun causes them to develop deeper-colored margins, whereas the winter color is green. 'Coppertone' is a grand cultivar with dependably orange foliage. The plant produces clusters of starry white flowers with pink *anthers* (pollen-containing lobes attached to stalks in the flower's center) in spring. Plants are about 6 inches (15.2 cm) tall, with hanging stems up to 14 inches (35.5 cm) long.

>> *Sedum allantoides:* Finger-shaped leaves of pale green to silver arch toward the tip of the plant, getting smaller as they go up the stem. Flower stems are branched, with small white blooms in open groups. Full height and width is about 4 to 6 inches (10.1 to 15.2 cm).

>> *Sedum (Hylotelephium) cauticola* **'Lidakense':** A memorable plant with wee rosettes in pink and sage-green hues, it grows 4 to 6 inches (10.1 to 15.2 cm) tall and spreads to 12 inches (30.5 cm).

>> *Sedum dendroideum* **(tree stonecrop):** This is a small, treelike sedum, suitable for raising in a pot. Its gray-brown "trunk" and stems hold clusters of green leaves (see Figure 10-25). It grows up to 2 feet (0.6 m) tall and half as wide.

FIGURE 10-24:
The golden sedum has the typical growth habit of this genus. Many are low-growing fleshy plants.

Photo by Steven A. Frowine

FIGURE 10-25:
This stonecrop resembles a miniature tree.

Photo by Steven A. Frowine

» *Sedum morganianum* **(burro's tail, donkey tail):** Smooth, thick gray-green foliage hangs heavily (see Figure 10-26), up to 3 feet (0.9 m) down, so show it off in a substantial pot. Because the leaves are rather easily knocked off, place this plant out of traffic.

» *Sedum* x *rubrotinctum* **(jellybean plant, Christmas cheer, pork and beans):** Chubby leaves about an inch (2.5 cm) long and ¼ inch (0.6 cm) wide taper at the ends. The tips are tinged with red (see Figure 10-27).

FIGURE 10-26: Donkey tail is a popular succulent for hanging baskets.

Photo by Steven A. Frowine

FIGURE 10-27: The long, succulent leaves certainly do look like jellybeans.

Photo credit Steven A. Frowine

Genus: *Sempervivum*

There are lots and lots of *Sempervivum* (hens and chicks, houseleeks), big and small, but common to them all are two distinguishing characteristics: They form clumps of compact rosettes of succulent foliage, and they have pointy leaves. Another giveaway to look for (although it's not always present when you're looking!) is the tiny independent offsets; when they appear, they can be carefully removed and given their own pots.

While sempervivums aren't a bit fussy, it's especially important to grow them in pots of well-drained potting mix, set them in a spot with bright, indirect light, and avoid overwatering. In other words, set them up and pretty much leave them alone. Note that their Latin name translates to always *(semper)* alive *(vivum)*!

Without further ado, here are a few favorites:

>> ***Sempervivum arachnoideum* 'Arctic White':** As the species name hints, this one features a spidery network of cobweb-like hairs. The plant size is about 4 inches (10.1 cm) in diameter.

>> ***Sempervivum x ciliosum*:** Frosty green leaves tipped in raspberry red have a fluffy look thanks to the presence of small hairs. The rosettes are 3 to 4 inches (7.6 to 10.1 cm) across.

>> ***Sempervivum* 'Eddy':** This one has unusual coloration: burgundy to ruby red. Rosettes spread to 12 inches (30.5 cm) in diameter.

>> ***Sempervivum* 'Gold Nugget':** What a color show this one has! It begins yellow-green and then warms up to fiery orange on rosettes that are only about 6 inches (15.2 cm) across.

>> ***Sempervivum* 'Reinhard':** 'Reinhard' has dramatic apple-green foliage with black tips. It grows up to 12 inches (30.5 cm) in diameter.

>> ***Sempervivum* 'Sugar Shimmer':** Hairy leaves touched with red tips present themselves in a perfectly symmetrical package. As you can see from Figure 10-28, it's low growing, and it produces plenty of offsets.

FIGURE 10-28:
The hairs on the leaves of 'Sugar Shimmer' sparkle in the sunshine.

Photo by Steven A. Frowine

Genus: *Senecio*

Because of their trailing stems, senecios are ideal for hanging baskets and tall urn-like containers, so they can spill over the sides. Good news: They're also tough. They can go for long periods without attention or even much water. However, they do need plenty of bright light.

WARNING

Plant parts are toxic to animals and humans, which is all the more reason to hang them aloft or set their pots up high, out of the way but still easy to admire.

>> *Senecio (Curio) radicans* **(string of bananas):** This curious-looking plant (see Figure 10-29) turns out to be quite easy to grow. Indirect sunlight and occasional soakings are all it needs. And those weird, wonderful leaves do look like little green bananas or fishhooks! Plants trail up to 2 feet (0.6 m) long.

>> *Senecio (Curio) rowleyanus* **(string of pearls, string of beads):** When happy, this is a remarkable trailing plant, letting its unique stems full of tiny, bead-like leaves hang down 2 to 3 feet (0.6 to 0.9 m).

TIP

If the pea-size "pearls" turn mushy and lose their color, you're overwatering, or the potting mix is too heavy and moisture-retentive.

>> *Senecio serpens (Curio repens)* **(mini blue chalk sticks):** This low-growing succulent has powdery, fingerlike, 1- to 2-inch (2.5- to 5-cm) blue-green leaves that face upward (see Figure 10-30). It forms a mat as it grows up to 12 inches (30 cm) tall and 30 inches (70 cm) wide. The tips of the leaves turn purple in strong light.

FIGURE 10-29: The common name, string of bananas, comes from the shape of the leaves, which resemble this fruit.

Photo by Steven A. Frowine

FIGURE 10-30:
In frost-free warm, dry climates, this succulent can be a groundcover.

Photo by Steven A. Frowine

THE HARDY BUNCH: SUCCULENTS THAT CAN TAKE THE COLD

Although succulents often are not cold-hardy and cannot survive cold winters, a few real tough guys don't mind the cold.

These are plants you can leave outdoors year-round. If you're willing to take a calculated risk, you can enjoy them on your deck, patio, or balcony well into autumn before you rescue them and bring them indoors for their winter rest.

Determining whether particular succulents are hardy enough for your area is a tricky call. The safest bet is to buy these plants from a local grower or supplier or a specialist online supplier who has experience and knows which succulents will survive your winter.

I planted an area around my mailbox with hardy succulents, mostly various sempervivums and sedums, and about 80 percent of them survived -2°F (-19°C) winter temperatures. The key to success is having confidence in your supplier — ideally, someone local who has experience with these plants and knows the varieties that are winter-hardy in your area.

To confirm that you can enjoy a specific plant outside as the temperatures begin to dip, cross-check the cold tolerance (hardiness zone) either by asking the supplier where you purchase your plant or by looking it up online or in a reference book. Don't find out the hard way by leaving it outside unadvisedly and witnessing its demise!

Saying Hi to Houseplant Cacti

Container-grown cacti are a special group, sure to win your heart once you delve in. While many are large landscape plants — even tall tree-size ones! — a number are small enough to enjoy a quiet life in a pot on a windowsill or shelf, in a corner of a bright room, or even on a deck, patio, or balcony, your climate permitting. These smaller cacti bring a mini-desert look to your home, and you can easily enhance their appeal by displaying them in attractive, colorful, or unusual pots.

For care tips, review the introduction of this chapter. The short version: These desert-dwellers need only what they're used to — namely, bright sunlight, sandy soil, and infrequent waterings.

When you go shopping for houseplant cacti, focus on these qualities:

>> **Find cacti that are interesting or beautiful.** Some have intriguing or unusual shapes that grab your attention. Some grow boldly upright, some are squat or rounded, and some have stems that can trail over the edge of a pot or hanging basket.

>> **Choose the size you want.** Cacti tend to grow slowly, so what you see is often what you get. If a plant is around 6 inches (15.2 cm) in diameter or a foot (30.5 cm) tall, it will pretty much occupy its allotted space and stay that way for a long time, expanding only slowly over the months and years.

TIP

>> **Don't depend on flowers or fruit.** The main reason to grow cacti is their form, shape, and color in their everyday appearance. Though flowers can be a pretty sight — especially when they emerge from a plain-looking plant — some cacti have to be quite old (a decade or more) to form and unfurl flowers. If the blooms are pollinated (a big *if*), unique-looking (and sometimes edible) fruit may follow flowering. My advice is to be happy with your houseplant cacti just the way they are and welcome flowers if they do appear. Post a picture on Facebook or Instagram so we all can see!

TIP

The curated list of cacti later in this chapter is meant to get you started. I can vouch that all the plants I mention are widely available and no trouble to care for. I make sure to point out the ones that bloom readily.

You may notice that common names, blessedly, tend to paint an accurate description. You may also observe that the same common name applies to different cacti. My advice is, worry more about how a plant looks than what it's called.

Getting to the point: Cactus spines and prickers

Most cacti have *spines* and *prickers*. You may be surprised to find out that these structures are actually modified leaves! They serve three important purposes:

>> They protect the cactus from nibbling creatures.

>> They radiate heat away from the stem during the daytime hours, helping to keep the plant cooler.

>> They collect valuable condensed water vapor (or dew) in the lower-temperature nighttime hours.

WARNING

A few cacti species have things called *glochids*, which are little cottony-looking patches containing many small spines. You don't want to get too close to these!

All these structures can conceivably hurt you — creating puncture wounds and even leading to skin infections. But just be sensible. Place your potted cacti where they can be admired but not brushed against, and you won't have any problems.

TIP

When you need to handle small plants, such as when you're potting, placing, or repositioning them, you may use heavy gloves or (why not?) kitchen or BBQ tongs. Grasp a large cactus carefully but firmly with a thick towel or folded newspaper.

WARNING

Do not try to pull out or clip off spines and prickers, which will end their benefits to the plant and create an entryway into the leaves for rot or insects.

Two can tango: Grafted cacti

You may come across an odd-looking cactus that seems to be two different cacti stuck together, one atop the other. That's exactly what it is! This is called a *grafted cactus*, made by splicing two cacti of similar circumference and encouraging them to grow as one. The bottom part tends to be a strong plant chosen for its sturdiness, while the top is more colorful or has an interesting shape. These are fun! Figure 10-31 shows a tray full of them to give you an idea of the possibilities.

FIGURE 10-31:
A sampling of
what you may
find of these
cacti oddities.

Photo by Steven A. Frowine

Genus: *Astrophytum*

The shape of this one, also known as star cactus or sea urchin cactus, is cool, whether it's viewed from across the room or, better still, from above. For example, *Astrophytum asterias* is olive green and dome-shaped with eight segments, each with tufty white hairs. Its maximum diameter is 4 inches (10.1 cm).

TIP

Note that this is a rare case of a cactus having no threatening spines. Position it accordingly.

Genus: *Cephalocereus*

The stout green columnar stem gets tall — up to 12 inches (30.5 cm) — in a pot but far shorter than it can get out in nature. It's easy to grow in a container and loves the sun.

Cephalocereus senilis is the one you find most readily. It's completely covered with long soft white hair, so it certainly earns its common name, old man cactus (see Figure 10-32). Don't expect flowers or fruit.

Photo by Steven A. Frowine

Genus: *Cereus*

Another tall, erect type of cactus, *Cereus* (torch cactus) has a nice blue–green hue and is lined with spiny ribs — very sculptural, as interior designers might say!

>> **Cereus forbesii or Cereus hankeanus:** This native of South America (Bolivia to North Central Argentina) is a shrubby branched cactus (see Figure 10-33) that can eventually get about 7 feet (2.1 m) tall. Honestly, it doesn't look like much until it shows its large funnel-shaped white, pink, and red flowers. It's also found in a spiral form — *Cereus forbesii* 'Spiralis' — that's much more interesting in stature than the straight species.

>> **Cereus peruvianus (Peruvian cactus, queen of the night):** This one can get an impressive 3 to 5 feet (0.9 to 1.5 m) tall with a thicket of gray-green to blue stems. Prevent leaning as it ages by rotating its pot from time to time. Once mature, it can send forth 4- to 6-inch (10.1- to 15.2-cm) white or pink flowers in summer . . . in the middle of the night.

>> **Cereus repandus (Peruvian apple cactus):** This is another tall grower, reaching 10 feet (3 m) or more, with three to five thick gray-green blades. Rotate the pot from time to time to prevent leaning. This species flowers at night in summer, producing cream-colored beauties. The flowers are pollinated by a certain kind of South American bat, so you won't be getting any Peruvian apples if you live on another continent.

FIGURE 10-33:
This plant looks
pretty mundane
until it displays
its spectacular
flowers.

Photo by Steven A. Frowine

Genus: *Disocactus*

These prickly-stemmed cacti hail from tropical areas, so they need more water (during their growing season, that is) than others, and they don't mind some humidity. They are *epiphytic* (plants that grow on the surface of another plant and derive their water and nutrients from the air or rain), so they're easy to take care of. In spring, they may produce funnel-shaped flowers up to 6 inches (15.2 cm) long.

>> ***Disocactus ackermannii* (red orchid cactus):** From a stout main stem, they grow long leaves with curved edges. The splashy flowers are bright red with yellow stamens (see Figure 10-34 and the color insert). Growth is both upward and outward; with a large pot and time, a plant can get 3 feet (0.9 m) or more wide and tall.

>> ***Disocactus crenatum* (crenate orchid cactus, queen of the night):** Another bushy, rather unruly member of this genus, prized for its gorgeous, fragrant creamy white flowers. The foliage is thick and leathery, with notched or scalloped edges. An especially broad-leafed cultivar is aptly called 'Beavertail'. The ultimate size of a pot-grown plant is 3 feet (0.9 m) wide and tall.

>> *Disocactus (Aporocactus) flagelliformis* (**rat tail cactus**): Very popular and easy to grow, this one has long, slender stems that froth and spill out of a pot or hanging basket, extending 3 to 6 feet (0.9 to 1.8 m). The crimson-pink blooms are abundant.

FIGURE 10-34: The brilliant red flower of this orchid cactus is an unexpected delight.

Photo by Steven A. Frowine

Genus: *Echinocactus*

This curious-looking cactus, commonly known as barrel cactus, slowly grows to form a small ridged ball with splayed spines covering its surface — a very geometric presentation. The contrast between the surface (green or gray) and the spines (yellow, gold, or brown) makes it a handsome plant. Repotting is stressful to this species, so give it a compatible-size container that it won't outgrow. It's a stunning houseplant.

Echinocactus grusonii (golden barrel cactus, mother-in-law's cushion) is a gorgeous green plant with golden spines (see Figure 10-35 and the color insert). Its mature size is about 8 inches (20.3 cm) around.

FIGURE 10-35:
Barrel cactus can grow to quite an impressive size.

Photo by Steven A. Frowine

Genus: *Echinocereus*

Here's a genus full of plants that are the right size for growing in pots and small spaces. In growth habit, they tend to be ribbed, cylindrical, and spiny. Also, they have some of the brightest and best flowers in the cactus world, provided they get plentiful sunlight. Flowers are usually in the 3-inch (7.6-cm) range and burst forth in everything from vibrant pink to bright yellow, bicolor, and more.

>> *Echinocereus coccineus* **(scarlet hedgehog cactus):** This one's a clump-former, and the sensational flowers are red to fiery orange. Mature size is about 18 inches (45.7 cm) tall.

>> *Echinocereus knippelianus:* Barrel-shaped with five to seven ribs, this one is dark green to bluish-green and nearly spineless, which is nice. Flowers are pink to magenta. It gets no more than 4 inches (10.1 cm) tall and wide.

Genus: *Echinopsis*

This is a large genus, with many different shapes and sizes, so I just alight on three favorites. Common to them all are the prickers, lots and lots of prickers — hence the common name, hedgehog cactus. A plus is that many of them bloom easily, sometimes on and off for most of the year. And, thanks to the efforts of hybridists, you can choose from many colors, including pink, red, orange, yellow, and white.

>> *Echinopsis chamaecereus* **(peanut cactus):** It's a cluster of green fingerlike branched stems, developing a trailing growth habit, so it may work best in a

hanging basket. It has ribbed stems and soft white bristles, and reddish-orange blooms literally cover the plant in late spring to early summer. Plant size is about 6 inches (15.2 cm) tall and 12 inches (30.5 cm) wide.

>> *Echinopsis eyriesii* **(sea urchin cactus):** This one has a bulbous, globular form; it's dark green and heavily ribbed with short spines. Best of all, it has proportionally huge scented white to pink flowers on short stalks. This cactus is around 6 to 12 inches (15.2 to 30.5 cm) high and less wide.

>> *Echinopsis oxygona* **(Easter lily cactus):** This native to Argentina and Brazil is quick growing with a gorgeous, fragrant 8-inch (20-cm) funnel-shaped white-to-pink night-flowering bloom. It can grow to 2 feet (60 cm) across and 1 foot (30 cm) tall. See Figure 10-36.

FIGURE 10-36: This cactus is attractive in its own right, but it really shines when it reveals its large white-to-pink flowers.

Photo by Steven A. Frowine

Genus: *Epiphyllum*

The flattened, succulent stems of *Epiphyllum* (orchid cactus, climbing cactus) get long (several feet/m) and hang down, so plants in this genus should be in an elevated pot or hanging basket. But it doesn't have spines!

TIP

These plants like their potting mix moist, but not soggy.

They live up to the orchid cactus name with their gorgeous big blooms. And I do mean *big* — some can be a foot (30.5 cm) or more across. There are tricks to induce blooming, but they vary with selection, so find out when you buy.

There's confusion associated with the nomenclature of the wild species and thousands of hybrids, so this genus gets tangled. Species bloom in spring; hybrids bloom in summer or fall. Just pick one you like and don't worry about it, I say. To save space and avoid unleashing all those choices on you, I'm describing just a couple, starting with the main star of the genus, the one that enthusiasts eagerly nurture and plan viewing parties around:

>> *Epiphyllum anguliger* also called *Disocactus anguliger* (zig zag cactus, fishbone cactus): This Mexican native has unique fishbone-shaped stems, but its main feature is the outstanding, impressive 2- to 8-inch (6- to 20-cm) white flowers that appear in the fall. They have an enchanting evening fragrance. It's usually grown in a hanging basket (see Figure 10-37).

>> *Epiphyllum oxypetalum* (queen of the night, Dutchman's pipe cactus): This cactus has long stems (up to 10 feet, or 3 m), so the plant needs to sit on something high or in a big, sturdy hanging basket. Its glorious night-blooming flowers — white with gold *sepals* (leaflike parts that surround the back of the petals)) — waft a sweet, gardenia-like scent and last only one night.

FIGURE 10-37 Even without its exceptionally beautiful and fragrant flowers, this plant's unique zigzag growing habit makes it a conversation piece.

Photo by Steven A. Frowine

Genus: *Ferocactus*

This is a small barrel-type cactus with prominent ribs and distinctive sharp spines. Bright indirect light is best, and you'll want to slow or withhold water during the winter months. Flowers, if they appear (no guarantees), are proportionately big, bright-colored, and saucer-shaped.

Ferocactus latispinus (recurvus) (crow's claw cactus, candy cactus, fishhook cactus, devil's tongue barrel cactus) is a stout little customer covered with red thorns. Someone thought it looked like a person sticking their tongue out, hence the last common name listed here. The contrast of the thorns against the gray-green barrel is striking. Flowers are funnel-shaped and purple to yellow. The mature size in a pot is about 12 inches (30.5 cm) high and a bit wider.

Genus: *Gymnocalycium*

When you want an easy small cactus houseplant, this genus, commonly called chin cactus, is often suggested. The stems generally don't have thorns, though tiny white ones may appear on the main stem and will flatten out.

TIP Indirect light is ideal for this cactus. Never overwater it.

>> ***Gymnocalycium baldianum* (dwarf chin cactus):** With a bulb-shaped but rather flattened growth habit, this one generates gorgeous coral-pink flowers. Mature size is about 4 inches (10.1 cm) high and a little bit wider.

>> ***Gymnocalycium mihanovichii* (moon cactus):** This charmer is the result of a graft. The top part is *Gymnocalycium* and is colorful with orange to reddish hues (meaning it cannot photosynthesize and thus needs the lower part to survive). The lower part is typically *Hylocereus*. It grows about 12 inches (30.5 cm) tall.

Genus: *Mammillaria*

This large genus is full of variety and includes some plants that are the right size for bright windowsills and other houseplant displays. Three of the best are described here. Mammillarias, or pincushion cacti, tend to have a compact growth habit. The name comes from the Latin word for nipple, which the *tubercles* (protuberances or bumps) are reminiscent of. The tubercles bear spines at their ends. These cacti flower freely, even when the plants are still quite young.

>> ***Mammillaria bocasana* (powder puff cactus):** This little clump-forming cactus is globe-shaped and covered with silky white hairs that hide hooked spines. In spring, a ring of small white flowers encircles it. It grows 5 inches (12.7 cm) tall and 3 inches (7.6 cm) wide. The flowers of var. *roseiflora* are pink.

>> ***Mammillaria spinosissima* (spiny pincushion cactus):** A cylindrical plant that's about 12 inches (30 cm) tall and 3 to 4 inches (7 to 10 cm) wide (see Figure 10-38), the spiny pincushion cactus displays petite 0.8-inch (2-cm) carmine pink flowers followed by purple fruits.

» *Mammillaria tetrancistra* (**common fishhook cactus**): This small globular or elongated plant is coated in the genus's signature white hairs that conceal spines. In a pot, it gets about 6 inches (15.2 cm) wide and, over time, forms clusters. Flowers come in white, yellow, pink, and red, depending on the variety.

FIGURE 10-38: The spiny pincushion cactus is a perfect size for most containers. Just watch out for its many thorns.

Photo by Steven A. Frowine

Genus: *Opuntia*

Opuntia, or prickly pear cactus, is a wide-ranging genus with bigger-than-a-house members and others that are sized appropriately to be houseplants (although the size can be substantial). Common to most are the flattened paddle-shaped leaves. Their flowers are lovely, but houseplants are unlikely to produce edible prickly pear fruits.

» *Opuntia basilaris* '**Baby Rita**' (**beavertail cactus**): A native of the Southwestern United States, it's low spreading (ranging 4 to 16 inches across) with wide, flat fleshy green-gray pads that have tiny thorns (see Figure 10-39). It has splendid 2- to 3-inch (5- to 7-cm) magenta flowers in the spring to early summer followed by small brown fruits.

» *Opuntia bergeriana (elatior)* (**red-flowered prickly pear**): Sunny and warm weather suits this shrubby cactus. Sporting oval pads with long yellow spines, it has memorable fiery red to red-orange springtime flowers. It can get too tall for a house or conservatory — perhaps growing to 10 feet (3 m) or more.

>> *Opuntia microdasys* **(bunny ears, polka dot cactus):** The common names couldn't be more perfect! This cactus has oval pads with tufts of yellow thorns, and it grows 2 to 3 feet (0.6 to 0.9 m) tall, spreading out over time if there's room in the container.

FIGURE 10-39:
Opuntia's pads are a favorite food in Mexico.

Photo by Steven A. Frowine

Genus: *Oreocereus*

Here we have a ribbed oval or columnar plant that, with time and the right location, branches. Its spines are yellow, and the plant is covered in long white hairs. It prospers in full sun.

>> *Oreocereus leucotrichus* **(old man of the Andes):** This is the most popular and recognizable species in this genus, and the common name definitely fits! It's absolutely covered in soft white hairs, which contrast beautifully with its red-pink springtime flowers. You can raise it in a pot to a size of approximately 2 to 3 feet (0.6 to 0.9 m) tall.

>> *Oreocereus trollii:* This smaller "troll" version looks much the same as the previous offering, though with fewer ribs. It gets only about 18 inches (45.7 cm) tall.

Genus: *Parodia* or *Notocactus*

Blue-green in color with spines radiating from prominent ribs, these handsome ball cacti make fine houseplants. Generally globe-shaped, they tend to become more columnar with age. Red, orange, yellow, or pink flowers bloom on mature plants in spring and summer. In my opinion, this genus contains some of the most elegant of all cacti.

TIP

Bright but indirect light is ideal.

>> *Parodia leninghausii* (**lemon ball cactus, golden ball cactus**): It may get its name from its (sharp!) golden spines (see Figure 10-40 and the color insert) or perhaps from its yellow blooms. Over time, it gets around 3 feet (0.9 m) tall.

>> *Parodia magnifica* (**balloon cactus**): Heavily ribbed and spiny (see Figure 10-41), this one has a spherical growth habit. When it's mature, pale yellow flowers appear on top like a bow on a gift-wrapped package. The mature size in a pot is 3 to 6 inches (7.6 to 15.2 cm) tall and a bit wider.

FIGURE 10-40:
Here is a perfect trio of lemon ball cacti.

Photo by Steven A. Frowine

Photo by Steven A. Frowine

Genus: *Rhipsalis*

Long, trailing segmented stems with no prickers make this genus, commonly known as mistletoe cactus or coral cactus, unique — and extremely suitable for a hanging basket or any pot it can spill out of. The stems may be adorned with small white or yellow flowers in winter or spring.

TIP

This cactus can't tolerate hot, direct sunlight, so morning sun or a west- or even north-facing windowsill is best.

Rhipsalis baccifera (mistletoe cactus) is the most widely grown, widely available species, with long, stringy stems. A cultivar called 'Horrida' has thick, fuzzy stems.

Genus: *Tephrocactus*

Naturally small and slow growing, these plants make fine houseplants. Their form is segmented and rather stubby, with a characteristic light or ashy color (*tephra* means *ash* in Greek). Some of them have long, dramatic but papery spines. This genus loves lots of light and should be allowed to dry out in the winter months.

Tephrocactus articulatus var. *papyracanthus* (papery-spined cactus) is the top houseplant choice. This one's spines look threatening but are thin, papery, and not at all sharp to the touch. It grows 4 to 12 inches (10.1 to 30.5 cm) tall.

'TIS THE SEASON: CHRISTMAS, THANKSGIVING, AND EASTER CACTI

Even people who don't know or grow houseplants are aware of these beauties. With their flattened, segmented succulent stems and showy, flaring flowers, these cacti are easy to grow and great for beginners. And nothing quite matches the thrill of watching a plant burst into glorious bloom — often, but not always, in time for a holiday — and then sustain the colorful show for many long weeks. These plants are durable and extraordinarily long-lived, some lasting for decades! They're also easy to raise from cuttings.

Though technically cacti, these plants don't hail from a hot, dry desert but rather from tropical Brazilian rainforests, where they adorn the branches of tall trees. From these origins, you can guess the care they need to thrive in your home or in a protected spot on your patio, deck, or sunporch:

- Filtered or dappled light rather than direct light, which bleaches out the leaves
- Some humidity (mist the plant occasionally when it's in a growth period)
- Water when the potting mix becomes dry

While they all appear quite similar, there's some variation in foliage and flowers. Within the different species and hybrids, more variation isn't unusual — sometimes because people have tweaked blooming to their desired timing (which may be done by experimenting with dry and lower-light periods). I have a friend whose red-flowered one likes to bloom around July 1. (She's Canadian, so she calls it her Canada Day cactus.) Here are the main ones:

- **Christmas cactus** (see the photo) is *Schlumbergera* x *buckleyi*. The flowers are red or hot pink and hang down.
- **Thanksgiving cactus** is *Schlumbergera truncata*. A distinguishing characteristic is pincer-like protuberances on each square leaf segment. It has soft pink flowers.
- **Easter cactus** is *Schlumbergera* or *Rhipsalidopsis gaertneri.* Look for trumpet-shaped flowers with pointy petals in hues of bright pink, dark red, orange, or cherry.

A few pro tips:

- Allow a yearly cool and dry rest period.
- Never move a plant once buds appear.

(continued)

(continued)

- Allow stems to harden/toughen up and buds to form outdoors in the summer months.

© Nadezhda Nesterova/Shutterstock

Chapter **11**

Easy Orchids: Don't Pass Up These Beauties

M any folks think growing orchids is an intimidating experience. Why is this? Possibly because it is one of the largest and most complex of all the plant families, with more than 25,000 species and 100,000 hybrids.

Orchids are found in most parts of the world but primarily hail from tropical climes. In this chapter, I am going to introduce you to some of the most commonly found and easiest to grow members of this fascinating family. I start out with the easiest to grow and most readily available orchid, which many gardeners think is the most satisfying one: the moth orchid. Then I deal with some of the others that are worth trying: slipper orchids, cattleyas, and a choice few others.

After you review this chapter, I hope you will take the plunge and try your hand at growing these unique and enchanting plants.

Becoming Familiar with the Basics of Orchid Culture

Orchids are not difficult to grow, but, like all plants, they have cultural requirements that must be met. In this section, I give you some fundamental orchid growing information, based largely on my own experience of growing orchids in a greenhouse, under lights, and in windowsills.

TIP

Check out the American Orchid Society's website at www.aos.org/ for cultural sheets with sound advice for growing all types of orchids.

Check out Part 2 for general growing information that's applicable to orchids, as well as other houseplants. Here, I list some specifics about growing orchids:.

» Light requirements are not much different than the other plants in this book. Moth orchids and slippers like low to medium light (about 1500 foot candles; see Chapter 5 for more detail on light). Cattleyas and their relatives like things a bit brighter, about 2500 footcandles.

» Most orchids are from tropical areas where ample air moisture is the norm, so around 50% humidity will be appreciated.

» Ventilation that provides a slow steady airflow results in fewer disease issues.

» Moth orchids are considered warmth-loving orchids and prefer day temperatures in the mid-70s to mid-80s°F(23 29°C) during the day and 15°F cooler in the evening. Slippers, cattleyas, and other orchids mentioned in this book prefer more intermediate temperatures: 65 to 75°F (18 to 23°C) during the day and about 15°F cooler in the evening.

» For fertilizing and watering guidelines, check out Chapter 6. Because orchids are slow growing, they have low fertilizing requirements compared to most other houseplants. When using water-soluble fertilizers, ¼ teaspoon of fertilizer per gallon of water works.

» Potting media used for orchids is a bit different than that used for other houseplants. Most consist of pine or fir bark and perlite. As a beginner, you are better off buying ready-made mixes available from orchid plant providers. Later, as you get more confident, you can blend your own.

>> Diseases and insects are not much of a problem with most orchids. Providing good sanitation and growing conditions will go a long way toward keeping your orchids healthy.

Repotting Orchids without Fear

Most beginning orchid growers are afraid to repot their orchids. Despite their reputation as elegant plants, orchids are tough. After all, they were first brought over from the tropics to Europe in the holds of ships and, miraculously, many of them survived the trip! In this section, I give you all the information you need to repot your orchids with confidence.

Knowing when to repot

Your orchid will tell you when it's the right time to repot. Look for these clues and situations to help you know when your orchid needs repotting:

>> When the orchid roots are overflowing the pot

>> When the plant itself is going over the edge of the pot

>> When the potting material is getting soggy and drains poorly

The ideal time to repot most orchids is when the plant starts new growth, usually right after it flowers. With certain orchids, you'll see a swelling at the base of the plant, which is the beginning of the new lead or shoot that will form the next stem, leaf, and flowers.

If you don't repot your orchid at this new-growth stage, the new roots and growths are easily exposed to breakage, and the new roots won't have any potting material to grow into. Therefore, they'll be more likely to dry out. If the orchid plant becomes too overgrown, you'll have trouble transplanting it later without damaging it.

Orchid potting — step by step

Here I explain how to repot a cattleya orchid:

1. **Remove the orchid from the pot.**

    You may need to use a thin-bladed knife to circle the inside of the pot to loosen the roots.

2. **Remove or cut off the old, loose, rotted potting material and any soft, damaged, or dead roots.**

3. **If the roots are healthy, firm, and filling the pot, put the orchid in a pot just one size larger than the one you removed it from, placing the older growth toward the back so the new lead or growth has plenty of room.**

    If the roots are rotted and in poor condition, repot the plant in a container of the same or one size smaller than it was removed from.

WARNING

    If you place a poorly rooted plant in too large of a container, the growing material will stay too damp, which will result in more of the roots rotting.

TIP

    Some orchid growers like to add a coarse material like broken clay pots, expanded clay aggregate, or Styrofoam in the bottom of the pots to improve drainage. You usually don't have to do this if you're using shallow pots.

4. **Place the plant in the pot so it's at the same depth as it was originally.**

    The new shoot should be level with the pot rim. See Figure 11-1.

5. **Press the fresh potting material into the pot and around the orchid roots with your thumbs and forefingers.**

    The orchid should be secure in the pot, so it doesn't wiggle — otherwise, the new roots won't form properly.

6. **Place a wooden, metal, or bamboo stake in the center of the pot and tie up the new and old leads with soft string or twist ties.**

TIP

The potting process for moth orchids and slippers is very similar to the steps I just outlined for a cattleya, except that the orchid should be placed in the *center* of the container rather than toward the back.

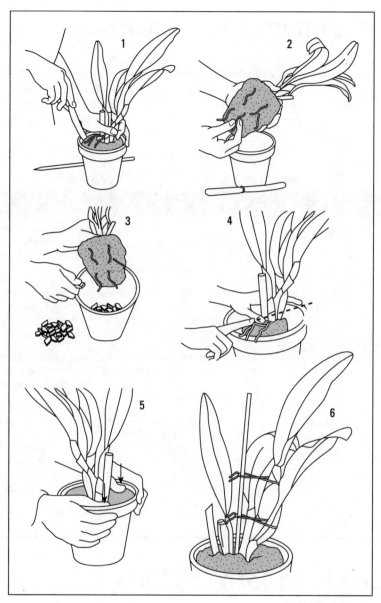

FIGURE 11-1:
Potting an
orchid — this
one is a type
of cattleya.

Understanding Orchid Names

Orchid names can be a bit complex and intimidating. They are more involved than other houseplant names. Here's an example of a hybrid orchid name: *Rhyncholaeliocattleya* Goldenzelle 'Lemon Chiffon' AM/AOS. (See the color insert for a photograph of this orchid.) Table 11-1 breaks down the name and explains its various parts.

TABLE 11-1 ## The Components of an Orchid's Name

Part of Name	Name	Comments
Genus	*Rhyncholaeliocattleya*	This genus combines two different genera — *Rhyncholaelia* and *Cattleya* — to result in the human-made name of *Rhyncholaeliocattleya.* The name is capitalized, in Latin, italicized, and frequently abbreviated *Rlc.*
Species	None	This is a hybrid that has several different species in its parentage, so no single one is listed. When an orchid hybrid comes from just one species, the species name will also be listed, lowercase, in italics, and in Latin.
Grex	Goldenzelle	All the resulting progeny from this cross are given a name that's known as a *grex.* Think of this as you and all your siblings having a label. The grex is always written in a language other than Latin, is capitalized, and isn't in italics.
Cultivar (cultivated variety)	'Lemon Chiffon'	This is a selection from this grex that was deemed, in some way, superior to the other members of the progeny. This name is always in any language other than Latin, is capitalized, is not italicized, and is in single quotes. There are frequently several or more cultivars in a grex. Think of the cultivar as one of your parents' children. You're all labeled with a grex, but the cultivar is you in particular.
Award Designation	AM/AOS	Award of Merit from the American Orchid Society

Meeting the Moth Orchids

Moth orchids (*Phalaenopsis*) are the fastest and easiest type of orchid to grow, and they offer everything that most orchid growers admire. They bloom for a long time — from many weeks to months. Their flowers are classy and borne on elegant arched branched flower stems frequently called "sprays". They come in a broad range of colors, and their foliage is a beautiful glossy or marbled green. They have very modest light requirements, and they grow well in temperatures commonly found in most homes.

Moth orchids are definitely the orchids to start with, and after you experience the great satisfaction they provide, you may decide to stick with them. The standard pink, white, and striped ones commonly sold in big-box stores and at flower shops are the essence of style, but in addition to these beauties, you can find many new and exciting colors, color patterns, and growth habits that increase their desirability. Although most aren't fragrant, some are.

After reading through this section, you'll understand why this type of orchid takes the prize for the one that most folks grow and admire.

TIP

In this section, I discuss the bare minimum about this huge group of fascinating orchids. To find out much more about them, check out my book *Orchids For Dummies*, 2nd edition (Wiley).

Examining the popularity of moth orchids

Moth orchids are by far the most popular type of orchid purchased and grown today, but that hasn't always been the case. During the Victorian era in England, when tropical orchids were the rage, moth orchids were hardly on the radar. Because moth orchids have succulent leaves, they were more perishable than some of the other orchids, which made them difficult to transport safely from their tropical climes to the greenhouses of England and Europe. During that time period, cattleyas, oncidiums, and other hardy orchids ruled the orchid market.

With improved and speedier transportation and superior growing techniques that produce better quality plants faster, the tides have changed. Now moth orchids are found everywhere — big-box stores, specialty growers, orchid shows, garden centers, botanical gardens, orchid societies, online, and mail-order companies.

You may be wondering what makes moth orchids more popular than other species. Here are some key reasons:

>> They're easy to grow.

>> You can start with standard phalaenopsis hybrids that any newcomer can be wildly successful with.

>> They cost less than they ever have.

>> Some emit lovely perfumes.

>> Because of the huge diversity of moth orchids, you'll never tire of them.

>> They don't require an expensive greenhouse to grow. They're happy with a windowsill or an artificial light setup.

>> They beautify your home and life.

>> They can live for a really long time.

Deconstructing the beauty of moth orchids

Moth orchids are beautiful plants, and in this section, I fill you in on exactly what to expect from them.

Attractive leaves

All the moth orchids have handsome foliage. This isn't true for many other types of orchids. Some moth orchids have leathery, glossy dark green leaves, whereas others flaunt exquisitely marbled dark green or gray-green leaves. Even when these plants aren't in bloom, they remain quite attractive.

Graceful flower shapes

The various types of moth orchid flowers have similar shapes, though many of the newer varieties have a very rounded look. Because moth orchids epitomize style, they're frequently used in flower arrangements and in simple, yet chic, corsages. Figure 11-2 shows you the names of the moth orchid flower parts.

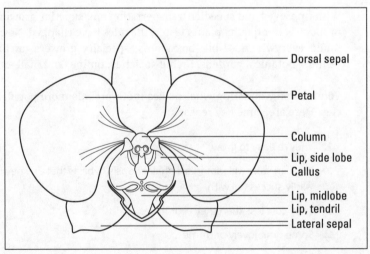

FIGURE 11-2: The parts of a moth orchid (phalaenopsis) flower.

© John Wiley & Sons, Inc.

ENCORE! ENCORE! A SECOND SHOW

One of the great features of moth orchids is their ability to produce a secondary flower spike that branches off the main one (as shown in the nearby figure). This will make your flower show last for months!

To make this happen, after the flowers have stopped blooming on the flower spike, feel along the bare spike to find the bumps where the flowers were. These knobby structures are called *nodes.* At the base of the nodes are resting flower buds. Your mission is to wake up one of these buds so it will produce another flower spike. Notice where the first flower opened on the stem, and go to the next node down, toward the base of the plant. Cut off the spent flower spike there. In most cases, you will stimulate the production of a secondary flower spike at this node.

Remember: Don't bloom your moth orchids to death! Sometimes moth orchids don't know what's good for them. They just keep blooming to the point of exhausting all their energy. If the orchid is a robust plant, this continual bloom is okay. But if the leaves are puckered and the plant looks worn out, or if the plant is very young and not yet established, you're better off cutting off the flower spike and enjoying it in a flower arrangement. This will give the plant some rest and an opportunity to put its energy into growing new roots and leaves so it will be strong enough to produce even more blooms in its next flowering.

© John Wiley & Sons, Inc.

Endless flower colors

White, pink, and candy-striped are the standard moth orchids most commonly found at flower shops and big-box stores as both potted plants and cut flowers. These traditional moth orchids seem to have reached the pinnacle of perfection in flower size and shape, and because of modern reproduction and growing methods, they're highly affordable. In fact, in Europe and certain large urban centers in the United States, they're commonly purchased as expendable flowering potted plants that are discarded after their many weeks of bloom.

The traditional colors are no longer the only options, though. In the last several years, a revolution in moth orchid breeding has occurred, resulting in an entirely new, diverse, and wonderful array of moth orchids that display flower colors and patterns unimaginable just a few years ago. Now these sensuous flowers come in all shades of red, orange, yellow, and dark purple. The harlequin types, with their unpredictable but always delightful patterns of color, have opened a virtual crayon box of color patterns with seemingly endless possibilities.

The following list examines some of the wide array of colors you'll encounter in moth orchids. Within these groups, you can find many variations, shades, and hues. Orchid breeders are constantly producing new flower colors and patterns.

>> **Shimmering whites:** Round, pristine white flowers (see Figure 11-3) epitomize the elegant look of moth orchids. Through breeding, the standard whites have reached such perfection in size, shape, substance, and texture that it's difficult to imagine how they can still be improved.

>> **Striped and spotted white moth orchids:** Striped moth orchids are sometimes referred to as *peppermint* or *candy-striped phalaenopsis* (see Figure 11-4). They have white flowers with stripes of dark pink or red that vary in intensity, number, and thickness.

   Today's hybrids with much larger flowers and more prominent stripes have surpassed older hybrids that were once considered such notable breeding accomplishments. Taiwanese breeders have recently introduced some superior striped hybrids.

>> **Semi-albas:** Many orchid growers would agree that by the 1980s, large flowering *semi-albas* (hybrids that have white flowers with red lips) had reached their peak. Although somewhat newer superior ones continue to be produced, the leaps in improvement are incremental. Interestingly, like the breeders of solid whites, many breeders of semi-albas are now concentrating on producing *multifloras* — plants that are compact with more small flowers — instead of larger-flowered standard-size hybrids.

FIGURE 11-3:
White moth orchids like this *Phalaenopsis* Cygnus 'Renaissance' are the epitome of elegance.

FIGURE 11-4:
Candy-striped moth orchids are striking.

Photo by Steven A. Frowine

>> **Pinks:** Most early pink moth orchid hybrids started off using the species *Phalaenopsis schilleriana* and *Phalaenopsis sanderiana* as parents for their desirable flower color. Pinks then started reaching the flower size of whites with better shape and color distribution. Progress toward larger, more intense flowers and an even distribution of color continues today.

For a breathtaking example of a sumptuous dark pink hybrid, see *Phalaenopsis* Ruey Lih Beauty in the color insert and Figure 11-5.

FIGURE 11-5:
Phalaenopsis Ruey Lih Beauty is one example of the rich, deep pinks found in some of the phalaenopsis hybrids.

Photo by Steven A. Frowine.

>> **Yellows and oranges:** Moth orchid breeders have the goal of producing yellow and orange hybrids with steadfast color and flower size equal to the white hybrids. Although they've made a lot of progress, most of the flowers today are a soft yellow. Some newer ones are brighter yellow and more colorfast, but they aren't as perfectly round or as large as the standard whites. Still, they're a delightful addition to any collection.

>> **Reds:** Red is a welcome addition to the color range of moth orchids. The quest for red hybrids continues to cause quite a bit of dissension among breeders regarding what constitutes a "good red." The hybrids of today have reached a high standard of strong, lasting color, good form, attractive flower presentation, and excellent substance. In general, the flowers aren't as large as the whites and pinks, nor do the plants have as many flowers, but orchid breeders are rapidly improving on both these scores.

>> **Harlequin moth orchids:** Harlequin moth orchid hybrids have some of the wildest and most unpredictable flower color patterns in the entire orchid world, as Figure 11-6 shows. A unique quality of these orchids is that flowers on the same plant are all slightly different in their markings. Some of these variations from flower to flower are caused by environmental conditions, whereas others are attributed to complex genetics.

REMEMBER

Flower color can be affected by environmental factors, including the temperature and light levels at which the plants are grown, especially during flowering. When temperatures are warmer (above 80°F [26°C] or so) as the flowers are forming, the pigmentation of the spotting and overall flower color are usually fainter; when the light is brighter, the spots tend to be smaller.

FIGURE 11-6:
A harlequin-
type orchid,
Phalaenopsis
'Sue Chin'.

Moth orchids with a scent

One complaint that some orchid lovers have voiced about moth orchids is that they may be beautiful, but they don't have any fragrance. Not true! Some species are wonderfully fragrant, and they have been used as parents to produce an array of sweet-scented hybrids. You likely won't find these fragrant moth orchids in the big-box stores, but they're available from specialty moth orchid suppliers and online.

Phalaenopsis Orchid World 'Bonnie Vasquez' AM/AOS is one of my favorite fragrant moth orchids. There are many different forms of this classic variety. Most have leathery, thick, long-lasting glossy yellow flowers brightly marked with red or maroon spots or stripes (see Figure 11-7).

FIGURE 11-7:
Phalaenopsis
Orchid World is a
group of moth
orchids that have
a delightful scent.

Some other fragrant moth orchids are *Phal. violacea*, *Phal. bellina*, *Phal.* Ambo Buddha, *Phal.* Perfection, *Phal* Sweet Memory, and *Phal.* Penang Girl.

Miniature moth orchids

Some of the glorious moth orchids you see in the stores make an impressive show with their 24- to 36-inch (60- to 90-centimeter) arching flower spikes, but these plants may not fit in the limited growing space you can provide. Luckily, diminutive moth orchids thrive in smaller environments. In fact, an entire group of moth orchids referred to as *novelties*, *minis*, *multifloras*, or *sweethearts* are very compact-growing plants sporting many flowers up to 2 inches (3 cm) across. I've grown several of these and find them to be a pure pleasure. They're commonly available and very reasonably priced at big-box stores and supermarkets. See Figure 11-8 for an image of the miniature moth orchid *Phalaenopsis* Sogo 'Twinkle'.

MOUNTING ORCHIDS

Many orchids that are found naturally growing in trees can be mounted instead of placed in pots. Mounting gives them perfect drainage, simulates their natural habitat, and can be an easy way to maintain them.

To mount your orchid, follow these steps (and refer to the nearby figure):

1. Place the plant on a small handful of moistened, squeeze-dried sphagnum moss.

2. Spread the roots around the sphagnum moss.

3. Place the orchid on the mount, which can be made of a long lasting hardwood like oak or a slab of tree fern, so its center points down for most monopodial (orchids that have one stem and grow in only one direction — up.).

   You can mount some sympodial types like cattleyas with the growing point facing up.

4. After the orchid is centered properly, wrap either stainless-steel wire or clear fishing line (monofilament) around the top and bottom of the mount to hold it in place.

   In several months, after the new roots have taken hold, you can remove the wire or line.

5. Hang the finished mounted orchid in a bright place in your greenhouse or near a window.

Because these mounts drain so rapidly, they need to be watered often, sometimes more than once a day during the hot summer months. It is usually easiest to water mounted orchids with a gentle spray in a sink.

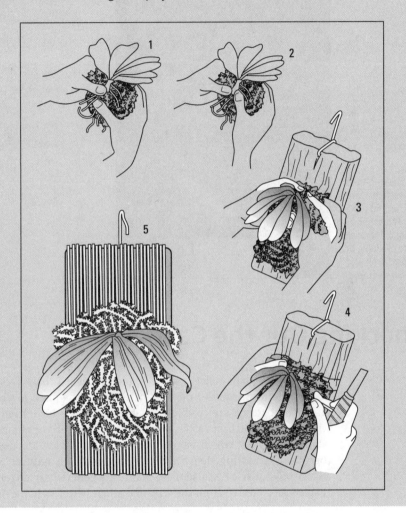

FIGURE 11-8: Many miniature moth orchids, like *Phalaenopsis* Sogo 'Twinkle', are available at most home and garden centers.

Checking Out the Cattleyas

In the 1800s, plant collectors and explorers risked their lives in steamy tropical outposts to bring South American cattleyas to the plant lovers of Europe. Today, all the best forms are readily available, and none have been collected from the wild. Instead, the best cattleyas are raised from seed or clones (see Chapter 8) in laboratory flasks, which is good news not only from a conservation standpoint (because harvesting doesn't result in destroyed natural habitats from field collecting) but also because these plants are generally stronger and more vigorous than those collected from the wild and adapt better to home-growing situations.

Until the skyrocketing popularity of moth orchids took off in the early 2000s, cattleyas were the undisputed orchid champs. They're still highly popular because they offer huge, often wonderfully fragrant flowers in a complete spectrum of colors and shapes on plants varying in size from a few inches (5 cm) to a few feet (60 cm) tall. To understand how the glorious flowers of cattleyas are constructed, see Figure 11-9.

In this section, I introduce you to a few of the many orchids in this illustrious group. All of them are readily available and easy to grow. You can see why they exemplify the beauty and fragrance that only orchids can offer.

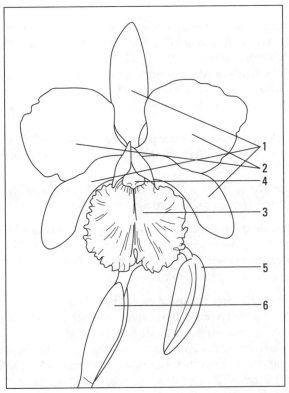

FIGURE 11-9:
The structure
of a typical
cattleya flower
(1 = Sepals; 2 =
Petals; 3 = Lip; 4 =
Column; 5 = Bud;
6 = Sheath).

REMEMBER

This group of orchids has undergone several name changes. Although many grow-ers and sellers still use the older names, some do use the newer names. To help you keep track of them, I list them by the older and more commonly used name and give the new name in parentheses to clarify some of the confusion.

Cattleyas grow best in moderate humidity and medium to bright light, with good air circulation and intermediate (55 to 66°F [12 to 18°C]) night temperatures (10 to 15 degrees higher during the day). For general cultural (growing) informa-tion, see Part 2.

The queens of the ball: Cattleya hybrids

A modern, standard-size cattleya hybrid in full bloom is a sight to behold! Thanks to the skill of orchid hybridizers and the ease with which cattleyas and their rela-tives have adapted to crossbreeding, today's hybrids are producing flowers in a breathtaking array of colors and heady fragrances.

REMEMBER

Note that the plants I've listed in this section are just the tip of the iceberg; many new hybrids are being produced and introduced every year. The range of flower color combinations seems endless. The United States used to be the premier breeder of the Cattleya Alliance orchids (those orchids that are related to cattleyas) but now Asia plays a major role, which is reflected in the names of some of the newer hybrids.

Because cattleya breeding has progressed to such a state of perfection, it's difficult to choose a bad one. Here are the most common flower colors you will find:

>> **Pristine whites:** White cattleyas are almost as classic as the lavender ones. The modern hybrids have full, round, fragrant flowers.

>> **Purples, pinks, lavenders, and blues:** Purple hybrids have been around for a long time. Any orchid in this color group is a good choice. The blue shades in cattleyas are newer. Most of the purples are highly fragrant. You can't go wrong with any of these hybrids.

>> **Hot reds and oranges:** Most of the red hybrids are compact growers because a common parent is one of the sophronitis, which are red, orange, or yellow dwarf plants native to Brazil. One to look for — either as plants you'll grow or in the parentage of the plants you're considering — is *Sophrolaeliocattleya (Cattlianthe) Jewel Box 'Scheherazade' AM/AOS* (now called *Cattlianthe* Jewel Box). It's an older hybrid that's still popular today because of its manageable size (see Figure 11-10), clear red flowers, and easy culture.

FIGURE 11-10:
Sophrolaeliocattleya (Cattlianthe) Jewel Box 'Scheherazade' AM/AOS remains a favorite.

>> **Sunny yellows:** Fine yellow cattleyas are a more recent development. Today's hybrids range from gold to butter yellow. Some are solid yellow, whereas others have dark red- or purple-splotched lips. *Brassocattleya* Goldenzelle 'Lemon Chiffon' (now called *Rhyncholaeliocattleya* Goldenzelle) is a worthy representative of how far yellow flowers in cattleya hybrids have come. It sports 6-inch (15-cm) lemon yellow flowers with a splash of deep red on the lip (see Figure 11-11). This is a winter bloomer and a frequent winner at orchid shows.

>> **Cool greens:** There's something refreshing about lime green flowers. Green cattleyas have their own following among orchid lovers. Some of their flowers have very fringed lips, usually inherited from the species *Rhyncholaelia digbyana* (formerly known as *Brassavola digbyana*). This unique species is also noted for its strong fragrance. Some of the greens have clear flowers, whereas others are blotched in purple. *Brassiocattleya (Rhyncholaeliocattleya)* Rio's Green Magic is a fine representative of this group (see Figure 11-12). This hybrid shows, with its deeply fringed lip, the influence of *Rhyncholaelia digbyana*. It has large 5-inch (13-cm) flowers.

FIGURE 11-11: *Rhyncholaeliocattleya* Goldenzelle 'Lemon Chiffon' AM/AOS is a gorgeous soft lemon yellow that highlights the advances in breeding.

© John Wiley & Sons, Inc.

FIGURE 11-12:
Rhyncholaeliocat-tleya Rio's Green Magic offers unique beauty and a sensuous fragrance.

© John Wiley & Sons, Inc.

>> **Splash petals and flares:** This group is commonly called *clowns* because of the sense of gaiety their wild color combinations arouse. They're marked with two or more splashes (or *flares*) of contrasting color, and the results can be quite dramatic. These days this group of cattleyas has received the lion's share of cattleya breeders' attention. Figure 11-13 shows one of the most popular clowns, *Potinara* Burana Beauty 'Burana' HCC/AOS (now called *Rhyncattleanthe* Burana Beauty). It's a compact grower that reaches about 12 inches (30 cm) tall. Its 3½-inch (9-cm) citrus-scented flowers are yellow with red flares, and it often blooms twice a year.

FIGURE 11-13:
Potinara (Rhyncattleanthe) 'Burana Beauty' HCC/AOS offers clusters of citrus-scented yellow flowers with red flares.

© John Wiley & Sons, Inc.

>> **Fashionable art shades:** This is a catchall category that includes cattleya-type hybrids that combine a range of pastel colors. Because most home orchid growers have space limitations, smaller-growing cattleyas are becoming more popular. Figure 11-14 shows a nice one named *Brassolaeliocattleya* Hawaiian Avalanche (now called *Rhyhncolaeliocattleya* Hawaiian Avalanche). This orchid shows off a delightful display of tropical color with its 6-inch (15-cm) apricot pink flowers that have a golden-orange fringed lip with a purple streak down the center.

FIGURE 11-14: *Rhyhncolaeliocattleya* Hawaiian Avalanche provides a riot of color.

© John Wiley & Sons, Inc.

Exploring the miniatures

For the past few decades, cattleya breeding has been focused on producing plants that are smaller in stature than the earlier large–growing hybrids. Now, small is in — at least in plant size. Previously, when cattleya orchids were primarily grown in commercial greenhouses for cut flowers and corsages, the objective was to produce very large blooms. The plants also tended to be sizeable. Although there's no denying that full-size cattleyas in bloom are impressive, unfortunately they also take up a lot of growing space. And for windowsill and under–light growers, where every square inch counts, this creates a problem. This is where *minicatts* (short for *miniature cattleyas*) come in.

Minicatts have no special cultural requirements that differ from the standard full-size plants. Because they're commonly planted in small clay pots, they tend to dry out more quickly than larger plants in bigger pots, so you need to keep a sharp eye on your watering to make sure they don't get too dry.

Laeliocattleya 'Angel Love' is a good example of a minicatt. This easy-to-grow fragrant hybrid (see Figure 11-15) has perfectly formed 4-inch (10-cm) lavender-pink flowers with a frilled lip and yellow inside the throat.

FIGURE 11-15: Miniature cattleyas like *Laeliocattleya* 'Angel Love' don't require much space and do well under lights or on a sunny windowsill.

A few other cattleya relatives of note

The orchids in this section are relatives of cattleyas (you can see the strong resemblance in the photos) and have the same basic growing requirements. Growing these will give you a greater variety of flower colors and shapes, and many of them are fragrant.

Genus: *Brassavola*

You can find several excellent *Brassavola* species, but the one that leads the pack because of its popularity and ease of growing (with the same cultural requirements as cattleyas) is *Brassavola nodosa* (shown in Figure 11-16). It's commonly called Lady of the Night because of its enchanting fragrance that permeates the evening. One to six spidery greenish-white flowers, from 3 to 6 inches (7.5 to 15 cm) across, are borne on a 6-inch (15-cm) flower stem. It's a clump-forming orchid.

FIGURE 11-16:
Brassavola nodosa, or Lady of the Night, has an enchanting evening fragrance.

Genus: *Prosthechea*

This group contains some of the easiest orchids to grow and bloom. Many of them are also fragrant. I group these together because they're closely related, and some growers still refer to them all as encyclias. Here are a couple that are very undemanding and rewarding:

» *Prosthechea cochleata* (now called *Encyclia*): Commonly called cockleshell or clamshell orchid because its upside-down flower lip resembles one, this unique-looking orchid (see Figure 11-17) is easy to grow and often blooms several times a year. The lip is streaked with purple, whereas the rest of the spidery flower is green.

» *Prosthechea radiata* (formerly called *Encyclia*): Its clusters of subtle creamy white cockleshell-type flowers with purple-striped lips (see Figure 11-18) aren't what make this orchid so popular — though they *could* be. Instead, its ease of growing and blooming and wonderful fragrance — which has been variously described as smelling spicy-floral or like coconut cream pie, lilac, cinnamon, and hyacinth — are what keep people coming back to this orchid.

FIGURE 11-17:
*Prosthechea
(Encyclia)
cochleata* blooms
more than
once a year.

FIGURE 11-18:
*Prosthechea
radiata* is another
cockleshell
orchid.

Trying On the Slipper Orchids

Lady's slippers aren't difficult to grow and are among the most rewarding orchids you'll find, making them a great orchid for beginners. They present a wide range of strikingly colored, frequently glossy flowers in many shapes. Some have petals that are elegantly twisted, whereas others are marked with hairs and warts. All slipper orchids are noted for very long-lasting blooms — the flowers usually last six to eight weeks. Many lady's slippers have gorgeous marbled foliage, which makes them stunningly beautiful, even when they aren't in bloom. Collectors of slipper orchids tend to be a fanatical lot — and it's easy to see why.

TECHNICAL STUFF

The official name of this group is *Paphiopedilum* 'Asian Lady's Slipper', but you'll probably hear them referred to as lady's slippers, just plain slipper orchids, or paphs. These orchids got their common name because of their pouchlike lip, or *labellum*, which resembles a lady's slipper (see Figure 11-19).

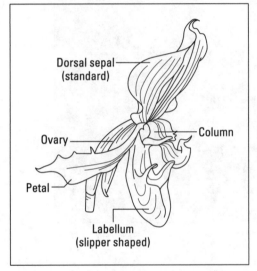

Dorsal sepal
(standard)

Column

Ovary

Petal

Labellum
(slipper shaped)

FIGURE 11-19: The parts of a lady's slipper orchid flower.

© John Wiley & Sons, Inc.

Giving your lady's slipper a good home

Although lady's slipper orchids are found in cold climates in North America, the ones that are most grown indoors are from the old-world tropics, like Southeast Asia. Almost all lady's slippers grow well in average home temperatures — 65 to 75°F (18 to 24°C) during the day, and 55 to 60°F (13 to 18°C) during the evening — and have modest humidity requirements.

Some lady's slippers are among the least demanding orchids when it comes to light, so they're very adaptable to growing on windowsills or under lights. (For more general plant-growing details, check out Part 2.)

Admiring marvelous *Maudiae*

What a fabulous group of lady's slippers these are. *Maudiae* is the name given to one of the first hybrids, created in 1901 between *Paphiopedilum callosum* and *Paphiopedilum lawrenceanum. Paphiopedilum* Maudiae and its offspring are noted for their exceptional vigor, ease of blooming (sometimes more than once a year), undemanding growing requirements, gorgeous foliage, and striking, gloriously colored flowers. Some have green-and-white flowers, whereas others are wine colored (called *vinicolors*). See Figure 11-20 and the color insert for an example of a wine-colored *Maudiae* type.

FIGURE 11-20: Vinicolor lady's slippers have flowers that are so shiny, they look like they've been lacquered.

© John Wiley & Sons, Inc.

Going big with modern lady's slippers hybrids

These lady's slippers are sometimes called *bulldogs* or *toads*. To tell you the truth, I don't know how they got branded with such odd nicknames! They look nothing like these two creatures to me. But they do sport wonderful huge flowers that last for weeks.

Another name for them is *complex hybrids*, which makes sense because their parentage is very convoluted, many times consisting of 20 or more parents.

All the orchids in this group have plain green foliage, and most of their flowers are huge and primarily round. They're basically categorized by their flower colors: spotted, green, white, yellow, red, pink, and shades of these colors. I have a spotted one that has been a delight: *Paphiopedilum* Langley Pride 'Burlingame' HCC/AOS (see Figure 11-21).

FIGURE 11-21:
Some hybrid slipper orchids are called bulldogs because of their massive flowers.

Taking a spin with the dancing ladies: Onicidiums

This group of orchids is referred to as *dancing ladies* because many of them have lips that are flared like a flounced dancing gown, and the tops of the flowers, with a little imagination, look like the arms and head of a person. Oncidiums are a joyful bunch of orchids that frequently display a flurry of flowers in the sunny yellow to orange-and-brown color range, although some shine in shades of pink, red, and green.

Hundreds of oncidiums are in existence, but just a handful are grown with regularity today. In general, they can be grown in the same conditions as cattleyas.

Oncidium 'Sharry Baby' is a good one to start with. This orchid (see Figure 11-22) is one of the most popular in the world, outselling all the other orchids. The number one reason: its very strong fragrance of chocolate or vanilla. It also blooms more than once a year, often around Christmastime. A mature plant has hundreds of ½-inch (1.5-cm) yellow-overlaid-with-burgundy flowers that have a flared white lip with purple markings.

It's a bone-tough plant that will thrive when others wimp out. I gave one to my neighbor, and with very little TLC, it performs dependably every year. This variety is available in many different color forms. If you have the space (it can grow more than 30 inches [75 cm] tall), you can't go wrong buying one.

FIGURE 11-22:
Oncidium 'Sharry Baby' is a favorite because of its luscious scent.

Growing miniature oncidiums or tolumnias

Until recently, these miniature plants that look very much like oncidiums were called *equitant* (or *variegata*). Plant *taxonomists* (people who name plants) are now huddling to decide whether these plants should be assigned to the genus *Tolumnia* rather than *Oncidium*.

Whatever you want to call them, they're darling little plants that are easy to grow. They have thick triangular leaves and grow best in a sunny spot with good air movement. They're often mounted on wood or cork but can also be grown in pots. Because they're small plants in small containers (see Figure 11-23), you must keep an eye on them so they don't dry out too severely.

FIGURE 11-23:
Miniature oncidiums or tolumnias are great for plant lovers with limited space.

Chapter **12**

Foliage Plants: Create an Indoor Tropical Paradise

oliage plants — those plants that are primarily grown for their attractive leaves — are by far the most popular and admired of all the houseplants. As far back as the Victorian era in England, keeping houseplants has been in vogue. At that time, parlor palms and ferns were a must-have for all "respectable" homes. Since then, houseplants have gone in and out of favor, and we're currently in a houseplant boom. Both younger and older folks are eager to find some new plant to add to their indoor oasis.

In this chapter, I introduce you to a variety of the most popular foliage plants that are easy to grow, readily available, and most attractive. Some are large display plants, and others fit on a tabletop. Their growth habits range from upright to viny. As you become a more experienced indoor gardener, you will discover many more other houseplants, but what I offer here is a good introduction to the wild world of exotic tropical foliage plants.

Examining Why People Grow Foliage Plants

It's no wonder that foliage plants are popular. They're easy to grow, and their gorgeous foliage can be as colorful as flowers. The indoor sanctuary you can create with these plants can relieve stress and connect you to nature. Superior growing and propagation techniques are constantly producing new and better-quality plants. Improved and speedier transportation means plants are available for purchase everywhere — big-box stores, specialty growers, home and garden shows, garden centers, botanical gardens, online, and mail-order companies. You may be wondering what makes foliage plants the most popular type of houseplant. Here are some key reasons:

>> They're easy to grow.

>> You can start with undemanding plants and later try some of the challenging plants as you get more adventuresome.

>> Most are very reasonably priced.

>> Because of the huge diversity of foliage plants, you'll never tire of them.

>> They don't require an expensive greenhouse to grow. They're happy with a windowsill or an artificial light setup.

>> They beautify your home and life.

>> They can live for a long time.

Introducing an Assortment of Foliage Plants

The variety of foliage plants available today boggles the mind. New plants are being produced all the time. In this chapter, I feature foliage plants that are proven, bread-and-butter houseplants as well as those that you can try if you want to stretch your plant repertoire.

Although these plants are grown for their foliage, they all flower when given enough light. However, the flowers are almost always insignificant, so I don't mention them in the description unless they're special or outstanding.

Most foliage plants are originally from a very similar environment, so their cultural (growing) requirements are alike. They enjoy moist air, modest air movement, bright but not direct sunlight, and temperatures that humans find comfortable — around 65 to 75°F (18 to 24°C), give or take 5 degrees in either direction. I've tried to avoid being too repetitive with the cultural requirements for the genera or individual plants I mention; you can assume that these relatively basic requirements pertain to all the plants discussed in this chapter unless otherwise noted. For more detailed information on cultural requirements, check out the chapters in Part 2.

Of course, there are many more foliage plants than I can list in this limited space, but the ones I describe will get you started with plenty of options to explore on your plant safari.

Large-growing foliage plants

I realize that the phrase *large-growing* is a bit vague and subjective. In general, this section includes houseplants that work as specimen or display plants in reasonably large growing areas like a sunroom or another bright living space. These houseplants are usually on the floor because their height, pots, and potting material make them too awkward and heavy to place on shelves, windowsills, or tables.

Genus: *Aglaonema*

The common name of this plant, Chinese evergreen, is quite misleading because it's in no way related to needled evergreen trees or shrubs. This is one of the toughies. It has a low demand for light and isn't too particular about humidity. It's somewhat slow growing, so it doesn't need to be repotted frequently (only about every couple years). On average, most aglaonemas grow to about 18 inches (45 centimeters) high and about as wide. Their spear-shaped leaves can be marked in silver or painted in red, yellow, or white.

>> *Aglaonema* **'Silver Queen':** This variety is one of the standards in the trade for good reason. It has conspicuous feather-like silver markings down the center of its leaves (see Figure 12-1) and is very undemanding in its culture. They are easily raised from stem cuttings, which you can read about in Chapter 8.

>> *Aglaonema* **'Siam Red':** Aglaonema varieties are getting spiffed up these days, and this one is a fine example. It sports green leaves brightly marked with red stripes on the margins and down the center (see Figure 12-2).

FIGURE 12-1: *Aglaonema* 'Silver Queen' is one of the most readily available Chinese evergreens.

FIGURE 12-2: *Aglaonema* 'Siam Red' is an example of the newer varieties. Easy-to-grow Chinese evergreens are workhorses for houseplant growers.

Genus: *Alocasia*

The plants in the *Alocasia* genus (common name African mask) are exotic beauties that add a touch of the tropics to any indoor plant collection. Some of the plants in this genus can be huge and are more appropriate for conservatories. I focus on those that are more in scale with most living spaces.

» **Alocasia x amazonica:** A distinctive plant with arrowhead-shaped dark green leaves marked with dramatic silver veins (see Figure 12-3). On average, one of these plants grows to about 2 feet (60 cm) tall. It prefers higher humidity (50 percent or better) and likes to stay moist; after all, it is a bog plant in its natural habitat. To keep it actively growing, try temperatures at 65°F (18°C) or higher.

» **Alocasia baginda 'Dragon Scale':** This one has the same basic growing requirements as *Alocasia* x *amazonica*, but it can get slightly taller. Its heavy-textured (scale-like) silver-marked leaves (see Figure 12-4) shine in bright light. This variety used to be rare but is showing up more frequently at plant specialty suppliers.

FIGURE 12-3:
Alocasia x
amazonica is a
striking plant that
used to be rare
but now is readily
available.

Photo by Steven A. Frowine

FIGURE 12-4:
Alocasia 'Dragon
Scale' is an
example of the
striking foliage
available in this
group of plants.

Photo by Steven A. Frowine

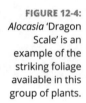

Genus: *Alpinia*

These ornamental gingers are a large and varied plant family. Many of them are too large to be houseplants, but others are good choices. Some are relatively hardy and can grow outdoors in areas where winter temperatures don't fall much below freezing. One of my favorites is *Alpinia zerumbet* 'Variegata' (shell ginger). It grows luxuriously outdoors in Florida, Mexico, and throughout the tropics. It can be big — about 3 feet (1 meter) tall and wide — but you can keep it in bounds by trimming it back. Its creamy white and green striped leaves (see Figure 12-5) are quite attractive. It produces fragrant shell-shaped flowers when it's grown in strong light; in lower light, it serves as a foliage plant.

Genus: *Araucaria*

The common name for this genus is monkey puzzle tree. Large specimens are found in Chile, but I'm featuring one that's native to Norfolk Island in the Pacific Ocean. *Araucaria heterophylla* (Norfolk Island pine) is a pyramidal soft-needled evergreen (see Figure 12-6) that can reach about 9 feet (2.7 m) but rarely gets that tall indoors. To keep it from getting leggy, give it very bright light exposure. Average household humidity and temperature ranges suit this plant fine.

FIGURE 12-5:
Alpinia zerumbet 'Variegata' lightens up any indoor garden with its variegated foliage.

Photo by Steven A. Frowine

FIGURE 12-6:
Norfolk Island pines are used as holiday trees in the tropics.

Photo by Steven A. Frowine

Genus: *Caladium*

Caladiums display an impressive array of dazzling foliage colors. They are frequently grown as shade-loving plants in outdoor gardens but also make colorful additions to an indoor garden.

Caladium lindenii (angel wings) also goes by the older name *Xanthosoma lindenii* 'Magnificum'. It hails from Colombia, and its dramatic leaf markings make it a standout. As you can see from Figure 12-7, it looks quite different from the garden variety of caladium. It reaches 2 to 3 feet (up to 1 m) high and does best in bright light, but not direct sunlight. As a tropical plant, it enjoys warm temperatures (70°F [20°C] or higher) and 50 percent or higher humidity.

FIGURE 12-7: This caladium has distinctive leaf markings.

Photo by Steven A. Frowine

Genus: *Cycas*

This plant genus from the Asian tropics has been around since prehistoric times. Although there are more than 100 cycads, only one is readily available and grown as a houseplant: *Cycas revoluta* (sago palm). This handsome cycad (see Figure 12-8) grows very slowly but can reach a spread of about 2 feet (60 cm). It's an undemanding houseplant that only asks for moderate humidity and bright diffused light.

FIGURE 12-8: This is a cycad, not a palm, but it does have a palmlike appearance.

Photo by Steven A. Frowine

Genus: *Dieffenbachia*

Dumb cane, the common name attributed to this genus of houseplants, comes from the fact that its sap can irritate or numb the tongue. The most common houseplant dieffenbachia is *Dieffenbachia seguine,* which is also known as *Dieffenbachia amoena.* It's one of the most popular large houseplants, undoubtedly because it displays large, attractively patterned leaves (see Figure 12-9 and the color insert) and is a fast, unfussy grower. It can grow to 5 feet (1.5 m), makes a strong statement in any indoor garden, and does well in bright diffused light and moderate humidity.

FIGURE 12-9:
Dieffenbachias are popular tried-and-true houseplants.

Photo by Steven A. Frowine

Genus: *Dracaena*

Several dracaenas are popular as large houseplants. I describe a few that are easy to find and widely admired. Aside from those I've listed, you can search out *Dracaena sanderiana (braunii)*. All plants in this genus have the same basic cultural requirements: bright light, moderate humidity, and room temperatures that are also comfortable for humans. In their native land, they can grow quite large, but as houseplants they're usually kept to about 6 feet (about 2 m).

>> ***Dracaena fragrans* (corn plant):** The shape of the foliage resembles the leaves on a corn stalk (see Figure 12-10), thus its common name. These plants are frequently sold as stalks with side branches. The leaves can be solid green or variegated.

FIGURE 12-10:
Dracaena fragrans is a sturdy, substantial plant.

Photo by Steven A. Frowine

- **Dracaena marginata 'Tricolor' (Madagascar dragon tree):** The spiky tufts of leaves are the primary feature of this plant (see Figure 12-11 and the color insert). It's found in forms with solid green leaves or with green, red, and white leaves (tricolor).

- **Dracaena reflexus (song of India):** Song of India is slow growing with appealing yellow-edged leaves (see Figure 12-12) that are borne in a whorl.

FIGURE 12-11:
A favorite of many houseplant enthusiasts, the Madagascar dragon tree isn't really a tree.

Photo by Steven A. Frowine

FIGURE 12-12:
Song of India is another popular dracaena.

Photo by Steven A. Frowine

Genus: *Fatsia*

Fatsia japonica (Japanese aralia, figleaf palm) has bold, glossy, palm–shaped green or variegated green and white leaves (see Figure 12–13 and the color insert). It grows up to 6 feet (2 m) high and wide. It only requires moderate humidity, average room temperatures, and filtered sunlight. A related houseplant with a similar appearance and cultural requirements is *Fatshedera*, whose parents are this plant and English ivy.

FIGURE 12-13:
Japanese aralia is
somewhat hard
to find but worth
the search.

Photo by Steven A. Frowine

Genus: *Ficus*

This huge genus of plants, which you may know as rubber plants, grow into substantial trees in the tropics and are also stalwart houseplants. All the plants in this genus can grow in full sun to bright diffused light. Because they're undemanding for humidity and comfortable in average household temperatures, they make easy-care houseplants.

WARNING

Unfortunately, these plants have the bad habit of dropping some of their leaves when they are moved from a humid spot to a drier location — such as when they have been on an outdoor summer vacation and move back to the drier air and lower light of their indoor home. Usually, they will recover with new leaves as they adapt. Don't panic and overwater the plants while they are recovering.

>> *Ficus elastica* **(rubber plant):** If you break one of its thick leaves, you'll see the white latex-like sap that gave this plant its common name. You can find rubber plants with solid dark green leaves or variegated leaves with white markings (see Figure 12-14). Both are handsome plants.

FIGURE 12-14:
The rubber plant
is a good-looking
and imposing
houseplant. This
is one of the
variegated forms
sometimes called
"Tricolor."

Photo by Steven A. Frowine

» *Ficus lyrata* (**fiddleleaf fig**): For a bold statement, you can't beat the fiddleleaf fig (see Figure 12-15). It can get quite large, which makes it great for a background plant or as a specimen in a sunroom or bright living room. More compact forms are available if you're short on space.

» *Ficus benjamina* (**weeping fig**): I'm mentioning this ficus because it's so commonly found. Unfortunately, it has a bad reputation for dropping leaves, so the other two in this list are better choices.

FIGURE 12-15:
The fiddleleaf fig is a very popular large-growing houseplant with fiddle-shaped leaves.

Photo by Steven A. Frowine

Genus: *Monstera*

Monstera deliciosa (Swiss cheese plant) is the only species within this genus that's commonly grown as a houseplant. The most curious thing about this Central American native is that its leaves form holes and cuts as they mature. This plant can get monstrous in size (10 to 15 feet [3 to 4.5 meters]!) so give it some room and a sturdy stake if you want to grow it to maturity. It's very undemanding in its cultural requirements. It comes in green or variegated green and white leaf forms (see Figure 12-16).

Genus: *Musa*

Unless you have a large sunroom or greenhouse, most of the plants in this genus are too tall for most homes. However, there's an exception: *Musa acuminata* 'Poquito' (red dwarf banana, poquito banana plant).

Red dwarf banana doesn't produce edible fruit but instead is grown for its attractive green leaves with red blotches (see Figure 12-17). It grows only 3 feet (1 m) tall and wide, and prefers full sun to partial shade.

Photo by Steven A. Frowine

Photo by Steven A. Frowine

Plant group: Palms

Frankly, most of the plants in this group are well suited only for large greenhouses and conservatories because of their massive size and need for bright light. A few can be happy in an indoor garden, though. Probably my favorite is *Phoenix roebelenii* (dwarf date palm, pygmy date palm), which is a small, slow-growing palm that peaks at about 6 feet (2 m) high. It doesn't demand the strong light or space of its much larger cousins. Its leaves are finely textured (see Figure 12-18).

A few other palms you can try for your indoor garden include *Beaucarnea recurvata* (ponytail palm), *Dypsis lutescens* (areca palm), *Chamaedorea elegans* (parlor palm), *Howea forsteriana* (kentia palm), and *Rhapis excelsa* (bamboo palm).

FIGURE 12-18:
The dwarf date palm is one of a handful of palms that are small enough for indoor gardens.

Photo by Steven A. Frowine

Genus: *Philodendron*

This is a large genus native to Central and South America with hundreds of species found in an array of sizes and leaf shapes. They're all easy plants that do well in moderate light, humidity, and temperatures. Here, I focus on a few star examples:

» *Philodendron* **'Birkin':** 'Birkin' is a relatively new philodendron that's a standout for the dramatic white stripes that show up as its leaves mature (see Figure 12-19). It's a slow-growing, compact plant that can ultimately reach about 3 feet (1 m) tall and wide.

» *Philodendron* **'Prince of Orange':** Sometimes folks think of philodendrons as ho-hum, boring plants. That certainly isn't the case with this beauty! Its leaves change color, starting off red, then maturing to coppery hues, and eventually settling to shades of green (see Figure 12-20). It's a real chameleon.

FIGURE 12-19:
The striped leaves of *Philodendron* 'Birkin' light up any houseplant collection.

Photo by Steven A. Frowine

Photo by Steven A. Frowine

Genus: *Polyscias*

A few species of this plant are popular, but the most readily available is *Polyscias fruticosa* (Ming aralia), which has a distinctive Asian look. Even small plants look like miniature trees with twisted stems and ornamental foliage (see Figure 12-21).

Photo by Steven A. Frowine

WARNING

If the humidity in its growing space is too low, it can drop some of its leaves.

Genus: *Radermachera*

Radermachera sinica (China doll) is the only species in this genus that's commonly sold as a houseplant. It was introduced into the trade in the 1980s. This is a fast grower with lush green leaves (see Figure 12-22). To keep it bushy, grow it in bright light and prune it regularly. It gets about 4 feet (1.2 m) tall and has no different growing requirements than other foliage plants.

FIGURE 12-22:
China doll is primarily grown for its foliage but will produce white or yellow flowers if given enough light.

Photo by Steven A. Frowine

Genus: *Schefflera*

Two species of this genus are popular: *Schefflera actinophylla* and *Schefflera arboricola*. The first, *Schefflera actinophylla* (umbrella tree), is the larger of the two, reaching 3 to 6 feet (1 to 2 m). Both sport stalks with 12 to 16 leaflets that produce a drooping canopy of leaves. *Schefflera arboricola* (dwarf umbrella plant), which you can see in Figure 12-23, seems to be more readily available these days, possibly because it has a more compact growth habit than its cousin. Both plants have no exceptional cultural requirements.

FIGURE 12-23:
The dwarf umbrella tree is smaller than its cousin, *Schefflera actinophylla*.

Photo by Steven A. Frowine

Genus: *Stromanthe*

Stromanthe sanguinea 'Triostar' is the star of this genus. Its green, cream, and pink variegated leaves (see Figure 12-24 and the color insert) make it an excellent choice to add color to any plant collection. It grows about 18 inches (45 cm) tall by 24 inches (60 cm) wide. To show off its full range of leaf colors, grow it in a very bright space. It prefers a more humid spot than some of the other houseplants.

Photo by Steven A. Frowine

Genus: *Thaumatophyllum*

Only one species from this genus is commonly cultivated as a houseplant: *Thaumatophyllum bipinnatifidum* (split-leaf philodendron). It looks something like a monstera with its glossy lobed green leaves (see Figure 12-25), but its leaves don't have holes. Like monstera, split-leaf philodendron can grow to be quite a large plant, up to 10 feet (over 3 m) tall, so it needs plenty of growing room and support for its stalk. It's a very undemanding plant to grow.

Photo by Steven A. Frowine

Genus: *Yucca*

This genus has species that are commonly grown outdoors as hardy garden plants. One tropical species that grows indoors is *Yucca elephantipes* (cane yucca), which makes a strong vertical statement in any indoor garden (see Figure 12-26). Like its outdoor cousins, the mature version produces white, bell-shaped flowers if it receives enough light. It grows 3 to 6 feet (1 to 2 m) tall and only requires bright light to grow best. Average room temperatures and humidity levels serve it fine.

Photo by Steven A. Frowine

FIGURE 12-26: This tropical yucca looks much like the hardy varieties you see in outdoor gardens.

Genus: *Zamioculcas*

Not long ago, this plant was rarely seen in garden stores, but now you can often find it in both its green and purple-black forms.

Zamioculcas zamiifolia (fern arum) is touted as a beginner plant because it's so forgiving in its cultural requirements. Its glossy, succulent leaves (see Figure 12-27) create quite an exotic and glamorous look. This happy companion to any of your houseplants grows to about 3 feet (1 m).

Photo by Steven A. Frowine

FIGURE 12-27: *Zamioculcas zamiifolia* used to be a rare plant, but its reputation for being undemanding has made it more common in most home stores.

Small-growing foliage plants

The small-growing foliage plants in this section are suitable for smaller growing spaces or as foreground plants. Even people in tiny houses, dorm rooms, or small urban apartments can find room for these plants.

Genus: *Asparagus*

Yes, these plants are related to the vegetable you enjoy eating with Hollandaise sauce. Two species in this genus are the most commonly grown. Both species look great as hanging plants and have a height and spread of about 2 feet (60 cm), and both are considered easy plants with no exceptional growing requirements. The foliage from both plants has long been used as a filler in floral arrangements.

>> ***Asparagus plumosus (setaceus)* (asparagus fern):** This graceful plant has very fine, feathery foliage that resembles a delicate fern, although it's not at all related to ferns. It can be a good substitute if you like the look of ferns but don't have the humid conditions that some of the more delicate ferns require.

>> ***Asparagus densiflorus* 'Sprengeri' (foxtail fern):** This plant seems to be more popular these days than the asparagus fern. Its arching stems with needlelike spring green leaves (see Figure 12-28) make the plant an attractive and tidy addition to your houseplant collection.

FIGURE 12-28: This plant has the fine texture of a fern but is related to the asparagus you eat.

Photo by Steven A. Frowine

Plant group: Bromeliads

Bromeliads form a large group of plants. They derive their nutrients and moisture from the air, so in nature they're most often found attached to trees. Bromeliads as houseplants roughly break down into two types: those that are noted for their flowers and those that are primarily grown for their foliage.

TIP

The center of a bromeliad is vaselike for collecting water and nutrients. Keeping it refilled with fresh water every 4 to 6 weeks is one cultural requirement. Some creatures, like small frogs, search out this damp oasis for their home. They sometimes hide as hitchhikers in these plants from the nursery where you purchased them.

Although some bromeliads can get 3 feet (1 m) or more across, most are smaller and fit well in an indoor garden. They all like bright diffused light, don't have excessive humidity requirements, and do well in average room temperatures. Mature plants eventually die after they flower but then produce sideshoots or babies that go on to become mature plants and repeat the cycle. Some bromeliads, such as the one in Figure 12-29 (and the color insert), have quite conspicuous and attractive *inflorescences* (flower spikes).

FIGURE 12-29: Some bromeliad inflorescences put on quite a show.

Photo by Steven A. Frowine

If you're so inclined, you can make it a hobby to specialize in these fascinating plants. I describe just a few of them here:

» *Aechmea* **(silver vase):** This genus of bromeliads includes several attractive species that have both ornamental foliage and flower spikes like the one shown in Figure 12-30.

» *Cryptanthus zonatus* **(zebra plant, earth star):** This one features distinctive silver banding on its leaves (see Figure 12-31) presented in a rosette form. Unlike most of the other bromeliads, zebra plant is *terrestrial* (it grows in the ground), so it is commonly grown in potting media in a container like most of the other plants in this chapter. It's smaller than many of the other bromeliads at about 10 inches (25 cm) high and 16 inches (40 cm) wide.

FIGURE 12-30: Many species of *Aechmea* treat you to both dramatic foliage and attractive inflorescences.

Photo by Steven A. Frowine

FIGURE 12-31: *Cryptanthus zonatus* is just one of many plants in this genus with striking foliage.

Photo by Steven A. Frowine

» *Neoregelia carolinae* **Tricolor (blushing bromeliad):** I'd say this is likely the most grown and admired bromeliad. Its green and white variegated outside leaves and brilliant red center leaves (see Figure 12-32 and the color insert) make it a showpiece in any indoor garden. Blue flowers in the center of the plant are merely a sideshow. It grows to about 18 inches (45 cm) high and wide.

» *Vriesea hieroglyphica* **(king of bromeliads):** With a mature spread of over 3 feet (1 m), this bromeliad is admittedly not a small plant. However, it's a slow grower, and it rarely reaches this size indoors. It's one of my favorite foliage-type bromeliads. The markings on its wide leaves look like some strange script (see Figure 12-33).

SOME PLANTS LIVE ON WATER FROM THE AIR

The moniker *air plant* applies to a type of bromeliad (the most common genus of these plants is *Tillandsia*), but it's a bit of a misnomer. In their natural habitat, they do collect moisture from the humid air, rain, and fog via their hairy leaves. If you visit any tropical or subtropical areas, you'll see these plants hanging on power lines or tree branches. They're frequently sold mounted on driftwood (as in the photo) or shells.

© Todd Boland/Shutterstock

They need little care aside from periodic watering. It's best to submerge the plant in warm distilled water for about 30 minutes once a week. Distilled water is recommended because these plants are used to rainwater and are sensitive to salts and other impurities that can be found in tap water.

FIGURE 12-32: Blushing bromeliad has green and white foliage with a red center that makes it shine in any plant collection.

Photo by Steven A. Frowine

FIGURE 12-33:
A specimen of king of bromeliads is truly regal.

Genus: *Calathea*

Calatheas are tropical plants with more than 300 members in their genus that mostly hail from Brazil; most are small enough to fit in your indoor garden. The foliage of these plants, which is dazzling with its dramatic markings and colors, develops best in humidity of 50 percent or greater. If the humidity is too low, the leaves sometimes develop brown edges. Other than that requirement, they do well in diffused light and average room temperatures.

>> *Calathea* **'Golden Gem':** This jewel has light green leaves irregularly painted in cream and gold (see Figure 12-34 and the color insert). In bright light it really shines.

>> *Calathea insignis (crotalifera)* **(rattlesnake plant):** An alternative name is *Goeppertia insignis*. This species is the one you're most likely to find offered for sale. The sword-shaped light green leaves with purple undersides have dark green markings and are quite stunning (see Figure 12-35). If the plant receives enough light, it produces yellow flowers. It grows about 2 feet (60 cm) tall.

FIGURE 12-34:
Calathea 'Golden Gem' is one of the outstanding newer calatheas.

>> *Calathea roseopicta* **(rose painted calathea):** This is a showstopper! The brilliant rose-pink color in the center of leaves bordered with green (see Figure 12-36) stops you in your tracks. It can reach about 3 feet (1 m) tall but is usually smaller indoors. To see this plant in full color, check out the color insert.

FIGURE 12-35: The striking leaf markings make this one of the most popular calatheas.

Photo by Steven A. Frowine

FIGURE 12-36: Brilliant foliage is the hallmark of this calathea.

Photo by Steven A. Frowine

Genus: *Colocasia*

Colocasia 'Hilo Beauty', which also goes by *Alocasia* 'Hilo Beauty' and *Caladium praetermissum*, is a newer hybrid with green leaves uniquely patterned with cream to chartreuse (bright green) flecks (see Figure 12-37) that are borne on bluish-black *petioles* (leaf stalks). It can reach over 3 feet (1 m) high, but it's not a fast grower. Like other members of this genus, it doesn't appreciate drying out. It will grow best in higher humidity — 50 percent or greater.

Photo by Steven A. Frowine

Genus: *Dracaena*

Most houseplants in this genus are covered earlier in this chapter in the large plant section, but there's at least one exception: *Dracaena godseffiana (surculosa)* (gold dust dracaena). Unlike its larger cousins, it's a small, shrubby plant rarely reaching 2 feet (60 cm) tall. It has glossy green leaves that look like they've been dusted with gold to creamy-white flecks (see Figure 12-38).

Photo by Steven A. Frowine

Plant group: Ferns (various genera)

It's difficult to imagine a tropical plant collection without these delightful foliage plants. It's a huge group of plants; I can only crack the surface. The many textures and shades of green that ferns add to your collection make them indispensable. Most ferns luxuriate in extra humidity — 50 percent or more — so rooms with higher humidity (like bathrooms) are a good place for ferns. They prefer bright, diffused light and do well in regular indoor temperatures.

Here are a few of my favorites:

- » *Adiantum raddianum* (maidenhair fern): This purely elegant beauty has delicate fronds with black stems (see Figure 12-39 and the color insert). It's a rather slow grower that can reach 2 feet (60 cm), but dwarf forms are available.

- » *Asplenium nidus* (bird's nest fern): When most folks think of ferns, they won't picture something like this. The bird's nest fern's leaves are strap-shaped and semi-erect (see Figure 12-40). This plant can grow to about 2 feet (60 cm) tall and wide, but it takes quite a while to reach that size.

- » *Nephrolepis exaltata* or *bostoniensis* (Boston fern): Another name for this one is sword fern. It's the fern you see in hanging baskets on porches throughout the United States in the summer (see Figure 12-41). No fern is tougher than this one! When it's moved from its summer outdoor growing area to an indoor space with lower humidity, some of its leaves can turn yellow and drop. Its height and spread can get 2 feet (60 cm) high and wide or even larger as it matures.

FIGURE 12-39: There is no more graceful fern than the maidenhair.

Photo by Steven A. Frowine

FIGURE 12-40: A very popular fern that's at home as a lone display plant or mingling with other houseplants.

Photo by Steven A. Frowine

FIGURE 12-41:
Most everyone is
familiar with
this fern.

Photo by Steven A. Frowine

>> *Pellaea (Hemionitis) rotundifolia* **(button fern):** This pixie fern is perfect for small spaces because it rarely grows larger than 12 inches (30 cm) high and wide (see Figure 12-42). It's less particular about humidity than other ferns, so it's considered one of the easier ferns to grow.

>> *Platycerium bifurcatum* **(staghorn fern):** One notable example of the diversity of plant forms you can experience with ferns is the staghorn fern. As the leaves mature, they strongly resemble deer or elk antlers (see Figure 12-43). This species is just one of many in the genus that are fascinating to grow. Unlike most ferns that grow in the ground, staghorn ferns are *epiphytic,* which means they grow on supports such as tree limbs. As house-plants, they're usually mounted on wood plaques, especially as they grow larger. They can get 2 feet (60 cm) wide and tall or larger, so they need to be mounted on substantial wood plaques and hung in a bright spot.

>> *Pteris cretica albolineata* **(variegated table fern):** This is another elegant, slow-growing fern with finely cut arching fronds (see Figure 12-44) that can reach 18 to 2 inches (46 to 60 cm) tall and wide.

FIGURE 12-42:
If you're looking
for a small fern,
this just may fit
the bill.

Photo by Steven A. Frowine

Photo by Steven A. Frowine

Photo by Steven A. Frowine

Genus: *Fittonia*

Fittonia argyroneura (albivenis) (nerve plant, mosaic plant) has strikingly dark green foliage that's veined in either brilliant white (see Figure 12-45) or red. Both forms brighten up any plant collection. Its relatively small size of 6 x 8 inches (15 x 20 cm) means it can be easily accommodated in most indoor locations. It does best in higher humidity — 50 percent or greater — but other than this requirement, it will be happy to live with any of your other plants.

Genus: *Hypoestes*

Hypoestes phyllostachya (polka dot plant) is a very fast-growing plant that has heart-shaped green leaves decorated with splotches in one of several colors — white, red, pink, or purple (see Figure 12-46). It's a small grower at about 10 inches (25 cm) high and wide. It can get a bit rangy as it gets older, but you can easily prune it back to make it bushier. It's happiest with humidity in the 50 percent range, bright light, and average room temperatures.

Photo by Steven A. Frowine

Photo by Steven A. Frowine

Genus: *Maranta*

This genus is somewhat like *Calathea* in that its members have striking, beautifully colored and marked leaves. They are in the same plant family and are natives of Brazil. Marantas are commonly referred to as prayer plants because their leaves fold up in the evening and reopen in the morning. This phenomenon also happens with calatheas. Like their cousins the calatheas, marantas perform best in 50 percent or more humidity, bright diffused light, and average room temperatures.

>> *Maranta leuconeura* **(prayer plant):** This may be the most commonly available maranta. It displays egg-shaped light green leaves with dark green markings or "rabbit tracks" on both sides (see Figure 12-47).

>> *Maranta makoyana, Calathea makoyana,* **or** *Goeppertia makoyana* **(peacock plant):** This maranta is admired because of the "wow" factor of its spectacular leaf markings (see Figure 12-48). It can reach up to 3 feet (1 m) tall but is usually much smaller when grown indoors.

>> *Maranta leuconeura* 'Tricolor' (herringbone plant): This plant's leaves are works of art. Each velvety oblong leaf looks like it has been exquisitely painted in shades of green and then highlighted with red veins (see Figure 12-49 and the color insert). A slow grower, it's similar in size to its cousin *Maranta leuconeura*.

FIGURE 12-47:
The leaves of the prayer plant close at night and open in the morning.

Photo by Steven A. Frowine

FIGURE 12-48:
The peacock plant struts its gorgeous leaves.

Photo by Steven A. Frowine

FIGURE 12-49:
The spectacular leaves of the herringbone plant are a remarkable sight.

Photo by Steven A. Frowine

Genus: *Monstera*

Most houseplants in this genus are giants suitable only for conservatories or large sunrooms (see the large-growing plant section earlier in the chapter), but there's one exception: *Monstera adansonii* (Swiss cheese plant). Like its big brother, *Monstera deliciosa*, it's from Central and South America. However, *Monstera adansonii* is much different in stature (see Figure 12-50). Indoors, it can reach up to 3 feet (1 m) high and wide. As it grows taller, it will benefit from a sturdy stake to support its stem and keep it from falling over. It's a very forgiving plant that's happy with about 50 percent humidity, average room temperatures, and bright diffused light.

FIGURE 12-50: This is a baby version of *Monstera deliciosa*.

Photo by Steven A. Frowine

Genus: *Peperomia*

More than 1,000 peperomias hail from the Neotropical region (Central America, the Caribbean, and South America). Some grow bushy, whereas others are more upright. They're all quite hearty plants with thick, sometimes succulent, sometimes textured leaves. They're a mainstay in most houseplant collections. Most grow about 4 to 8 inches (10 to 20 cm) high. They're some of the easiest houseplants to grow because they ask only for modest humidity, bright diffused light, and average room temperatures. Here are a few favorites:

>> *Peperomia argyreia* **(watermelon peperomia):** The pattern on its leaves is reminiscent of a watermelon rind (see Figure 12-51 and the color insert).

>> *Peperomia caperata* **(ridged peperomia):** Its heart-shaped dark green to purplish leaves (see Figure 12-52) have pleats like a ridged potato chip. It's a small plant that grows to about 8 inches (20 cm) wide and tall.

Photo by Steven A. Frowine

Photo by Steven A. Frowine

>> *Peperomia obtusifolia (emarginulata)* **(baby rubber plant):** This plant got its name because its leaves are thick and fleshy like the larger rubber plant *(Ficus elastica)* I describe earlier in this chapter. It's most common in its variegated form, with leaves that are green at the center and white at the edge (see Figure 12-53). This plant grows more upright than some of the other peperomias, reaching up to 12 inches (30 cm) tall. It's a slow grower.

>> *Peperomia puteolata* **(parallel peperomia):** This species has thick, leathery leaves, and unlike many of the peperomias, it's a trailer. In its natural habitat, it's a forest groundcover. Its dark green leaves are veined in green and white (see Figure 12-54). It grows to about 18 inches (45 cm) tall.

FIGURE 12-53:
This is the
variegated form
of the baby
rubber plant.

Photo by Steven A. Frowine

FIGURE 12-54:
This peperomia is
a desirable
choice for a small
trailing plant.

Photo by Steven A. Frowine

Genus: *Pilea*

Pilea is another genus of small plants with more than 600 members that are easy to grow. Most have succulent leaves and grow well in bright diffused light, moderate humidity, and average room temperatures.

>> *Pilea cadierei* (aluminum plant): This species is by far the most common and easiest to grow in this genus. It can reach 2 feet (60 cm) but is usually much smaller in an indoor garden. Its green leaves are serrated and painted with silver patches (see Figure 12-55 and the color insert).

>> *Pilea peperomioides* (Chinese money plant): Another popular pilea that looks quite different from the aluminum plant is the Chinese money plant, which has roundish succulent leaves shaped like coins.

Photo by Steven A. Frowine

Genus: *Plectranthus*

Plectranthus ciliatus (Indian borage or Swedish ivy) is in the mint family. It's not a fussy plant, and it's willing to withstand dry locations. It has a sprawling growth habit, which makes it a desirable choice as a hanging plant. The green and white variegated leaf form is most common, but others have plain green leaves or gold variegations (see Figure 12-56 and the color insert). It has a tubular white flower. It grows about 1 foot (60 cm) high and spreads to about 3 feet (1 m).

Photo by Steven A. Frowine

Genus: *Sansevieria*

I don't believe there's another houseplant that can take as much abuse as *Sansevieria*. It can take strong light or survive low light conditions. It's drought-tolerant and comes in many different leaf color combinations and heights. It seems like the only way you can kill it is to overwater it.

> » ***Sansevieria cylindrica (Dracaena angolensis)* (African spear plant or cylindrical snake plant):** This plant's long, fleshy leaves with pointed tips

(see Figure 12-57) can reach 4 to 6 feet (1.2 to 2 m) tall, which makes it stand out from the other snake plants.

>> ***Sansevieria trifasciata* or *Dracaena trifasciata* (snake plant):** If you have only one houseplant, this may be it. It's as common as a penny. It has long, swordlike leaves that can grow 3 feet (1 m) or more tall. The stiff leaves have green-patterned centers with edges of cream or yellow.

>> ***Sansevieria trifasciata* 'Golden Hahnii' (golden bird's nest snake plant):** This mutation of the preceding plant looks the same but is a diminutive form. It comes with solid green leaves or variegated green and yellow leaves like the one shown in Figure 12-58. It grows to about 1 foot (30 cm) tall.

FIGURE 12-57: This unusual snake plant is less common than the others.

Photo by Steven A. Frowine

FIGURE 12-58: This is one of the smaller sansevierias. All of them are noted for having a tough constitution.

Photo by Steven A. Frowine

Genus: *Saxifraga*

Although plenty of plants from this genus are grown as hardy perennials, only one representative is commonly grown as a houseplant: *Saxifraga stolonifera* or *Saxifraga sarmentosa* (mother of thousands, strawberry begonia). The first

common name stems from the fact that it produces seemingly countless miniature plants, or *offsets*, on thin runners. It grows about 9 inches (22 cm) high and
can have runners that trail for about 3 feet (1 m). It's a perfect choice for a cool
eastern window or any area with bright diffused light because it can tolerate temperatures down to 40°F (4°C). It comes in an olive green–leafed form or one that's
variegated in green and white (see Figure 12-59). The variegated form is slower
growing than the solid green form; it's also less tolerant of cooler temperatures.

FIGURE 12-59:
The strawberry
begonia is neither
a strawberry nor
a begonia, but
can be grown
indoors or
outdoors in
milder climates.

Genus: *Scindapsus* or *Epipremnum*

These plants are familiar to most houseplant growers. Their many names can be
confusing. Sometimes they're called *Scindapsus* or philodendron, but most commonly they go by pothos. They're plants with heart-shaped leaves and stems that
sprawl. You can train them up a post, let them wander off on their own, or plant
them in a hanging basket. They come in various leaf colors, including plain green,
green and white, and golden. They're among the easiest houseplants to grow, so
they'll be at home in most indoor garden settings.

>> *Scindapsus aureus* **(golden pothos):** This pothos is as bright as sunshine! This
species comes with green leaves speckled in gold or pure yellow gold like the
one shown in Figure 12-60 and the color insert. Like all plants in this group, it
has no special cultural requirements.

>> *Scindapsus* **or** *Epipremnum* **'N'Joy':** The green and white variegations of the
heart-shaped leaves are striking (see Figure 12-61 and the color insert). This
hybrid was discovered at the University of Florida in 2002, and has been
sought out ever since for hanging baskets or as potted plants.

Photo by Steven A. Frowine

Photo by Steven A. Frowine

Genus: *Seleginella*

Seleginella (creeping moss) are mosslike plants that thrive in high humidity, so they're often planted in terrariums. Except for their humidity requirement, they're easy to care for in bright diffused light and average room temperatures.

Selaginella martensii is the one species that many plant suppliers sell. It has a delicate appearance (see Figure 12-62) and is an upright grower to about 1 foot (30 cm).

Genus: *Strobilanthes*

Strobilanthes dyerianus (Persian shield) wows you with its glowing purple foliage (see Figure 12-63). The purple is most vibrant in very bright light. Unfortunately, the purple sheen becomes more silver and muted as the plant matures. Persian shield is rather fast growing and can reach 3 feet (1 m) or more. Pruning it back periodically will keep it in bounds and stimulate new young foliage that will be brighter.

FIGURE 12-62: *Selaginella* is often planted in terrariums because it loves high humidity.

Photo by Steven A. Frowine

FIGURE 12-63: Persian shield becomes vibrant purple when it's grown in full sun.

Photo by Steven A. Frowine

Genus: *Tradescantia*

It's difficult to imagine any houseplant collection that doesn't have at least one of these plants. Some are grown as potted plants, while others perform well in hanging baskets. These plants fit in most growing environments with no unusual requirements, except, like most foliage plants, they prefer bright diffused light, not direct sunlight.

Tradescantia spathacea (boat lily or Moses-in-the-cradle) is grown as a care free groundcover in the tropics but can also serve as an attractive container plant indoors. The variegated form that has green, white, and pink leaf markings is especially attractive (see Figure 12-64). It typically grows to about 1 foot (30 cm).

Vines and climbers for foliage and flowers

Vines and climbers add different dimensions to an indoor garden. They provide both vertical and horizontal elements, as well as offer foliage texture and color and, in some cases, plentiful flowers.

FIGURE 12-64:
Boat lily, also known as Moses-in-the-cradle, requires very little care to perform well.

Photo by Steven A. Frowine

Genus: *Abutilon*

Abutilon (flowering maple) contains species and hybrids that have plain green foliage and others that are variegated with flowers in red, white, and yellow. Most are very ornamental. They can grow rapidly, so pruning them back periodically will restrain their size and make them bushier. Some grow upright, but others are vining. Abutilons aren't particular about humidity and do well in average room temperatures, but they need bright light to flower well. Plants can grow 2 to 3 feet (0.6 to 0.9 m) tall and wide, depending on the species or hybrid. Because some of these can grow quite tall and have heavy pendulous flowers, they can benefit from staking.

Abutilon hybrida is one of the vining forms. With leaves speckled in gold and showy flowers (see Figure 12–65 and the color insert), it makes a striking hanging basket.

FIGURE 12-65:
The common name for this beauty, flowering maple, is misleading because it isn't related to a maple, but its leaf has a similar shape.

Photo by Steven A. Frowine

Genus: *Chlorophyllum*

Chlorophyllum comosum (spider plant) must be the number one plant for college dormitories. And since taking care of plants isn't usually a high priority for students, that gives you a good idea of the plant's durability. It gets its common name from all the "spidery" offshoots or babies it produces. It's most often grown as a hanging basket (see Figure 12-66). It requires little care and grows 1 to 2 feet (0.3 to 0.6 m) tall and wide.

FIGURE 12-66: If you want a hanging basket that can survive less-than-ideal growing conditions, try a spider plant.

Coplay/Shutterstock

Genus: *Cissus*

Although more than 3,000 species of viny plants populate this genus, only a few are ornamental enough for a spot in your indoor garden. Some are valued in their native lands for their medicinal properties.

Cissus discolor (begonia vine, tapestry vine) is my favorite species in this genus because of its intricately patterned silvery leaves with green midveins (the raised veins in the center of the leaf that are also called midribs) and red or deep pink edges (see Figure 12-67 and the color insert). The leaves are borne on long, wiry weeping stems, so it's well suited as a hanging plant, or you can train it to climb up a pole. The underside of the leaves is a dark purple. A green-leaved species named *Cissus rhombifolia (alata)* (grape ivy) is a rugged plant that's commonly used in hanging baskets.

Genus: *Clerodendron*

This genus contains more than 100 members that are small shrubs as well as vines; however, only one is regularly grown as a houseplant. The others are much larger and grow as shrubs in tropical areas.

FIGURE 12-67:
Begonia vine isn't related to the begonia but does have leaves that resemble some of the rex begonias.

Photo by Steven A. Frowine

Clerodendron thomsoniae (bleeding-heart vine) is my favorite of the bunch. It's a climber that can be grown as a container plant or in a hanging basket. It has heart-shaped leaves and unique 1-inch (2.5-cm) flowers that have a white *calyx* (a modified leaf) from which a scarlet flower emerges (see Figure 12-68). The white part of the flower lasts for months. It needs a very bright spot to flower well. You can prune it back heavily to keep it in bounds.

FIGURE 12-68:
This is a desirable vine for both its attractive foliage and interesting flowers.

Photo by Steven A. Frowine

Genus: *Ficus*

Earlier in this chapter, I introduced you to some large treelike ornamental figs. The one I talk about here is a far cry in stature from its big brothers.

Ficus pumila (creeping fig) is nothing like what most folks think of as a ficus or fig. It's a climber you can see covering walls in tropical countries or in conservatories. It's a dainty plant with 1-inch (2.5-cm) leaves borne on clinging stems that can be trained up any vertical support or grown in a hanging basket (see Figure 12-69). It has no exceptional cultural requirements, so it's happy in most indoor environments.

Photo by Steven A. Frowine

Ficus pumila minima is a form with smaller leaves, and another form has variegated green and white leaves.

Genus: *Gynura*

This is another genus containing plants that are often used for medicinal purposes. Only one plant in this genus is commonly grown as a houseplant.

Gynura sarmentosa (procumbens) (passion vine) is a vine with leaves covered in purple fuzz (see Figure 12-70). It's a vigorous grower that needs to be trimmed back when it gets out of hand. Its leaves won't turn purple and will stay green if it doesn't receive enough light. It is often grown in hanging baskets and requires no exceptional care. It's in the daisy family, so it does have pom-pom flowers, but they really aren't much to look at and are usually removed to keep the foliage growing well.

FIGURE 12-70: The passion vine quickly grows into a hanging plant specimen.

Photo by Steven A. Frowine

Genus: *Hedera*

You don't have to be an indoor gardener to know *Hedera helix* (English ivy). In outdoor gardens, its aggressive growth habit can make it a real pest. However, in an indoor container, you can easily control it by cutting it back whenever you want. It's a trailer, with leaves that vary tremendously in size, shape, and coloration (see Figure 12-71).

FIGURE 12-71: The various forms of English ivy work well as complementary plants in container or hanging basket combinations.

Photo by Steven A. Frowine

WARNING

It's quite difficult to kill this plant, so you can couple it with any other houseplants you have, but be aware that you may need to keep its growth in check.

Genus: *Hemigraphis*

This genus is sometimes listed as *Stobilanthes,* which I discuss earlier in this chapter. The two species I mention here are still usually referred to as *Hemigraphis.*

Hemigraphis alternata (purple waffle plant) is the member of this genus that's most commonly available, and its selling point is its silvery-purple leaves (see Figure 12-72). It's a compact climbing plant used in containers or hanging baskets. It's very undemanding, which makes it a good companion for other houseplants.

Another species, *Hemigraphis exotica,* is sometimes available. It's similar to purple waffle plant, except its leaves are puckered.

Genus: *Hoya*

Some folks collect hoyas because they're such an interesting vining plant. They offer a variety of unique balls of flowers that are often very fragrant. Their thick, leathery succulent leaves come in various shades of green or variegated in green and white.

FIGURE 12-72:
The purple leaves of this plant make it popular as both a houseplant and a groundcover.

Photo by Steven A. Frowine

Hoya pubicalyx (wax plant), which is native to the Philippines, is practically indestructible as a houseplant. Its only requirement is a bright spot. If you're lucky enough to experience this beauty in full bloom, you'll find its honey fragrance heavenly and its clusters of star-shaped pink flowers (see Figure 12-73 and the color insert) spectacular. Its thick green leaves are speckled in silver. With vines that can grow to 3 feet (1 m) or longer, this hoya is perfect in a hanging basket.

FIGURE 12-73:
Hoyas are vigorous flowering vines with delightfully scented blooms.

Photo by Steven A. Frowine

Another common form, *Hoya carnosa,* is similar to *Hoya pubicalyx.* If you become a hoya connoisseur, you may want to pursue a few species that have some of the largest flowers in the genus, such as *Hoya lautercachii* and *Hoya macgillivrayi.*

Genus: *Nepenthes*

These exotic plants are naturally found in the jungles of the African and Asian continents. It's quite amazing how they form carnivorous pitchers on the end of their leaf tendrils. Nepenthes were Victorian-era darlings that shared space with other tropical beauties like orchids in private conservatories. Some of the rare sought-after species and hybrids have pitchers large enough to trap and digest rats.

These plants used to be available only through specialty suppliers, but now you can frequently find them in home and garden and grocery stores. Because they're vines, they're usually grown in hanging baskets. For more information on these and other carnivorous plants, check out the nearby sidebar "Carnivorous plants: They actually eat bugs!"

Nepenthes alata (pitcher plant) is a species from the Philippines that's commonly available. Its pitchers are about 7 inches (23 cm) long (see Figure 12-74 and the color insert).

FIGURE 12-74: Pitcher plant is an attractive and intriguing houseplant.

Photo by Steven A. Frowine

CARNIVOROUS PLANTS: THEY ACTUALLY EAT BUGS!

There's something ironic about plants that eat bugs — it's such a turning of the tables. As a child, I was fascinated with these plant "creatures." In fact, my first science fair project was a terrarium of carnivorous plants. The truth is, I still marvel at them and have a large pot of pitcher plants and Venus flytraps in my garden.

The trick to growing carnivorous plants is realizing that some are tropical and can be grown indoors year-round, whereas others are temperate and need a cool rest period during the winter. Almost all these plants are from boggy areas, which means you should never allow them to dry out. It's best to water them with rainwater or distilled water because they're very sensitive to water impurities. These plants perform best in full sun.

If you really get into carnivorous plants — and it's difficult not to — search out some books on them. Most of these plants can be grown in a 5:1 ratio of sphagnum moss to sand. Here are a couple broad categories of carnivorous plants:

- *Dionaea muscipula* (Venus flytrap): If you know any carnivorous plants, you know this one (see the photo). The amazing thing is that this exotic plant isn't native to some far-off tropical land but comes from the Carolinas in the United States! Consequently, it requires a rest period during the winter, when it can be placed outdoors where winter temperatures don't go below 20°F (–6°C). Not giving them this required dormancy is probably the most common reason these plants perish. The traps get bright crimson if exposed to full sun.

- *Drosera* (sundews): This is the largest group of carnivorous plants with almost 200 species. Some are from temperate areas, whereas others are tropical. They all trap their prey with sticky tentacles that ensnare and then envelop and suffocate their victims.

Photo by Steven A. Frowine

Genus: *Mandevilla*

Mandevilla splendens (mandevilla vine, trumpet vine) is also called *Dipladenia splendens.* Mandevilla plants seem to be for sale at every home and garden store these days. They're mostly available during the summer to be grown outdoors as hanging plants, and they're popular because they produce bright red, white, or pink flowers all summer (see Figure 12-75). Because they're tropical, they cannot take freezing temperatures, but they're an ideal plant to move indoors to enjoy when summer's warm weather fades.

Most mandevillas sold today are hybrids with trade names. Some of the most popular are *Mandevilla* 'Alice Du Pont' and *Mandevilla* 'Sun Parasol Crimson'. They flower best in full sun.

Photo by Steven A. Frowine

Genus: *Senecio*

This is a rather confusing genus because it contains flowering vines and succulents (which I introduce in Chapter 10). Here, I discuss a tropical vine from this genus.

Senecio confusus (Mexican flame vine), which also goes by *Pseudogynoxys chenopodioides*, has brilliant orange-red daisylike flowers that stand out like flames against its fleshy arrow-shaped dark green leaves (see Figure 12-76 and the color insert). It is fast-growing and will flower continuously if it's given enough light. It can get quite tall, reaching about 10 feet (over 3 m), so it needs to have a sturdy support.

Photo by Steven A. Frowine

Genus: *Tradescantia*

The number of plants in this genus seems almost limitless! Some are at home in containers, whereas others show off best in hanging baskets. The leaves vary tremendously in color and size. They're all tough plants, which is a big reason they're so popular. I've listed just a few representatives of this large group:

» ***Tradescantia fluminensis* 'Variegata' (spiderwort, variegated inch plant):** This one has beautiful variegated green and white foliage with graceful drooping stems (see Figure 12-77). You can't ask for a more perfect hanging basket.

» ***Tradescantia sillamontana* 'White Fuzzy':** This is the teddy bear of spiderworts. The leaves are covered with soft, white hairs (see Figure 12-78). It flowers like most of the other tradescantias, producing small pink blossoms if it's grown in bright light.

» ***Tradescantia zebrina* (zebra plant):** This is one of the most common tradescantias. Its leaves are striped in silver and white with dark purple edges (see Figure 12-79) and undersides that shimmer in the sunlight.

FIGURE 12-77: Just about every indoor plant grower has one variation of spiderwort.

Photo by Steven A. Frowine

FIGURE 12-78: The leaves of 'White Fuzzy' are covered with white hairs.

Photo by Steven A. Frowine

FIGURE 12-79:
Zebra plant is another popular spiderwort.

Photo by Steven A. Frowine

HOUSEPLANTS THAT CAN TOLERATE LOW LIGHT

Light is what gives plants their energy. Without light, they can't exist; however, some plants can survive in much lower light than others. Most of these plants have adapted because they're naturally found in the deep shade of a jungle. For the most part, they're foliage plants that seldom flower. (To flower, most plants need more light energy than low-light habitats provide.)

Here are some plants that can survive in lower-light settings. Note that I'm not saying they won't thrive with brighter light, but they can tolerate low light better than most. The following plants are described earlier in this chapter:

- *Aglaonema* (Chinese evergreen)
- *Dieffenbachia* (dumb cane)
- *Dracaena* (corn plant, dragon plant)
- *Hedera helix* (English ivy)
- *Monstera adansonii* (Swiss cheese plant)
- *Nephrolepis bostoniensis* (Boston fern)
- *Philodendron*
- *Sansevieria* (snake plant)
- *Scindapsus* (pothos)
- *Zamioculcas zamiifolia* (fern arum)

Chapter **13**

Flowering Plants: Dazzling Additions to Your Indoor Garden

Who doesn't like plants that flower? It's like icing on the cake, right? You always feel a buzz of anticipation when a flower bud shows up with the promise of a new bloom.

Flowering plants add a whole new dimension to your indoor garden. They complement your foliage plants with the delightful, brilliant colors that only flowers can deliver. Because of the boom in houseplant interest, more new and unusual flowering plants are showing up on the plant scene, especially from specialty plant growers.

In this chapter, I describe quite a few flowering plants that can add visual interest to your indoor garden and give you the basics on caring for them.

Understanding the Conditions Flowering Plants Need to Thrive

Most flowering plants for indoor gardeners are from very similar tropical or semi-tropical environments, so they share cultural (growing) requirements with their cousins, the tropical foliage plants. (See Chapter 12 for lots of info about tropical foliage houseplants.) Probably the biggest difference between foliage and flowering plants is the light requirement. Flowering plants need a lot of light; in fact, it's difficult to give them too much light. Most relish full sun or at least very bright but indirect sunlight. Without it, they may grow lush foliage but won't flower or will flower very poorly.

Some of the plants in this chapter are grown as shrubs in their tropical homes, but you can usually prune them to restrain their size for your indoor garden and keep them manageable.

Flowering plants enjoy moist air, modest air movement, and temperatures that humans find comfortable — around 65 to 75°F (18 to 24°C), give or take 5 degrees in either direction. I've tried to avoid being too repetitive with the cultural requirements I give for the genera or individual plants in this chapter; you can assume that these relatively basic requirements pertain to all the plants discussed here unless noted otherwise. For more detailed information on cultural requirements, check out the chapters in Part 2.

Introducing a Parade of Flowering Plants

Flowering plants add welcome color and excitement to your indoor garden. The various green shades of foliage plants are a perfect backdrop for vibrantly colored flowers. Here is a sampling of some of the most popular and best performing flowering plants.

Genus: *Abutilon*

Abutilon (flowering maple) has members that grow upright and members with vining, pendulous foliage. Most of the upright forms are hybrids, and that's what I describe here. There are many upright hybrids to explore. Here are a few that you may enjoy that are easy to grow and bloom like gangbusters if they are happy.

>> *Abutilon* 'Red Glory': 2½-inch (6.4-centimeter) deep red flowers

- » *Abutilon* 'Red Tiger': Dangling yellow flowers with red veins

- » *Abutilon* 'Star Sprite': 1-inch (2.5-cm) orange petals with darker veins

- » *Abutilon* 'Victorian Lady': 2-inch (6-cm) double pink flowers

- » *Abutilon* 'Victor Reiter': 3-inch (8-cm) soft orange flowers

Genus: *Acalypha*

This genus is most noted for its pipe cleaner–style flower, but some are grown more for their brightly variegated foliage. A few can grow into shrub-like plants, whereas others are smaller.

Acalypha wilkesiana (Jacob's coat) is prized for its serrated heart-shaped leaves painted in various shades of copper, red, gold, and pink (see Figure 13-1). It's a fast grower and can reach 2 to 4 feet (60 to 120 cm) wide and tall. Its flowers are like chenille.

FIGURE 13-1: Gorgeous leaves are the hallmark of Jacob's coat acalypha, but they also have chenille-like reddish streamer flowers.

Photo by Steven A. Frowine

Acalypha hispida (chenille plant) has *catkins* (tubular flower clusters) that are very long lasting. These soft, fuzzy flowers (see Figure 13-2 and the color insert) tempt you to stroke them like a cat's tail. It's very easy to grow these plants in containers or hanging baskets. They can reach the size of a small shrub but can be easily kept in bounds by pruning. The oval leaves are light green and 6 to 8 inches (15 to 20 cm) long.

FIGURE 13-2:
The chenille
plant's curious
flowers always
attract attention.

Genus: *Alpinia*

Many species in this genus are far from compact-growing plants, so they require quite a bit of space to reach their mature size. Some are grown for their variegated foliage (see *Alpinia zerumbet* in Chapter 12), whereas other species like *Alpinia purpurata* have outstanding flowers (see Figure 13-3).

FIGURE 13-3:
The red
inflorescence of
red ginger really
stands out
against the bright
green leaves.

Alpinia purpurata (red ginger) is a large plant that reaches 4 to 6 feet (1.2 to 1.8 meters) tall. Commonly seen in all tropical climates, it has lustrous evergreen foliage, and its *inflorescences* (flower spikes) are usually red, although they can be pink or magenta. Prune it often to keep it reasonably sized.

Genus: *Anthurium*

This is a very large genus of mostly foliage plants. However, one species that breaks the mold has flowers that are synonymous with Hawaii.

Anthurium andreanum (flamingo flower) has a "flower" (technically a *bract*, or modified leaf) that's usually bright red, although it's also found in other shades of red as well as pink and white. The actual flower is the long tail-like spike in the center of the bract (see Figure 13-4 and the color insert). Flamingo flower is popular because it's so unusual, and it lasts a very long time. It's a favorite with flower arrangers. The standard form grows 12 to 18 inches (30 to 45 cm) tall and wide, but it's also available in dwarf forms.

FIGURE 13-4:
Flamingo flower, a favorite plant in Hawaii, can be a welcome addition to your houseplant collection.

Photo by Steven A. Frowine

Genus: *Aphelandra*

The most readily available member of this genus is *Aphelandra squarrosa*, which is known by the common name zebra plant. It's an exceptional plant both for its striking dark green leaves with contrasting white ribs as well as its bright yellow bracted flowers (see Figure 13-5 and the color insert). This is another shrubby plant that needs to be pruned if it outgrows its growing space.

Photo by Steven A. Frowine

FIGURE 13-5:
Striking foliage and a brilliant yellow flower are hallmarks of zebra plant.

Genus: *Beloperone*

More than 30 species populate this genus of tropical perennials or small shrubs from Mexico and South America, but only one is commonly cultivated indoors. Their flower colors can vary from yellow to pink to orange.

Beloperone guttata or *Justicia brandegeeana* (Mexican shrimp plant) gets its name from its reddish-pink bracts shaped somewhat like a delectable seafood (see Figure 13-6). Small white flowers emerge from the bracts. It can grow 1 to 3 feet (0.3 to 1 m) tall and wide.

TIP

To keep it compact, cut it back regularly. It requires strong light to produce blooms.

Genus: *Bougainvillea*

The two things I remember about bougainvillea from when I lived in Hawaii and Mexico are how brilliant the flowers are in the dry season and what wicked thorns they have. The gardeners there said pruning bougainvillea is like fighting with cats.

FIGURE 13-6:
The Mexican
shrimp plant is
easy to grow.

Photo by Steven A. Frowine

The fact that bougainvillea show the best color when it's dry and bright tells you they require full sun and don't like cold, dark, and wet conditions. Bougainvillea can grow as vines or shrubs and may require aggressive pruning to keep it in bounds. They come in a range of colors — red, pink apricot, white (see Figure 13-7) — and some have variegated green and white foliage.

FIGURE 13-7:
Bougainvillea can
be a colorful
addition to your
plant collection,
but watch out for
their vicious
thorns.

Photo by Steven A. Frowine

Genus: *Brugmansia*

Brugmansia (angel's trumpet) can be grown indoors during cold months and placed outdoors on your patio or deck during the summer. It goes dormant and the leaves fall off when it starts to get cool (below 50°F [10°C]). At that point it's best to place the plant in a cool (not freezing) dark space and water it sparingly until spring, when strong light and warmer temperatures return.

Its elegant dangling trumpet flowers (see Figure 13-8 and the color insert), which range from 6 to 12 inches (15 to 30 cm) long and come in shades of pink, yellow, and white, are delightfully fragrant and attract hummingbirds.

FIGURE 13-8: Angel's trumpet is a dramatic addition to your plant collection that you can enjoy on the patio during the summer.

Photo by Steven A. Frowine

Genus: *Brunfelsia*

This genus contains about 50 species of tropical shrubs, but only one is cultivated as a houseplant. *Brunfelsia guttata*'s common name — yesterday, today and tomorrow — refers to its unusual flowering process: The flowers change color as they mature. When they open, they're violet-blue (see Figure 13-9); the next day, they turn pink before eventually fading to white. The plant can reach 3 feet (about 1 m) tall and wide but can be pruned to keep its size manageable and encourage flowering. Like most tropical shrubs, it blooms best in very bright conditions.

FIGURE 13-9:
Brunfelsia treats
you to a different
color flower
every day.

Photo by Steven A. Frowine

Genus: *Burbidgea*

Five different species of the ginger family hail from Borneo, and one plant from this genus is sometimes available as a houseplant. *Burbidgea schizocheila* (golden brush ginger) really shines in bright light because of its brilliant yellow-to-golden torch-shaped flowers (see Figure 13-10). It's a compact upright grower reaching 12 to 18 inches (30 to 45 cm) high and wide, making it an excellent container plant. It is more cold-tolerant than many tropical plants and can take temperatures down to 40°F (4°C).

FIGURE 13-10:
Golden brush
ginger has
unusual sunny
flowers.

Photo by Steven A. Frowine

Genus: *Canna*

The plants in this genus are known for their various flower colors, but some have spectacular foliage (see Figure 13-11 and color insert). Like brugmansias, discussed earlier in this chapter, cannas go dormant when the light is reduced and the temperature drops at the onset of winter. To care for these plants, follow the cultural recommendations for brugmansias.

Photo by Steven A. Frowine

Genus: *Cestrum*

This genus of more than 150 species includes small shrubs from the neotropics (Central America, the Caribbean, and South America) and the southernmost part of the United States. One species is commonly available in the trade.

During the day, shrubby *Cestrum aurantiacum* (jessamine, night-blooming jasmine) treats you to an abundance of small tubular sun-yellow flowers with star-shaped ends (see Figure 13-12), but the real treat comes at night when it releases its sweet fragrance (which is meant to attract pollinating moths). It can grow to 6 feet (about 2 m) tall and wide but rarely grows this large indoors.

Photo by Steven A. Frowine

Genus: *Clerodendrum*

This genus has about 150 species and can be found in perennials, shrub, or tree forms. See the vine section in Chapter 12 for information on and an image of *Clerodendrum thomsoniae.*

If you want a clerodendrum that can be grown indoors, look for *Clerodendrum ugandense* or *Rotheca myricoides* 'Ugandense' (blue butterfly bush), which is from Africa. Its unique two-toned 1½-inch light and dark blue or lavender flower looks a bit like a petite butterfly (see Figure 13-13). The bush gets to be about 4 to 5 feet (1.2 to 1.5 m) tall and wide.

Genus: *Clivia*

Clivias have long strap-like leaves and can grow in low-light conditions but won't flower well unless they're given strong diffused light. Most clivias have orange to orange-red flowers (see Figure 13-14), but there's a treasured form with buttery yellow blooms that's the envy of many houseplant lovers.

Clivia minata (natal lily) is the most common species of this genus that grows as a houseplant. Some folks complain about not being able to get it to flower. This is usually due to one of two things: not providing enough light or not giving it a cool, dry rest period during the winter.

FIGURE 13-13:
When this
clerodendrum is
in full flower, it
looks like it's
covered with
small blue
butterflies.

Photo by Steven A. Frowine

FIGURE 13-14:
Clivias are rugged
plants with
attractive foliage
and bright orange
flowers.

Photo by Steven A. Frowine

TIP

During the dormant period, water should be withheld until the foliage almost wilts, and the plant should be moved to an area like a sunporch where the temperatures are around 50°F (10°C) for 6 to 8 weeks. This will encourage the plant to set flower buds.

Genus: *Costus*

Although these plants have technically been assigned to a family that doesn't include true gingers, they still go by the common name spiral ginger. They have cone-shaped inflorescences with colorful bracts that overlap. In their native lands, they're valued for various medicinal uses.

Costus comosus var. *bakeri*, previously known as *Costus barbatus* (red tower ginger), is a native of Costa Rica. It's a large-growing costus most suited for spacious areas because it can reach almost 6 feet (about 2 m) tall. Its yellow flowers poke out from red bracts (see Figure 13-15).

FIGURE 13-15: A relative of the ginger family, this costus is a special houseplant.

Photo by Steven A. Frowine

Genus: *Crossandra*

Only one species of this genus is commonly grown as an outdoor bedding plant or an indoor tropical plant. *Crossandra undulifolia*, previously called *Crossandra infundibuliformis* (firecracker plant), adds welcome color to a tropical plant collection. When grown in an environment with adequate humidity and very bright light, it will be covered with radiant orange flowers (see Figure 13-16 and the color insert). Although it can grow to the size of a small shrub, it's usually much smaller, about 12 inches (30 cm), in an indoor garden.

TIP

To keep it flowering longer, pinch off the spent blooms.

FIGURE 13-16:
Crossandra
sports attractive
glossy green
foliage and bright
orange flowers.

Photo by Steven A. Frowine

Genus: *Curcuma*

This is another member of the ginger family. Only one species from this genus, which used to be quite rare, has become available in the trade and is showing up in big-box stores. *Curcuma alismatifolia* (Siam tulip, Java tulip) hails from Thailand. When it's in flower (see Figure 13-17), it's a real star. It relishes very bright, but not direct, sunlight and grows to about 2 feet (60 cm) tall.

FIGURE 13-17:
Siam tulip has
a shocking
pink flower.

Photo by Steven A. Frowine

TIP

During the low light of winter, it goes dormant and drops its leaves. When this happens, just keep it on the dry and cool (but not freezing) side until the brighter light and warmer temperatures of spring and summer return.

Genus: *Duranta*

This beautiful blue-flowering shrub native to Central and South America has only one species that's commonly grown outdoors in tropical to subtropical climates or indoors as a houseplant. *Duranta erecta* (golden dewdrop) is glorious when it's covered with light or dark blue, violet, or white star-shaped flowers (see Figure 13-18) offset by its attractive glossy green foliage. It flowers best in full sunlight. It can get quite large, so it needs to be pruned periodically to keep it manageable indoors. It produces drooping clusters of yellow to orange berries after the flowers drop.

FIGURE 13-18:
Any plant with violet flowers like duranta is always a welcome addition to your houseplant collection.

Photo by Steven A. Frowine

Genus: *Euphorbia*

This is a huge genus that encompasses cacti, succulents, and very hardy perennials (see Chapter 10 for information about and images of the succulent form), but the one I present here is a plant most people know by its common name: poinsettia.

When we lived in Mexico, where poinsettias are native, we were surrounded by poinsettia "trees," which presented their welcome red flowers (really modified leaves, or *bracts*) like clockwork around Christmas. Now, in the United States and many other countries, poinsettias are synonymous with this winter holiday.

When you see *Euphorbia pulcherrima* in the wild, you can appreciate how plant breeders have changed the poinsettia into the festive potted plant that most people are familiar with. It comes in untold variations of red, red and white, speckled, pink, and white (see Figure 13-19 and the color insert). Some are even rose types with double flowers. They're available as topiaries, large potted plants, or miniatures. Recent efforts to make this plant a year-round houseplant by breeding various color forms have been unsuccessful, and poinsettias seem destined to be a one-act holiday player.

FIGURE 13-19:
For some folks, poinsettias are synonymous with the winter holidays.

TIP

Poinsettias aren't poisonous. This persistent misinformation has been around for decades. That's not to say that they're good eating. It just means that poinsettias, like other houseplants in this book, are sold as ornamental rather than edible plants.

WARNING

Even though poinsettias themselves aren't poisonous, be aware that these houseplants, like others, may have pesticide residue on their leaves, so it isn't a good idea for you or your pets to munch on any houseplant leaves or flowers. Some of the succulent euphorbia relatives of the poinsettia can be toxic to animals (see Chapter 10).

HOW DO I GET MY POINSETTIAS TO REFLOWER FOR THE HOLIDAYS?

Eventually, when the winter holidays have passed, your poinsettia will lose its colored bracts. This may take longer than you imagine — 2 to 6 months! If you haven't already done this, move your poinsettia to a very bright spot. You can trim it back quite a bit — prune off half to a third of it — if it has gotten leggy. Milky sap will leak from the cut stems, can cause skin irritation to some folks. The sap will soon harden and dry. Eventually, in several weeks or so, new sideshoots and leaves will develop. Continue to nurture the plant along with your other houseplants, providing regular watering and fertilizing. It will now serve as an attractive foliage houseplant.

When fall approaches, around the end of September, you must go into action. Poinsettias in nature are triggered to color up when the days get shorter, so to trick the plant into starting this process, you must artificially produce short days. This isn't as difficult as it sounds. Put your plant in a completely dark place, like a closed closet, in the early evening so it's in the dark for 14 hours. Then, return it to its regular growing spot. Continue doing this for 8 weeks. After this period, the plant will have gotten the message, and it will start coloring up so you can enjoy its bright colors again for the holidays.

Because it's the modified leaves that have the color variations (the flowers are those little yellow things in the center), poinsettias maintain their color in all but the most adverse conditions. If you want to keep your plants in top shape longer, put them in a cool (55 to 65°F [13 to 18°C]) room with bright light. They demand very little to survive — modest humidity, average room temperatures, and water when the potting material is dry.

Genus: *Fuchsia*

There are about 50 species and hundreds of hybrids in the *Fuchsia* genus. The flower shapes and colors vary immensely, but most are either red, purple, or white. Flowers may be a single hue or multicolored. Fuchsias can be grown as potted plants, in hanging baskets, or in treelike forms called *standards*. Some of them are more persnickety than others, especially when it comes to high temperatures. Some hybrids with the brightest, largest multicolored flowers resent temperatures much above 70°F (21°C), whereas others are more resilient.

TIP

Fuchsias can get rangy and benefit from periodic pruning to keep them shapely and vigorous. Removing spent flowers encourages new ones to form. They enjoy bright but filtered light.

Fuchsia hybrida, a general name given to many hybrids of the *Fuchsia* genus, is mostly associated with those that have large multicolored flowers (see Figure 13-20). These are the ones that benefit most from cool, bright growing conditions.

FIGURE 13-20:
Fuchsia hybrids are a great indoor plant if you can provide a bright, cool spot.

Fuchsia 'Gardenmeister Bonstedt' (see Figure 13-21) is the fuchsia for you if you've watched your others wilt in heat and light that's too bright. It may not be as flamboyant as other fuchsias, but it's a toughie that flowers and flourishes where others fail. It's an upright grower that reaches up to 3 feet (1 m) high and wide. It can be grown outdoors during the summer, where its tubular red flowers attract hummingbirds.

Genus: *Gardenia*

For a heavenly, unforgettable scent, no other plant can beat gardenia flowers. Unfortunately, gardenias have a bad rap as being very temperamental and live up to their reputation by dropping their buds. It can be very frustrating. This bad habit has been attributed to low humidity, extremes in temperature, or potting material that gets too dry between waterings.

TIP

To do well, gardenias require bright but not direct sunlight, cool evening temperatures (60 to 65°F [15 to 18°C]) to set buds, and well-drained but moist potting mix. Is this plant worth all that effort? Yes, without a doubt!

FIGURE 13-21:
There's no more
dependable
fuchsia than
'Gardenmeister
Bonstedt'.

Photo by Steven A. Frowine

Gardenia jasminoides (gardenia, cape gardenia) is the gardenia that most people picture when this plant is mentioned. It's a bushy plant with glossy dark green leaves and creamy white double flowers (see Figure 13-22) that emit an enchanting fragrance.

FIGURE 13-22:
Can anything
match the
fabulous
fragrance of a
gardenia?

Photo by Steven A. Frowine

TIP

Remove spent flowers to encourage further flowering.

Genus: *Globba*

Another member of the ginger family contains about 100 species that are smaller in stature than many of the others in this family and generally require less light to flower. Like some of the other gingers, it can go dormant during the winter but will start new growth in the spring with warmer temperatures and brighter light.

The most commonly available species is *Globba winitii* (dancing girl ginger). It has flower spikes with red bracts and yellow flowers (see Figure 13-23). They appear in the summer through the fall, giving the plant a whimsical look unlike any of the other gingers. It grows to 1 to 2 feet (30 to 60 cm) tall.

FIGURE 13-23: Dancing girl ginger has delicate, fascinating flowers.

Photo by Steven A. Frowine

Genus: *Heliconia*

This genus features some spectacular but huge plants that were great in our outdoor gardens in Mexico and Hawaii but aren't practical for growing indoors in anything other than a very large sunroom or conservatory. Fortunately, a few small-growing varieties are compact and manageable. They add a real tropical touch to any houseplant collection.

Heliconia 'Golden Torch' (dwarf yellow heliconia), which is shown in Figure 13-24 and the color insert, is relatively small growing compared to others in this genus, usually getting only about 3 feet (1 m) high. Its smooth leathery leaves are about 1 foot (30 cm) long and have an erect 8-inch (20-cm) inflorescence featuring a bright yellow bract and small flower. It's a very undemanding plant and a dependable grower, happy with average humidity and bright diffused light. It's popular as a long-lasting cut flower.

FIGURE 13-24:
Dwarf yellow
heliconia is one
of the few
heliconias small
enough for most
indoor gardens.

Photo by Steven A. Frowine

Genus: *Hibiscus*

The color range found in hibiscus hybrids is simply astounding! No other plant says "tropical" more than this plant. In their native lands, they can grow to sizable shrubs, but you can easily keep them at a reasonable size by pruning. Dwarf hybrids can be enjoyed in indoor gardens of modest space.

TIP

When given as much sun as possible, they flower best, rewarding you with a constant display of bold flowers that vary in size from 2 to 10 inches (5 to 25 cm). They won't go dormant during the winter, but they don't bloom heavily unless they receive supplemental light. (See Chapter 5 for more information on artificial light sources.)

Hibiscus rosa-sinensis is the name given to many hibiscuses. Figure 13-25 shows just one example of the shape of hibiscus flowers.

Genus: *Ixora*

Ixora (West Indian jasmine) are common shrubs in Florida but also work in a bright indoor garden. They come in a wide range of colors and will display clusters of four-petaled flowers all year if given enough light. They can grow to be 10 feet (3 m) tall or more as a shrub but can be pruned to maintain a manageable size. Small forms that peak at about 6 feet (about 2 m) are available.

FIGURE 13-25:
This is a typical
hibiscus flower.

Photo by Steven A. Frowine

Ixora carnea or *Ixora coccinea* (flame of the woods, jungle geranium) is a shrub that has glossy, leathery oblong leaves and semiglobular clusters of tubular red flowers (see Figure 13-26). It can reach 6 feet (about 2 m) or more, but you can prune it to keep it smaller.

FIGURE 13-26:
Flame of the
woods is
welcome in
anyone's indoor
garden because
of its free
flowering.

Photo by Steven A. Frowine

Genus: *Jatropha*

This genus is shrubby in its natural habitat in the Caribbean and can even grow to the size of a small tree. However, it seldom reaches this height in an indoor garden.

Jatropha podagrica or *Jatropha peregrina* (spicy jatropha, firecracker jatropha) is the only species grown as a houseplant. It has clusters of star-shaped 1-inch (2.5-cm) scarlet flowers held upright above lobed leaves (see Figure 13-27). It frequently grows with multiple trunks but rarely gets over 2 feet (60 cm) tall indoors.

Photo by Steven A. Frowine

If you place this plant outdoors during the summer, you'll find butterflies are attracted to its bright flowers.

TIP

Genus: *Justicia*

This genus is also known as *Jacobinia*. *Justicia carnea* (Brazilian plume, king's crown) is the only species from this genus available for houseplant lovers. It's a small shrub that reaches about 4 feet (1.2 m) tall but can be kept shorter with pruning. The 8-inch (20-cm) bright pink crested inflorescence with tubular flowers is quite eye-catching (see Figure 13-28 and the color insert).

Given bright conditions, Brazilian plume flowers multiple times a year.

TIP

FIGURE 13-28:
Brazilian plume is
crowned with an
abundance of
bright pink
tubular flowers.

Photo by Steven A. Frowine

Genus: *Medinilla*

This genus from the Philippines consists of broad-leaved evergreen shrubs, some of which have breathtakingly beautiful pendulous inflorescences.

The most commonly available, *Medinilla magnifica* (showy medinilla, rose grape), has 14-inch (35-cm) pendulous flower spikes (referred to as *panicles*) of bracts and grape-shaped flowers that are a remarkable electric pink (see Figure 13-29). The plant has ribbed dark green foliage and can reach 2 to 4 feet (60 to 120 cm) tall and about as wide. It prefers humidity of about 50 percent and very bright diffused light.

Genus: *Mussaenda*

Native to the tropics and subtropics of Africa and Asia, this midsize shrub isn't commonly found in plant shops. *Mussaenda erythrophylla* (summer poinsettia, red flag bush) puts on twice the show with small flowers and long-lasting bracts in contrasting colors. Figure 13-30 shows a plant with star-shaped white flowers backed with larger red poinsettia-like bracts. It's quite an attractive combination. This shrub can get large in its natural habitat but can be restrained indoors with pruning.

FIGURE 13-29:
The flower spikes
on this shrub are
simply
magnificent.

Photo by Steven A. Frowine

FIGURE 13-30:
Red flag bush
adds radiant
color to your
indoor garden.

Photo by Steven A. Frowine

Genus: *Nerium*

Oleander is a popular shrub that is cultivated in all subtropical and tropical areas but is especially at home in warm Mediterranean countries. It loves a lot of sun and toasty temperatures. Many plants in this genus naturally grow to be quite large shrubs, but there are dwarf forms. When given bright, warm growing conditions, they'll bloom continuously with funnel-shaped flowers in a wide array of colors — purple, red, pink, or white. Figure 13-31 shows a dwarf form that's about 2 feet (60 cm) tall and wide.

FIGURE 13-31:
Oleander is found and enjoyed around the world.

WARNING

The sap from oleander branches can be irritating to some folks.

Genus: *Pachystachys*

This genus of tropical shrubs has only one representative in the houseplant trade. The dazzling yellow bracts topped with tubular white flowers of *Pachystachys lutea* (lollipop plant) are its trademark feature that makes it stand out in a crowd (see Figure 13-32). It can grow to 3 to 4 feet (1 to 1.2 m), although its attractive dark green foliage can be managed by pruning. Lollipop plant is closely related to *Beloperone* (Mexican shrimp plant, described earlier in this chapter), and you can see some similarity in the construction of the flower heads.

Genus: *Pentas*

Plants from this genus are winners as summer bedding plants as well as indoor plants because of their vibrant star-shaped flowers. They're small shrubs, growing to about 3 feet (1 m) at maturity. They flower best if given strong light. Only one species from this genus is commonly grown as a houseplant.

FIGURE 13-32:
Lollipop plant
provides
luminous color in
your houseplant
collection.

Photo by Steven A. Frowine

Pentas lanceolata (Egyptian star flower) has tubular star-shaped 4-inch (10-cm) clusters of soft pink to intense red flowers (see Figure 13-33) offset by dark green foliage. Outdoors, hummingbirds and butterflies love this plant. It grows to about 1 foot (30 cm) tall.

FIGURE 13-33:
Pentas are
appreciated for
their abundance
of flowers.

Photo by Steven A. Frowine

Genus: *Plumbago*

This genus has more than 10 species of shrubs that are native to various tropical lands. Although there's a white-flowering plumbago native to Florida called

Plumbago zeylanica (doctorbush), the one that's most common is *Plumbago auriculata*.

A houseplant collection never has enough sky-blue flowering plants, but *Plumbago auriculata* (cape plumbago) can fill that void. This native of South Africa has clusters of cool blue flowers (see Figure 13-34) that are always on display if the plant receives strong light. It's a compact mounding shrub that gets 1 to 2 feet (30 to 60 cm) tall and somewhat wider.

Genus: *Plumeria*

You never forget the sweet fragrance of plumeria (also known as frangipani). It reminds me of when I lived in Hawaii, where plumeria *leis* (floral wreaths or necklaces) are standard welcoming gifts to visitors.

Even though plumeria grow to the size of small trees in tropical climates, they are available in dwarf forms suited to small growing spaces. Plumeria have large clusters of waxy tubular flowers in various colors (see Figure 13-35 and the color insert). They are *deciduous,* not evergreen, so they go dormant in the winter, and their leaves drop even in their natural habitat. However, they spring back to life during the longer, brighter, warmer days of spring and summer.

FIGURE 13-35: Because of their luscious colors and sweet scent, frangipani are favorites for leis.

Photo by Steven A. Frowine

Genus: *Rosa*

Roses probably aren't the first plant you think of as belonging with your other houseplants, and most of them aren't well suited to growing indoors because of their rangy growth habit and the fact that most of the standard varieties require cold overwintering temperatures. Even though most of us think of roses as being an outside garden plants, there are types that serve well as houseplants. The ones appropriate for growing indoors are miniature roses. They aren't as delicate as you may imagine; rather, they're tougher than standard roses in terms of their resistance to disease, and they don't require as much of a cooling-off period. So, if roses are your passion, give miniatures a try. They come in a wide range of colors, and some are fragrant. They grow 6 to 12 inches (15 to 30 cm) high.

Genus: *Ruellia*

Despite the common name wild petunia, this genus isn't related to petunias, although the flowers do look similar. This genus is rather large, but only a few species are cultivated for horticultural use.

Ruellia simplex (Mexican bluebell) is a woody plant grown as an annual in colder climates, but it can also be an indoor plant. Although the flower does resemble a petunia in shape (see Figure 13-36), the plant's growth habit is quite different. It's an upright grower reaching 2 to 3 feet (60 to 90 cm) tall and about as wide; a dwarf form is also available. Its purple-blue flower contrasts beautifully with its dark green to purple-green lancelike foliage. It needs full sun to flower well.

FIGURE 13-36:
Ruellia's flower looks much like a purple-blue petunia.

Photo by Steven A. Frowine

Genus: *Spathiphyllum*

Although more than 40 species of this plant exist, only a few are cultivated as houseplants. Their flowers resemble jack-in-the-pulpits, with their catkin-like structure in the center, called a *spadix*, which houses the tiny nondescript flowers. The showy white part of the plant (the *spathe*) is a modified leaf.

This genus contains some of the toughest houseplants you can grow, which is why you see them for sale just about everywhere and often find them in the usually less-than-ideal growing environment of many offices. They'll bloom in low-light spaces when no other plant will.

Spathiphyllum wallisii or *Spathiphyllum clevelandii* (peace lily) is the species you're most likely to find in stores. The peace lily is common in houseplant collections because it always delivers. The standard form gets about 2 feet (60 cm) tall, but you can find dwarf varieties if you have limited space. The spoon-shaped spathe is about 5 inches (13 cm) long and 3 inches (8 cm) wide. The 6-inch (15-cm) dark green lance-shaped foliage is attractive (see Figure 13-37).

Genus: *Tabernaemontana*

Tabernaemontana is a genus of shrubs frequently mistaken for jasmine because of their sweetly scented white flowers. *Tabernaemontana divaricata* (crepe jasmine, pinwheel flower) is the most popular species. It's an evergreen shrub from Southeast Asia with 6-inch (15-cm) glossy green leaves and clusters of 2-inch (5-cm) waxy pinwheel-shaped flowers (see Figure 13-38). It grows about 5 to 6 feet (1.5 to 2 m) tall.

Photo by Steven A. Frowine

Photo by Steven A. Frowine

Genus: *Tibouchina*

Royal purple flowers are the claim to fame for tibouchinas. Although some species can be as large as a tree, the species grown outdoors in warm climates or indoors as houseplants are much smaller. Their stiff, dark green leaves have distinctive parallel veins (see Figure 13-39).

FIGURE 13-39:
Princess flower
sports regal
purple flowers.

Photo by Steven A. Frowine

Tibouchina urvilleana (glory bush, princess flower), a Brazilian native, can be trained to a tree form for ornamental purposes, but it's most often pruned and grown as a small shrub. It will continue to flower if it gets strong light.

Genus: *Zantedeschia*

It wasn't long ago that the only calla lilies were mostly the white-flowered species *Zantedeschia aethiopica*. This tall-growing (up to 3 feet [1 m]) species is still popular for its long-lasting cut flowers, which are a pristine white (symbolizing the essence of purity to some). Its glossy arrow-shaped dark green foliage speckled in white is also quite ornamental. Callas tend to prefer damp potting material because they are bog plants.

Hybridizers have developed new callas with flowers in many luscious colors borne on dwarf plants that are perfect in containers. Figure 13-40 shows, one of the new brightly colored calla hybrids.

Photo by Steven A. Frowine

FIGURE 13-40: Calla lilies come in an assortment of rich colors like this gorgeous hybrid.

Genus: *Zingiber*

The ginger family of plants is huge. Some of these Southeast Asian plants are treasured all over the world for their culinary value (primarily *Zingiber officinale*), whereas others are grown for their ornamental flowers and foliage. I've already mentioned a few popular houseplants in this family. Here, I introduce you to another.

Although *Zingiber zerumbet* (shampoo ginger) is edible, it's very bitter, so its real attribute is its interesting inflorescences. When I lived in Hawaii, I became very familiar with this plant because it was treasured both for its ornamental flowers and for its practical use as a shampoo. The sap-like ginger-scented liquid from the mature inflorescence will suds up when poured into damp hair. (I tried it, and it works!)

Indoor plants are usually about 3 feet (1 m) tall and wide. The globular, pine cone–shaped orangey-red inflorescence (see Figure 13-41) is about 8 inches (20 cm) long.

FIGURE 13-41:
Shampoo ginger
has both a
beautiful and a
practical side.

Photo by Steven A. Frowine

Chapter **14**

African Violets and Their Kin: Almost Always in Flower

African violets *(Saintpaulia)* are part of a large family of plants called *gesneriads*. The plants in this family are mostly tropical, but a few can take colder climates. In this chapter, I focus on those that like warmer indoor environments.

I've been an admirer and grower of gesneriads for many years, and it baffles me that more houseplant lovers aren't very familiar with this great group of plants. Maybe their family name has something to do with it. Gesneriad does kind of have a nasal sound to it, so maybe it isn't very inviting. With the small sample of plants I cover in this chapter (there are so many more you can explore), I show you why these plants deserve your attention.

Understanding Why Gesneriads Should Be More Popular

Recently, amateur and professional plant breeders — particularly in the United States, England, and Eastern Europe — have released a flood of new and exciting hybrids of various gesneriads. These plants are perfect companions to other tropical houseplants because they have the same basic growing requirements as many plants in your indoor garden. They also offer a huge range of flower colors and shapes and leaf colors and patterns.

TECHNICAL STUFF

In nature, some gesneriads are *epiphytes* (grow on trees), some are *terrestrial* (grow on the ground), and some are *lithophytes* (grow on rocks).

Here are some key reasons I think more people should add gesneriads to their indoor garden:

>> They're easy to grow.

>> They're easy to flower. They need less light than almost any other flowering houseplant.

>> Most are very reasonably priced.

>> There are more than 3,000 species, plus many hybrids, so you never run out of new ones to try.

>> They're happy with a windowsill or an artificial light setup.

>> Most are compact plants that take up very little growing space.

Introducing the Main Players in This Genus

It's lucky, for simplicity's sake, that most gesneriads have the same basic cultural (growing) requirements as most other tropical houseplants — moist air, modest air movement, bright light of an eastern or southern exposure filtered through a sheer curtain or appropriate artificial lights (see Chapter 2), and temperatures around 65 to 75°F (18 to 24°C), give or take 5 degrees in either direction. I note any plants that have different growing requirements as I tell you about them in the following sections. For more detailed information on general cultural requirements, check out the chapters in Part 2.

Generally, the gesneriads with very hairy leaves resent water touching their leaves, especially if the water is very cold or hot. Watering your plants from the top may result in unsightly splotches on the leaves.

As I mention earlier in this chapter, this is an enormous family of plants. I focus only on the stars in this group that I have grown.

Genus: *Achimenes*

This genus, which has the common name magic flowers, includes more than 25 species and even more hybrids. They display clustered flowers in an array of colors — red, purple, yellow, and various pastels. Some are weeping forms great for hanging baskets, whereas others grow upright (reaching 6 to 12 inches [15 to 30 centimeters]) and are suited for containers.

TIP

Achimenes plants require more light than some of their cousins, so for the best flowering, give them very bright light but no direct sunlight. To make them bushier (as shown in Figure 14-1), I pinch (or cut back) the top few inches of the new growth when the plants are several inches tall.

FIGURE 14-1:
This is a beautiful pastel-colored upright *Achimenes* called 'Sweet and Sour'.

Photo by Steven A. Frowine

Genus: *Aeschynanthus*

Most plants in this genus have a trailing habit and are commonly planted in hanging baskets. They have red, yellow, or orange flowers borne in clusters. Their foliage is succulent and dark green.

Aeschynanthus parviflorus (lipstick plant) is the species that's usually available. It grows best with higher humidity (50 percent or higher) and bright diffused light, and it performs well in a hanging basket. It has brilliant red flowers that resemble tubes of lipstick (see Figure 14-2) and appear from the *calyx* (base of the flower).

FIGURE 14-2: Look at the red buds on this plant, and you can see why it was given its common name.

Photo by Steven A. Frowine

Genus: *Chirita*

Beautiful foliage is the hallmark of this genus. Even when its petite tubular flowers aren't in bloom, it's stunning. Plants in this group are diverse, and hybrids of this species are commonly grown today.

Chirita sinensis (also called *Primulina dryas*) is from Hong Kong. It's a beauty with 6-x-2-inch (15-x-5-cm) fuzzy green leaves marked with silver. Its light lilac tubular flowers are pretty insignificant compared to its dramatic foliage (see Figure 14-3). The plant reaches about 6 inches (15 cm) high and somewhat wider.

Chirita tamiana (also called *Deinostigma tamiana*) is a small-growing plant with leaves that are only about 1 inch (2 cm) in diameter (see Figure 14-4). Unlike some of the others in this genus, this one has dainty and charming flowers. Its diminutive size makes it ideal as a terrarium plant. See Chapter 5 for more information about making your own terrarium.

FIGURE 14-3:
Chiritas
have become
more popular
because of their
attractive leaves,
compact growing
habit, and cheery
flowers.

Nikiforov Volodymyr/Shutterstock

FIGURE 14-4:
This miniature
chirita is perfect
for terrariums.

Photo by Steven A. Frowine

Genus: *Chrysothemis*

Plants in this genus of six species get up to 18 inches (45 cm) tall. Their leaves are very dark green. The flowers tend to be small and short lasting, but the calyx is persistent and stays in color for quite a while.

Chrysothemis pulchella (sunset bells) is the species you'll most likely find. It has handsome, shiny reddish-green leaves, and its flower has an orange calyx with a yellow and red *corolla* (the top part of the flower). See Figure 14-5.

FIGURE 14-5:
Sunset bells is a taller-growing gesneriad worth adding to your collection.

Genus: *Columnea*

Columneas are native to North and South America and are noted for their upright colorful tubular hooded flowers. Figure 14-6 shows a typical columnea flower *(Columnea multiflora)*. Most are trailing plants (see Figure 14-7), so they make stunning hanging baskets. Because of their popularity, hybrids abound.

FIGURE 14-6:
A closeup of the hooded flower of a columnea.

Photo by Steven A. Frowine

Genus: *Corytoplectus*

This gesneriad isn't that common. It's an erect grower, and like *Chrysothemis*, its flowers are small and yellow, and its foliage is toothed and shiny green. The plant can be pinched to make it branch out.

Corytoplectus cutucuensis (see Figure 14-8) is somewhat rare but is worth searching for. Its foliage is a gorgeous velvety dark green with lighter green to white markings in the center and along the veins of the leaves. The small red flowers form dark pearl-like fruits.

Karen J Fernandez/Shutterstock

Genus: *Episcia*

This genus of about 35 species and quite a few hybrids is most noted for plants with beautifully patterned multicolored foliage. However, some also have delightful flowers. Most are trailing plants well-suited for hanging baskets or wide containers.

Episcias are more sensitive to cold temperatures and low humidity than some of the other gesneriads, so they appreciate temperatures of about 75°F (24°C) (55°F [13°C] or lower means death for them!) and moist air with 55 percent humidity or higher. The gorgeous varieties with pink, white, and green foliage (see Figure 14-9), like 'Cleopatra' and 'Pink Brocade', will grow well only in high humidity, so are best grown in a terrarium.

FIGURE 14-9: Some of the episcias, such as 'Ember Lace', have gorgeous variegated green, pink, and white foliage.

Photo by Steven A. Frowine

Episcia cupreata (flame violet) is one of the episcias with varied leaf forms and patterns. It lives up to the name *flame violet* with its dazzling orange-red flowers (see Figure 14-10).

Genus: *Kohleria*

Of the lesser-known gesneriads, *Kohleria* is one of my favorites. They're found in a wide range of heights, leaf colorations, and flowers. The newer hybrids are prolific bloomers that tend to be more compact growing than others in the species. If they're grown in ideal conditions, they bloom almost constantly.

TIP

The taller forms can be pruned to encourage branching. When mine get rangy, I cut them back several times, and they just keep popping back with new growth and flowers.

FIGURE 14-10:
If you have a warm, humid, bright spot, *Episcia cupreata* is a good choice.

They aren't particular as far as humidity goes and are happy in a home environment with average temperatures but bloom best in very bright diffused light.

The *Kohleria* hybrid shown in Figure 14-11 and the color insert has the compact growth habit and heavy flowering found in many of these wonderful plants.

Photo by Steven A. Frowine

FIGURE 14-11:
Kohleria is one of the lesser-known African violet relatives that deserves more attention because it's almost always in flower.

Kohleria 'Marta' is another compact-growing variety. In Figure 14-12, you can see the beautifully marked fuzzy flowers.

FIGURE 14-12:
Close up, you can
see the amazing
details of the
flowers of
Kohleria 'Marta'.

Photo by Steven A. Frowine

Genus: *Nematanthus*

The plants in this genus from Brazil grow shrubby in the wild. They have succulent leaves and sport flowers that have a swollen pouch. Most of them have a rambling growth habit, so they're usually grown in hanging baskets.

Nematanthus gregarius (goldfish plant, guppy plant) is one of the popular plants in this genus. Its attractive, succulent shiny green leaves are enough of a reason to grow goldfish plant, but its long-lasting, hard, waxy orange-to-yellow flowers are a charming bonus (see Figure 14-13). It is slow growing and rarely reaches 24 inches (60 cm) high and wide.

FIGURE 14-13:
This plant's
flowers look like
little goldfish
swimming among
the thick glossy
green foliage.

lennystan/Shutterstock

Genus: *Pearcea*

Pearcea is a rather small South American genus of about 20 species. Its outstanding features are its decorative dark green leaves with lighter contrasting midveins (branched lateral ribs) and unique ball-shaped red flowers (see Figure 14-14).

Dr Morley Read/Shutterstock

FIGURE 14-14: This gesneriad has gorgeous foliage topped with ball-shaped flowers that look like red berries.

Pearcea hypocyrtiflora is a native of Ecuador. It isn't a beginner's plant and can be hard to find, but it's worth searching out if you're up for a challenge. It can be persnickety and does best in an enclosed container like a glass bowl or terrarium, where it receives high humidity and isn't exposed to drafts. It's a small plant, usually not growing over 6 inches (15 cm) tall.

Genus: *Saintpaulia*

Saintpaulia (African violet) is hands down the most popular genus in the gesneriad family. This African native is found and admired in homes all over the world. Why is it so popular? Because it's relatively undemanding in its light and humidity requirements, and it comes in so many different leaf shapes, sizes, and colors with a range of flower colors and patterns unmatched by any of the other gesneriads.

Years ago, African violets seemed to be considered old-fashioned, but not anymore. Thanks to the efforts of amateur and professional plant breeders, exciting new hybrids are being introduced constantly, and these plants now have a dedicated following of houseplant lovers across all age ranges.

As far as the plant forms go, you can find African violets in everything from miniature or *teacup* varieties that are comfortable in 2-inch (5-cm) pots to standards that can get 12 inches (30 cm) or more across to trailing forms and plants in sizes in between. Although some specialists enjoy growing the original species of these plants, many enthusiasts are drawn to the hybrids for their larger, more dramatic flowers and ease of growing.

Here are some cultural tips for this popular group of gesneriads:

>> African violet leaves are succulent and hairy and tend to retain any water that falls on them, so be careful not to get water on the foliage to avoid unsightly leaf spotting, as shown in Figure 14-15. This is especially true if the water is much warmer or colder than the surrounding air temperature.

>> African violets are particular about their watering requirements. They like to be moist but not wet or waterlogged. So, should you water from the top or the bottom? Both can work. Some growers have found that self-watering pots are the easiest way to meet this plant's watering requirements. See Chapter 6 to get more information about watering, and check out Chapter 7 for details on self-watering pots.

>> Thrips are a particularly fearsome pest on African violets because they damage the flowers and leaves. Even more important, they are *vectors* (carriers) of two dreaded viral diseases, *Tomato spotted wilt virus (TSWV)* and *Impatiens necrotic spot virus (INSV)*. See Chapter 9 for controls for this pest. Also check the African violet websites and online forums for the most up-to-date information and controls for this pest.

FIGURE 14-15: The white marks and patches on this African violet's foliage are the result of cold or hot water pooling on the leaves.

Photo by Steven A. Frowine

The best way to prevent TSWV or INSV from infecting your collection is to buy only from vendors recommended by plants societies or those online suppliers that have high ratings (at least mid-90's). If you still aren't sure, talk to the grower to find out how they are preventing these viruses from contaminating the plants they sell. Also, it's always a good idea to quarantine your newly purchased plants for several weeks before adding them to your collection.

>> The other two pests that can sometimes bother African violets are mites and mealybugs. Check Chapter 9 for controls for these pests.

>> One common disease African violets get is powdery mildew. Again, see Chapter 9 for disease-control measures.

>> African violets are some of the easiest gesneriads to propagate from leaf cuttings. Check out Chapter 8 for more information on how to do this. If you get carried away, you can start many leaf cuttings at once in a container holding a mix of half perlite and half sphagnum peat moss, as shown in Figure 14-16. Cover the container with a plastic lid or plastic wrap to hold in humidity until new plants sprout from the leaves. Then the new plants can be potted up.

Be aware that African violets do mutate, so for some leaf cuttings, the result may not look exactly like the parent. You may create a new variety!

>> Varieties with lighter foliage tend to require less light than those with darker foliage.

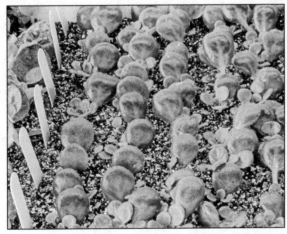

FIGURE 14-16: You can start many African violet cuttings at once.

Photo by Steven A. Frowine

>> If a plant receives too much light, the growth will be stunted or bleached-out looking; too little light, and the leaves will be stretched, and you'll get little or no flowering.

>> Most African violet growers prefer nonporous pots made of ceramic or plastic materials. Porous clay pots usually dry out too quickly and can become encrusted with minerals or covered with algae.

>> African violet potting mixes should be moisture-retentive but also well-draining. To obtain this ideal, which seems contradictory on the surface, I usually use a mix of half sphagnum peat moss and half perlite. Some folks use one-third sphagnum peat moss, one-third perlite, and one-third vermiculite. Of course, you can purchase commercial African violet potting mixes if you don't want to formulate your own. See Chapter 7 for more info on potting materials.

>> Their temperature requirements of 65 to 75°F (18 to 24°C) are the same as most of the other houseplants.

>> Humidity of around 50 percent will suit them fine.

>> To keep your plants symmetrical, which seems to be the ideal (except for the vining types), you have to be vigilant about removing sideshoots or suckers as they appear. The removed sideshoots can be used like leaf cuttings to propagate the variety.

>> To keep them actively growing and flowering, repot your African violets every year or so, but don't be too eager to transplant them in much larger pots. They bloom best when they are somewhat *pot-bound* (tightly fitted to their pot).

>> As with all plants, remove the spent leaves and flowers. This will stimulate new growth and flowering.

Don't let all the tips I listed scare you off from growing African violets. I'm just trying to cover the bases so you can handle the most common issues in growing them.

The *Saintpaulia* genus is so diverse that it's impossible to give you a true sense of all the varieties in this short introduction. Just go online or visit some African violet growers — you'll be wowed by what's available. Figure 14-17 shows a commercial African violet greenhouse to give you some idea of the wide array of African violet varieties you can choose from.

Photo by Steven A. Frowine

Figures 14-18 through 14-21 show just a few African violets that I have enjoyed growing. *Saintpaulia* 'Cajun's Blueberry Hill' in Figure 14-18 is also in the color insert.

Photo by Steven A. Frowine

Genus: *Seemannia*

This small genus, which used to be in genus *Gloxinia,* is from the Andes. Plants have showy, long-lasting red or yellow tubular flowers and are compact with narrow leaves that grow in a rosette.

Photo by Steven A. Frowine

Photo by Steven A. Frowine

Seemannia sylvatica (Bolivian sunset) has red tubular flowers and shiny dark green leaves (see Figure 14-22). It's sometimes used as an annual groundcover during the summer and seldom grows over 6 inches (15 cm) tall. It only requires moderate temperatures and humidity but will bloom best with very strong diffused light.

Photo by Steven A. Frowine

Khairil Azhar Junos/Shutterstock

Genus: *Sinningia*

Second only to African violets (*Saintpaulia*) in popularity, the genus *Sinningia* offers houseplant enthusiasts many wonderful choices. Although some aficionados grow the species, the hybrids are what catches most people's fancy. The variety of flower colors and types and growth habit are quite varied from miniatures 1" (2.5cm) or so across to those 1 foot (30 cm) or more in diameter. They need a bit more light than African violets to flower well, but their modest temperature and humidity requirements are much the same as their cousins.

Sinningia speciosa is much better known by its common name, florist gloxinia. Botanists decided that it really doesn't belong in the genus *Gloxinia*, so it was reassigned to the genus *Sinningia*. A florist gloxinia in full flower is a glorious sight! I've grown these for years, and I'm always excited when they bud up and eventually open their spectacular bell-shaped flowers.

These plants went out of favor for a while, probably because they can take up a bit of space and houseplant growers mistakenly thought that they bloomed only once a year. Many plants were discarded after they flowered, which is too bad because they'll put on another show relatively quickly if handled correctly. (See the "Getting florist gloxinias to rebloom" sidebar later in this chapter for more information.)

Florist gloxinias come in single (Figure 14-23 and the color insert) and double flower (see Figure 14-24) forms. For a closeup of the gorgeous flowers of *Sinningia* 'Dainty Dot', see Figure 14-25.

FIGURE 14-23:
Although most plant lovers know it as florist gloxinia, the proper name for this gorgeous plant with bell-shaped flowers is *Sinningia speciosa*.

Photo by Steven A. Frowine

FIGURE 14-24:
Double-flowered florist gloxinias put on quite a show.

Photo by Steven A. Frowine

GETTING FLORIST GLOXINIAS TO REBLOOM

As I mention earlier in this chapter, many indoor gardeners love these plants when they're in flower but don't know what to do with them when they're done flowering. Many growers say you should let the plant go into dormancy. Allow the foliage to die back, and only periodically add a small amount of water to keep the *tuber* (swollen underground stem) from drying out while you wait for it to send up new shoots. This method works, but you must be careful not to overwater it while it's dormant, or the tuber will rot.

Another method I've used that gets much quicker results is to cut back the foliage to just two sets of leaves. Water the plant sparingly to keep the foliage from wilting. New growth will start up, and the plant will flower once more in several weeks. You may consider repotting the plant in fresh potting media when the new growth begins.

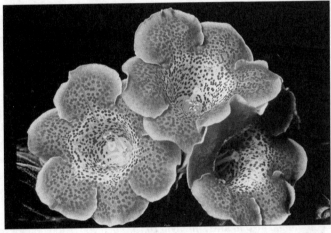

FIGURE 14-25: The huge single flowers of this *Sinningia* 'Dainty Dot' are spectacular.

Photo by Steven A. Frowine

Other sinningias are also worth growing. They may not have the huge flowers of florist gloxinia, but they offer other charms. They have a multitude of flowers and are small growing, which may be easier for you to accommodate. Most of them will bloom repeatedly if you handle them as I've described in the nearby sidebar. Here are a few I have enjoyed:

>> ***Sinningia leucotricha* (Brazilian edelweiss):** This is an oddity among sinningias because it grows in conditions that succulents like. The silvery-white hair on its foliage (see Figure 14-26) feels as soft and velvety as a dog's ear. The fragrant tubular orange flowers are a bonus. It's slow growing and prefers to be in a well-drained medium like the potting mix used for cacti and succulents.

FIGURE 14-26:
Brazilian
edelweiss is a
good partner with
succulents.

Photo by Steven A. Frowine

» *Sinningia speciosa* **'Regina':** This plant is elegant for both its exquisite dark green foliage with prominent silvery veins and its royal purple slipper-shaped flowers. It grows about as large as the other florist gloxinia hybrids. It's a stunner.

» *Sinningia* **'Dollbaby':** Anyone can make space for this compact-growing (under 6 inches [15 cm]) hybrid. It has been around since the '60s but is still popular. It has 1-inch (2.5-cm) lavender slipper-shaped flowers with light yellow markings in the throat (see Figure 14-27). It's one of the easiest to grow and most available of the semi-miniature types of sinningias. Because of its small dimensions, it will fit in a terrarium, although it's at home with any of its gesneriad cousins.

» *Sinningia pusilla* and *Sinningia concinna:* If you're looking for miniscule or micro sinningia species, these two can fit in a thimble-size pot or small terrarium.

» *Sinningia* **'Prudence Risley':** This is one of my all-time favorites. Figure 14-28 shows a plant I've had for years. It treats me to round after round of oodles of pinkish red, tubular flowers. It grows about 8 inches (20 cm) tall and wide. After my plant flowers, I just cut it back to a few inches from the tuber, and it sprouts new growth and flowers again within several weeks.

Genus: *Smithiantha*

This Mexican genus of about six species is noted for its velvety, hairy green-to-red leaves and pyramidal flower spike covered with lovely pendulous bell-shaped flowers. Like the African violet, its leaves are easily marked or damaged by cold water. Most of the species tend to be quite large plants, but breeders have given us hybrids of a more manageable size. Figure 14-29 shows an example of the smaller growing hybrids, *Smithiantha* 'Little One'.

Photo by Steven A. Frowine

Genus: *Streptocarpus*

Don't be put off by the unfortunate name *Streptocarpus,* which sounds like a throat disease! This is a genus from Africa with intriguing species. Although some plant collectors grow the species, most houseplant growers are bowled over by the new hybrids that are the result of diligent work by hybridizers from the United States, England, Poland, Russia, and Ukraine. I'm over the moon for these newer hybrids. The range of flower colors! The abundance of huge flowers!

With sufficient light and moderate care, streptocarpus can flower almost constantly, especially if they're grown under lights. (See Chapter 5 for more on lighting options.) If you're growing them on a windowsill during the winter when the light is weaker, they will stop blooming until they're exposed to more light in the spring.

I've listed just a sliver of the hybrids available, but hopefully enough to get you to search for these marvelous hybrids:

>> *Streptocarpus* **'Constant Nymph':** This is an older hybrid, but Figure 14-30 gives you an idea of how these plants can develop into awesome specimens.

>> *Streptocarpus* **'Kaleidoscope':** This plant is part of a group of hybrids called *Fantasy streptocarpus* because of their multicolored flowers. Figure 14-31 shows one of my plants that always gets oohs and aahs from friends.

>> *Streptocarpus* **'Neil's Samson':** The plant shown in Figure 14-32 (and the color insert) has bloomed for me almost constantly. Its countless 3-inch (7.5-cm) speckled and dark-veined pink flowers are a wondrous sight.

FIGURE 14-30:
Streptocarpus
can make
spectacular
specimens.

Photo by Steven A. Frowine

FIGURE 14-31:
Streptocarpus
'Kaleidoscope' is
part of a group
called Fantasy
streptocarpus
because of their
fantastic flower
patterns.

Photo by Steven A. Frowine

TIP

Streptocarpus can be easily propagated by leaf cuttings — with either entire leaves or edges of the leaves. The midvein of the leaf can be removed and laid sideways in the potting media or pointed wedges of the leaves can be used (see Figure 14-33). For more information on propagation from leaf cuttings, check out Chapter 8.

FIGURE 14-32: *Streptocarpus* 'Neil's Samson' never disappoints.

Photo by Steven A. Frowine

FIGURE 14-33: Multiplying your favorite streptocarpus via leaf cuttings is easy.

Photo by Steven A. Frowine

Chapter **15**

Begonias: Brilliant Flowers, Gorgeous Foliage

B egonias hail from all parts of the tropics — Asia, Africa, and Central and South America. A few even grow in cold climates. They represent a large genus of almost 1,500 species. Some are grown as houseplants, whereas others are grown outdoors as bedding plants. Some grow upright; others trail. Some grow in trees; others grow on the ground. Some are minuscule plants usually grown in terrariums, and others grow much larger as *subshrubs* (low shrubs or perennials with woody stems) or shrubs. Their leaf types, shapes, and colors are varied.

Begonias have long held a special place in the hearts of plant lovers, and this chapter covers the most popular types. After reading through this chapter, you'll understand why begonias have been and continue to be must-haves in every indoor garden.

Examining Why People Grow Begonias

Begonias have been admired as houseplants for quite a while — since the mid-1800s in Europe and the 1920s in the United States. One reason for their popularity is that they don't require as much light as some of the other houseplants. Another is that no other foliage plant can match the brilliant and varied colors found in some begonias. They're also outstanding among flowering plants. The tuberous begonias have impressive flowers that can compete with roses and camellias.

Because of the houseplant craze we're experiencing today, the increased demand for begonias has resulted in new species and hybrids being discovered and introduced. That makes this genus of plants even more desirable.

Here are some of the reasons begonias score so high in the desirable plant category:

>> If you pick the right ones, they're easy to grow.

>> The standard, readily available varieties are good for beginner indoor gardeners. With more experience, you can graduate to some of the more challenging species.

>> They're reasonably priced.

>> They're readily available. You can find the basic varieties at home-supply stores, grocery stores, and garden centers and the more exotic ones at specialty suppliers.

>> They come in such a variety of sizes that they fit in any growing space.

>> The gorgeous foliage colors and patterns found in begonias are almost endless.

>> They don't require an expensive greenhouse to grow. They're happy with a windowsill or an artificial light setup.

>> They beautify your home and life.

>> They're easy to propagate, so you can share your favorites with your friends and family.

Understanding Basic Care of Begonias

Begonias don't require more special care than most of the other houseplants in this book, but in this section, I review the fundamentals of growing them. I mention exceptions to these cultural guidelines as I discuss the individual types of begonias.

Potting your begonias

Begonias can be grown in plastic or clay pots. For smaller plants especially, plastic or ceramic pots can be a better choice because they don't dry out as quickly as terra cotta. Most begonias greatly resent dryness. Larger begonias can benefit from being planted in heavy ceramic pots (with drainage holes in the bottom) because they can be top heavy and prone to toppling over.

A well-drained but moisture-retentive potting mix is best for begonias. Most commercially available potting mixes are acceptable. Don't buy potting soil because it is usually too heavy and won't drain well, which will lead to rotting roots.

Regulating humidity

Because most begonias are from humid environments, they appreciate at least a modest humidity of 40 to 60 percent. Some of the very tender species require higher humidity, and these types are frequently kept in enclosed growing spaces like terrariums to meet this requirement.

Watering correctly

Here are some guidelines for how to properly water your begonias:

>> To check the moisture in the potting mix, push your finger into the mix up to your first knuckle. If it doesn't feel moist and your finger comes out dry, you may water your begonia.

>> When you water, don't wet the foliage; only wet the potting mix.

>> Be especially careful not to water too often when the air temperature is low because during this time begonias grow much slower and use less water.

WARNING

>> *Never* let your begonia sit in a saucer of water for more than 10 minutes or so. If any excess water remains, dump it out. Otherwise, your plant's roots can rot.

>> Wilting leaves are a sign that a plant *needs* water.

Providing light

Begonias need bright, diffused light but not direct sunlight. To bloom well, flowering begonias require more light than the foliage types. The smaller-growing begonias are great candidates for growing under lights.

During the summer, I grow many of my begonias on my patio with a 50 percent shade cloth over them as shown in Figure 15-1.

FIGURE 15-1: I grow some of my begonias on hanging shelves on the patio under a 50 percent shade cloth.

Managing temperature requirements

Most begonias love tropical temperatures, so average room temperatures or higher (below 90°F [32°C] and above 55°F [13°C]) suit them fine. Tuberous begonias don't appreciate the heat as much as the cane and rex types. (Read more about each type of begonia later in this chapter.)

For general cultural information on begonias and other houseplants, like growing under lights, pests and their controls, fertilizing guidelines, and propagating techniques, check Part 2.

Meeting the Begonias

Get ready to enter the world of bodacious begonias. The begonias I list in the rest of this chapter only touch the surface of what's available in this wondrous genus.

Trying to categorize begonias is a real challenge because there are so many! I settled on a nontechnical but practical way of organizing them for this chapter. These are the three categories I use:

>> Foliage begonias

>> Flowering begonias

>> Shrub or cane begonias

Foliage begonias

This group is noted for its sensationally colored foliage, but that doesn't mean they don't flower. However, the flowers aren't the main show — the leaves are. Most begonias in this category are also referred to as *rhizomatous begonias* because their stems (or *rhizomes*) creep along the ground.

I admit that this category of begonias is more challenging than some in terms of culture. One of the biggest issues is correct watering — they will easily rot if overwatered. They're also very sensitive to colder temperatures. However, any extra care they require is totally worth it. Their leaf colors and patterns are breathtaking. When you're looking for plants in this group, you can easily recognize them by their brightly colored foliage. But they often aren't labeled or are sold under the broad category of *rex begonias*, so don't worry much about their names. Just enjoy them for their splendid beauty.

The following sections provide details about a few foliage begonias, some with names and some without.

Begonia 'Connie Boswell'

This majestic hybrid is a popular large-leafed rhizomatous begonia. The silvery leaves are deeply lobed with lavender markings along the edges and center veins (see Figure 15-2). Although this plant is primarily grown for its sumptuous foliage, it does produce small fragrant pale pink flowers in the spring.

FIGURE 15-2:
This well-known
begonia is fancied
for its lustrous
leaf colors.

Photo by Steven A. Frowine

Begonia 'Escargot'

The foliage on this begonia is a conversation piece because of its spiral snail-like pattern that's accentuated by silver and brown markings (see Figure 15-3). It's designated as a rex hybrid.

FIGURE 15-3:
The curlicue in
the center of the
leaves is a
popular feature
of this begonia.

Photo by Steven A. Frowine

TIP

This plant's small pink flowers are just a sideshow. In fact, some folks think that the flowers of many rex hybrids detract from their curious leaves, so they remove them to allow all the plant's energy to go toward producing more leaves.

Begonia masoniana

This is a classic among begonia lovers, and there's no way this striking begonia native to China and Vietnam can be confused with any other. The reddish-brown iron cross–like pattern in the center of its rough-textured fuzzy light green leaves (see Figure 15-4) is a dead giveaway. It gets about 1 to 2 feet (30 to 60 cm) high and wide, making it a perfect container plant.

FIGURE 15-4:
Begonia masoniana (iron cross begonia) is one of the most admired rex begonias.

Photo by Steven A. Frowine

Begonia rex and hybrids

These are some of the most popular begonias because of their brilliantly colored foliage (see Figure 15-5). There are many types on the market, but most are not labeled with their hybrid name. These are called rhizomatous begonia because they grow from their rhizome, which is a stem that grows on the surface of the soil. Miniatures are just about 3 inches (7.6 cm) to over 2 feet (60 cm) high and wide. The varieties of this begonia have flowers, but for the most part, they are not very significant; it is the spectacular foliage that gives these begonias their appeal.

Begonia 'Tiger Paws'

If you don't have much growing space, this begonia is a great choice. It's one of the smallest of the rhizomatous begonias, growing only 10 inches (25 cm) high. Figure 15-6 shows its green leaves with chocolate-colored markings and white eyelash-like hairs on the edges. The undersides of the leaves are red. It has small white flowers that aren't very significant.

Begonia 'Winter Queen'

Large, beautifully marked spiral leaves make this begonia a standout (see Figure 15-7). Its lush leaves are about 6 inches (15 cm) across and 8 inches (20 cm) long. It grows upright from its rhizome.

FIGURE 15-7:
Brilliant white
markings contrast
against a dark
green leaf on this
standout.

Photo by Steven A. Frowine

Flowering begonias

The flowering begonias can put on quite a show. Some have small flowers but are prolific bloomers, whereas others are quite showy with larger flowers. In general, flowering begonias prefer a spot that's a little brighter than foliage begonias need; otherwise, they're happy with the same home as the leafy types. Their foliage is pretty, but their flowers are the main attraction. In this section, I discuss the most commonly available begonias in this group.

Begonia boliviensis

Hanging baskets are where these begonias shine. Although the species is only red flowering, hybrids come in different shades of red, pink, and white. This plant grows upright about 1 foot (30 cm) and then cascades over the edge of its container. The number of blooms it produces (see Figure 15-8) more than makes up for the small size of the flowers. It's a very dependable bloomer.

Begonia 'Elatior' hybrids

Prolific masses of brightly colored pink, yellow, orange, or white flowers are the hallmark of these begonias, which are also called *Begonia x hiemalis* and *Begonia reniformis* (see Figure 15-9 and the color insert). They're usually winter bloomers that provide welcome color in the cold months, but they're also sold in the spring for outdoor planting. Within this group are hybrids called *Reiger begonias*, which are considered superior to the species because of their heavier flowering and resistance to disease, especially powdery mildew. They vary somewhat is size, but most are about 1 foot (30 cm) high and wide.

FIGURE 15-8:
This cascading begonia comes in various colors.

FIGURE 15-9:
For spectacular flowering you can't beat these begonias.

TIP

Because begonias are so colorful, they are fun to mix with your other houseplants. In the color insert, notice how the yellow-flowered begonia complements the yellow in the foliage of the adjacent croton leaves.

Begonia semperflorens

Begonia semperflorens (sometimes known as *Begonia cucullata* and wax begonia) must be the toughest and most common begonia out there! It can take partial or full sun, and as long as it gets enough light, it never stops blooming. It comes in a variety of leaf colors, from light green to dark green to bronze-red. The range of flower colors is also broad, including all shades of red, pink, and white. It's widely enjoyed as a bedding plant but can serve admirably as an addition to your indoor garden. They vary in size but generally peak out at 1 to 1.5 feet (30 to 45 cm) high and wide. See Figure 15-10.

FIGURE 15-10:
This begonia is a popular bedding plant, but also works well as an indoor plant.

Photo by Steven A. Frowine

Begonia tuberhybrida

The queens of the flowering begonias, the tuberous begonias, have sumptuous flowers (see Figure 15-11) that mimic the shape of roses, camellias, and carnations and are available in upright or cascading growth habits. They take more effort to grow than some of the others in their clan because they need to be started from *tubers* (root-like stems) in the early spring in a warm, bright spot indoors. Alternatively, you can purchase them as already-started plants. Grow them in a partially shady spot out of direct sunlight, and protect them from significant wind because their large, heavy blooms make them prone to blowing over.

They go dormant in the fall when their leaves turn yellow and eventually drop. Then they require storage in a frost-free, cool, dry location until they can be started again the following year. Yes, they're more trouble than some of the other begonias, but I grow them every year and am always happy that I do.

FIGURE 15-11:
A tuberous
begonia in full
bloom is a
spectacular sight.

Photo by Steven A. Frowine

Shrub or cane begonias

These big begonias can grow several feet tall but can be contained with judicious pruning. They're some of the most forgiving begonias, which makes them easy to grow. Because they can get quite tall, they're great as background plants. Most of them have very attractive foliage and some have striking flowers. Many are great to grow in large pots that sit on the floor. These begonia can grow to be 5 feet (1.5 meters) or more.

Begonia corallina

There are slew of begonias in this category. All of them have triangular wings (thus their common name, angel wing begonia), as you can see in Figure 15-12 and the color insert. Many angel wing begonias can get quite tall, most of them produce a flurry of small red, pink, or white flowers, and their foliage can be quite attractive. Some of the most recognizable are corallina hybrids.

Begonia 'Miss Mummy'

I've just become aware of how popular this begonia is. After seeing its dark, purple-black leaves, which look like they've been sprinkled with silver dust (see Figure 15-13) and have deep red undersides, I can see why. It's an upright grower that displays pendulous white clusters of flowers in the spring.

TIP

Begonias can be easily propagated by leaf or stem cutting. See Chapter 8 for details.

FIGURE 15-12:
You can see by the shape of its leaves how angel wing begonia got its name.

Photo by Steven A. Frowine

FIGURE 15-13:
There's no more striking begonia than this one.

Photo by Steven A. Frowine

4

The Part of Tens

Choose the easiest houseplants to grow.

Beware of the most common ways houseplants die.

Find answers to the most commonly asked questions about houseplants.

Chapter **16**

Ten Common Reasons Houseplants Die (and How to Avoid 'em)

S ooner or later, everyone loses a few houseplants to the Grim Reaper, but some causes of death take more houseplant lives than they should. Being on the lookout to prevent the problems I spotlight in this chapter will save many of your plants from a premature death.

Overwatering

Overwatering is the biggest killer of houseplants. Some people just can't keep themselves from doing it. Watering is lots of fun, and you feel like you're doing something to help your houseplants when you're watering them. Unfortunately, sometimes you're speeding them toward an early end.

TECHNICAL STUFF

When plants die from overwatering, it isn't really the result of too much water. The problem is too little air. There's only so much open space in any potting material, and water naturally displaces air. If you add water too often, there's no room for air, which your houseplant needs for healthy root growth. If it doesn't get enough air, the roots rot and die.

If overwatering is a common problem for you, consider switching your potting material to something that drains faster and doesn't retain as much water, as I discuss in Chapter 7. In addition, see Chapter 6 for tips on how to properly water your plants and an emergency treatment to try if any of your overwatered plants start going downhill.

Underwatering

Ironically, just as overwatering is a big houseplant killer, so is underwatering. In both cases, improper watering leads to root damage from dehydration (see Chapter 6 for more details). Because houseplant potting material drains much more rapidly and tends to hold less moisture than growing media commonly used for other plants, some people tend to underwater. Also, remember that fresh potting material dries out much more quickly than older potting material does.

TIP

Be sure to premoisten your potting material before you use it. Doing so makes it more water-retentive. Also, some potting materials retain water longer. Check out Chapter 7 for houseplant potting tips and information.

Too Much Light or Heat

Light and heat are related to one another. Frequently, excessive light leads to high temperatures. When houseplants receive too much light, heat starts to build up inside their leaves. Think of the leaf's skin (called the *epidermis*) as a plastic bag with very small holes in it. Inside this plastic bag is the leaf tissue. When excessive heat gets trapped inside the leaf, it literally cooks the tissue, destroying it. Large black circular dead spots form, or in extreme cases, the entire plant collapses. After this damage is done, it can't be fixed.

TIP

When the plant is in full light, feel the leaf surface with your hand. If it's hot to the touch, move the plant to a location where it gets less light. See Chapter 5 for more information on light and temperature requirements for houseplants.

Leaving Houseplant Foliage Wet Overnight

Leaving plant foliage wet overnight is asking for trouble in the form of leaf spots and crown rot disease. (The *crown* is the growing point of the plant.) Water your houseplants in the morning or early afternoon so the leaves have plenty of time to dry before nightfall, and ensure that no water is left sitting in the crown.

If you can catch leaf spots or crown rot early, you may be able to save the plant. But after the disease (which shows up as soft, mushy tissue that eventually turns black) gets to the crown, it's goodbye to your plant. For more information on plant diseases and their control, see Chapter 9.

Too Much Fertilizer

Applying too much fertilizer will dehydrate your plant's roots. Signs of too much fertilizer are black root tips or black or brown leaf tips. When you fertilize, be careful not to apply more than the recommended dosage, and use fertilizer only when the plant is actively growing and when the potting material is damp. If you aren't sure how much fertilizer to apply, err on the low side. For more details on fertilizing houseplants, see Chapter 6.

Insect Infestation

Catching insect problems in the early stages is extremely important. If you realize that your houseplant is completely covered with an insect like scale or mealybugs, getting rid of all these critters is very difficult, and you'll need multiple insecticide sprayings to get them under control.

TIP

If you have a severe infestation, trashing the plant for the sake of others in your collection can be the best approach; you don't want to expose your other plants to these bugs.

For more information on common plant pests and their control, check out Chapter 9.

Improper Use of Pesticides

When pesticides are used properly, they're safe for both you and your plants. However, if they're applied at excessive concentrations or when the plants are dry or the air temperature is too high, severe damage to the plant can result.

Also, many pesticides contain an oil that can cause leaf damage, especially if the material is applied when the plant is exposed to bright, hot sunlight.

As a result, use care with these materials and always read the label before applying them. See Chapter 9 to find out what to try before resorting to pesticides and which pesticides are safest and most effective to use.

Purchasing Sick Plants

Some houseplant growers are Florence Nightingale types who feel it's their mission to save a plant that looks sick. So they buy it, usually at a deep discount. In most cases, these plant lovers don't get a deal at all.

TIP

I highly recommend you resist the temptation to buy an unhealthy houseplant and try to nurse it back to health. If a plant is in poor condition and the leaves are wilting or shriveled (which usually indicates dead or damaged roots), it's often on an unstoppable death spiral, and the likelihood of your nurturing it back to robustness is slim to none.

WARNING

Another issue with bringing an unwell plant into your home is that you risk spreading the problem to the plants you already own. Trying to save a sickly plant isn't worth the risk of potentially contaminating your home garden.

Poor Water Quality

In certain parts of the United States, notably in the West, local water has a high salt and mineral content (known as *hard water*), which can be very damaging to houseplants. Watering your plants with hard water can cause the same problems as overfertilizing (see the section "Too Much Fertilizer," earlier in this chapter).

TIP

If you have doubts about the quality of your water, hire a company to test it. Better yet, use a lab that tests for high *soluble* (dissolved) salts because they're usually the most harmful to plants. Also, don't water your houseplants with water that has been treated with a water softener because it usually has a high salt content. Instead, use rainwater or distilled or deionized water. You also can install a reverse osmosis system to provide high-quality, salt-free water. These units are available from home stores, hydroponic suppliers, or online. For more information on water quality, see Chapter 6.

Inadequate Ventilation

Houseplants don't appreciate stale air. When air isn't circulating, fungal and bacterial diseases flourish. Moving air also evaporates moisture on leaves (which causes disease problems). Air movement reduces temperature stratification. In other words, it blends hot air that normally goes up with colder air that comes down.

To make your houseplants happy, invest in an overhead ceiling fan or oscillating fan to keep the air gently moving. A fan can make a great difference in the health of your houseplants. For more on ventilation, see Chapter 5.

Chapter **17**

The Ten Most Frequently Asked Questions about Houseplants

This entire book covers everything you need to know about houseplants, but in this chapter, I answer some of the most common questions that beginning houseplant growers have.

Are Houseplants Difficult to Grow?

Houseplants aren't difficult to grow — they just have requirements that are somewhat different from the outdoor plants you may be more familiar with. Thanks to modern plant breeding and selection, many of the houseplants available for would-be houseplant lovers are vigorous growers that are adaptable to a wide range of growing situations.

Selecting the right houseplant for your environment is one of the keys to success. See Chapter 2 to get information to help you choose plants that will do well for you.

Why Should I Grow Houseplants?

Every human living space can benefit from the beauty of houseplants. They're a huge group of plants with similar horticultural requirements. This means that, no matter where you live, most of the houseplants in this book will suit your growing area. Also, because there are so many foliage colors, plant sizes, and flower forms, you're sure to find houseplants that satisfy your taste and lifestyle.

Growing houseplants is more than merely cultivating plants. Being a plant parent can introduce you to a new community. You'll join a guild of avid (if not fanatical) houseplant enthusiasts who share your interests. Soon, you may become a member of one or more plant societies or online forums (see the appendix), and you may visit different houseplant growers and attend various plant shows. You'll form new friendships with others who share your passion.

Do I Need a Greenhouse to Grow Houseplants?

Absolutely not! Years ago, houseplants were reserved for wealthy people who could afford elaborate greenhouses with a staff of professional horticulturists. Although a few of these places are still around today, most people now grow houseplants on windowsills and under fluorescent lights in their own homes. I've grown most of my houseplants that way and have been pleased to produce plants and flowers that look as good as those grown in a greenhouse. So, don't despair: If you have a sunny window or a place to set up some lights (and many types of growing lights are now available — check out Chapter 5), you, too, can grow these fascinating plants.

Are Houseplants Expensive?

They don't need to be. Sure, if you're bound and determined, you can spend thousands of dollars on rare forms of houseplants, but most of the plants in this book can be purchased for very modest prices at big-box stores, garden centers, specialty plant suppliers, or grocery stores. They usually cost less than a flower arrangement from the florist, and a houseplant lasts much longer. They're really quite the bargain.

How Long Will Houseplants Live?

The short answer is that many houseplants can survive for years if you give them the proper care. The life span varies depending on the type of houseplant. You may decide to trade or discard some plants if they get too large for their space. Of course, that's up to you.

What Makes a Plant a Houseplant?

When many people see houseplants, they can't imagine what so many diverse plants have in common that makes them all houseplants. They look so different! Most houseplants have tropical or semitropical origins, and most cannot withstand cold weather, especially frost. But essentially, any plant that you decide to grow indoors can be considered a houseplant.

Are Any Houseplants Cold-Hardy?

Most houseplants are from tropical or semitropical areas and are intended to be grown indoors in most of the United States. In warmer states, like parts of California, Texas, and Florida, some houseplants can be grown outdoors as long as you provide protection from the cold in winter. Be sure to check the hardiness recommendations from the various plant information sources listed in the appendix.

Are Houseplants Fragrant?

Some houseplants are fragrant, but most aren't. In the plant profile chapters — especially Chapter 13, where I cover flowering plants — I point out which plants have enchanting fragrances. Some of the orchids in Chapter 11 are also sweet-scented, as are a few of the cacti and succulents in Chapter 10.

Where Can I See the Best Collections of Houseplants?

Many public botanical gardens and conservatories display a large sampling of houseplants. For some particularly outstanding exhibits of tropical plants, I recommend the following gardens:

» **Atlanta Botanical Garden,** 1345 Piedmont Avenue NE, Atlanta, GA; website: www.atlantabg.org

» **Biltmore Conservatory,** One Lodge Street, Asheville, NC; website: www.biltmore.com/visit/biltmore-estate/gardens-grounds/conservatory/

» **Fairchild Tropical Botanic Garden,** 10901 Old Cutler Road, Coral Gables, FL; website: https://fairchildgarden.org/

» **Frederik Meijer Gardens and Sculpture Park,** 1000 East Beltline Avenue NE, Grand Rapids, MI; website: www.meijergardens.org/

» **Garfield Park Conservatory,** 300 N. Central Park Avenue, Chicago, IL; website: https://garfieldconservatory.org/visit/

» **Longwood Gardens,** 1001 Longwood Road, Kennett Square, PA; website: https://longwoodgardens.org/

» **Los Angeles County Arboretum & Botanic Garden,** 301 N. Baldwin Avenue, Arcadia, CA; website: www.arboretum.org

» **Missouri Botanical Garden,** 4344 Shaw Boulevard, St. Louis, MO; website: www.missouribotanicalgarden.org/

» **New York Botanical Garden,** 2900 Southern Boulevard, Bronx, NY; website: www.nybg.org

» **Phipps Conservatory and Botanical Gardens,** One Schenley Park, Pittsburgh, PA; website: https://www.phipps.conservatory.org/

» **San Diego Zoo,** 2920 Zoo Drive, San Diego, CA; website: https://zoo.sandiegozoo.org/activities/botanical-tours

» **The Huntington Library, Art Museum, and Botanical Gardens,** 1151 Oxford Road, San Marino, CA; website: https://huntington.org/botanical-gardens

» **United States Botanic Garden,** 100 Maryland Avenue SW, Washington, DC; website: www.usbg.gov/

If you live outside the United States or are traveling to another country, check out one of the gardens on these websites:

» **Canada:** `www.botanicalartandartists.com/botanic-gardens-in-canada.html` or `www.botanicalartandartists.com/botanic-gardens-in-canada.html`

» **United Kingdom:** `www.greatbritishgardens.co.uk/botanical-gardens.html` or `www.greatbritishgardens.co.uk/botanical-gardens.html`

» **Australia:** `www.botanicalartandartists.com/botanic-gardens-in-australia.html` or `www.botanicalartandartists.com/botanic-gardens-in-australia.html`

Anytime I travel anywhere, I'm always on the lookout for a botanical garden to visit. Those in tropical climates are a treat, and those in cold climates almost always have conservatories displaying a wide range of tropical beauties. Check out a list of botanical gardens around the world at `https://en.wikipedia.org/wiki/List_of_botanical_gardens`.

What Are the Best Materials to Use to Repot or Transplant My Houseplants?

In general, you are better off with commercial potting mixes or one that you make yourself. Using garden soil is *not* a good choice because it generally doesn't drain well and can contain insects and disease organisms. For detailed information on potting materials check out Chapter 7.

Appendix

Plant Societies and Resources

Plant societies are always my go-to for knowledgeable information. They have no axe to grind, so they tell you the way it is without the marketing hype. The resources I share in this appendix are just a sample of what's out there. As you explore information online, you'll find others. Also, be on the lookout for houseplant interest groups in your area. It's always fun to find other folks to talk plants with.

For a great local source of information, check out your closest land-grant university (www.nifa.usda.gov/about-nifa/how-we-work/partnerships/land-grant-colleges-universities). Also, Master Gardeners — volunteers affiliated with the land-grant school's Cooperative Extension Service — can be very helpful. You can find a list of those people at https://mastergardener.extension.org/contact-us/find-a-program/. Check out your local garden centers, conservatories, botanical gardens, and tropical plant suppliers; many of the staff can provide a wealth of information.

I haven't listed any specific sources of houseplants and supplies because it would become quickly outdated as suppliers leave and new ones join the game. Plant societies usually keep updated source lists and recommend only suppliers that pass muster.

Plant Societies

Most countries around the world have plant societies of one type or another. You can find a directory of international plant societies, organizations, and resources at https://botany.org/home/resources/international-plant-societies-organizations-and-resources.html.

Here are some of the most prominent ones:

- African Violet Society of America: `https://africanvioletsociety ofamerica.org/`

- American Begonia Society: `www.begonias.org/`

- American Fern Society: `www.amerfernsoc.org/`

- American Hibiscus Society: `www.americanhibiscus.org/`

- American Orchid Society: `www.aos.org/`

- Australasian Plant Society: `www.anzplantsoc.org.uk/`

- British Cactus and Succulent Society: `https://bcss.org.uk/`

- British Pteridological Society: `https://ebps.org.uk/`

- Bromeliad Society International: `www.bsi.org/new/`

- Cactus and Succulent Society of America: `http://cactusandsucculent society.org/`

- Epiphyllum Society of America: `www.epiphyllums.org/`

- The Gesneriad Society: `https://gesneriadsociety.org/`

- International Aroid Society: `www.aroid.org/`

- International Hoya Association: `www.international-hoya.org/links.html`

- International Palm Society: `https://palms.org/`

- Orchid Society of Great Britain: `www.osgb.org.uk/`

- The Plumeria Society of America: `https://theplumeriasociety.org/`

- Royal Horticultural Society: `www.rhs.org.uk/`

- Sedum Society: `www.cactus-mall.com/sedum/`

- Southern Ontario Orchid Society: `https://soos.ca/`

- Succulent Society: `www.succulent-society.com/`

- Toronto Cactus & Succulent Club: `www.torontocactus.club/`

- Tropical Fern & Exotic Plant Society: `www.tfeps.org/`

Online Plant Forums

Online plant forums seem to be an endless source of houseplant information. Just make sure the information supplied is accurate. You'll find much anecdotal information out there that nobody has vetted. For most dependable information, use the other sources that I have mentioned in this appendix. They're your best bet.

Plant ID Apps and Websites

Several good (and free) plant ID apps are available, but I recommend these two:

>> iNaturalist: www.inaturalist.org/

>> Pl@ntNet: https://plantnet.org/en/

A third alternative, if you know the name of a specific plant and want the nitty-gritty on it, is the Missouri Botanical Garden's Plant Finder website. It can't be beat. You can find it at www.missouribotanicalgarden.org/plantfinder/plantfindersearch.aspx.

Local or Regional Plant Suppliers

Plant suppliers in your town or region can also be great sources of info. I strongly encourage you to patronize your local garden centers and nurseries, which have dedicated themselves to supplying high-quality plants and information on how to grow these plants.

Sometimes, these suppliers charge a little more than a big-box store, but you're paying for their knowledge and the care they take to give you the healthiest plants they can. These suppliers actually know the names of the plants you're buying and have firsthand experience growing them. For most of these growers and suppliers, plants aren't just a business; growing plants is their passion. They carry plants that are never found in the big-box stores, so if we don't patronize them, we'll greatly reduce the variety of plants available to us.

TIP

To find other plant aficionados, attend some of the houseplant programs given at plant stores, botanical gardens, arboreta, and adult education programs at community colleges. Many plant groups are on Facebook; you can find them by typing the common or Latin name of the plant group in the Facebook search bar.

Online and Mail-Order Suppliers

The internet and mail-order suppliers are another super source of information, as well as plants. These sources can be invaluable for some of the more unusual plants that aren't available locally. The better suppliers have excellent informational sites. Just do a general online search with your browser using the names of the houseplants that you are interested in. Facebook, Etsy, and eBay are also good places to search using the common or Latin name. Plant societies frequently list preferred suppliers on their websites.

Index

C

cachepots, 110

cacti. *See also* succulents

  Astrophytum genus, 195

  Cephalocereus genus, 195–196

  Cereus genus, 196–197

  choosing between, 193

  Christmas, Thanksgiving, and Easter, 207–208

  cultural requirements, 158–161

  Disocactus genus, 197–198

  Echinocactus genus, 198–199

  Echinocereus genus, 199

  Echinopsis genus, 199–200

  Epiphyllum genus, 200–201

  Ferocactus genus, 201–202

  grafted, 194–195

  Gymnocalycium genus, 202

  Mammillaria genus, 202–203

  Opuntia genus, 203–204

  Oreocereus genus, 204

  overview, 157–158, 193

  Parodia or *Notocactus* genus, 205–206

  Rhipsalis genus, 206

  spines and prickers, 194

  Tephrocactus genus, 206

  terrariums for, 86, 87

Caladium genus, 242–243

Caladium praetermissum (*Colocasia* 'Hilo Beauty'), 259–260

Calathea genus, 258–259, 264

calcium, fertilizer containing, 104

calla lilies (*Zantedeschia* genus), 316–317

candy-striped phalaenopsis, 218, 219

cane begonias, 354–355

cane yucca (*Yucca elephantipes*), 252–253

Canna genus, 294

cape plumbago (*Plumbago auriculata*), 311–312

carnivorous plants, 279–281

cattleya orchids

  Brassavola genus, 230–231

  hybrids, 225–229

  maintaining, 210

  miniatures, 229–230

  overview, 224–225

  Prosthechea genus, 231–232

  repotting, 212–213

Cattlianthe Jewel Box, 226

ceiling fans, 48, 83–84

Cephalocereus genus, 195–196

Cereus genus, 196–197

Ceropegia genus, 167

Cestrum aurantiacum (jessamine/ night-blooming jasmine), 294–295

chemical controls for insects and diseases, 148, 153–154

chemical sterilization of tools, 142

chin cactus (*Gymnocalycium* genus), 202

China doll (*Radermachera sinica*), 250–251

Chinese evergreen (*Aglaonema* genus), 239–240

Chirita genus, 322–323

Chlorophyllum comosum (spider plant), 275

Christmas cactus (*Schlumbergera x buckleyi*), 207–208

Chrysothemis genus, 323–324

Cissus genus, 275, 276

Clerodendrum genus, 275–276, 295, 296

climbers. *See* vines and climbers

climbing cactus (*Epiphyllum* genus), 200–201

Clivia genus, 295–296

cloning plants. *See* vegetative reproduction

clown cattleyas, 228

cockroaches, 147, 149

coir, in potting mixes, 117

cold-hardy houseplants, 192, 367

collections of houseplants, viewing, 368–369

Colocasia 'Hilo Beauty' (*Alocasia* 'Hilo Beauty'), 259–260

color combinations, creating, 124

color echo, 57

Columnea genus, 324–325

common names, 2, 7–8

companion plants, 33, 57, 58, 123–124

complex hybrids, 234–235

composted bark, in potting mixes, 116

'Connie Boswell' begonia, 347–348

conservatories, 368–369

containers. *See also* repotting

  for African violets, 332

  for begonias, 345

  choosing plants for, 121–124

  creative, 113–114

  overview, 109–110

  practical concerns when choosing, 110–111

  preventing fertilizer deposits on, 108

  removing plants to assess watering, 100

  roominess of, in relation to watering, 95

  self-watering, 18, 112, 114–115

  standard materials for, 111–113

  for succulents and cacti, 158–159

  type of, in relation to watering, 94–95

  washing out before reusing, 18

cool-mist humidifiers, 47

coral cactus (*Rhipsalis* genus), 206

Corytoplectus genus, 325

Costus genus (spiral ginger), 297

Cotyledon genus, 168

Crassula genus, 168–169

creeping fig (*Ficus pumila*), 276–277

creeping moss (*Seleginella* genus), 272, 273

crepe jasmine (*Tabernaemontana divaricata*), 314–315

Crossandra undulifolia (firecracker plant), 297–298

crown rot disease, 361

Cryptanthus zonatus (zebra plant/earth star), 255, 256

cultivar names, 10, 11, 214

Curcuma alismatifolia (Siam tulip/Java tulip), 298–299

cut flowers, arranging, 59–62

cutting tools, 35–37

cuttings
    for arrangements, 61
    as form of propagation, 32
    propagating through, 126–129, 331
    taking in September, 19

Cycas revoluta (sago palm), 243

D

dancing ladies (*Onicidium* genus), 235–236

death of houseplants, avoiding, 359–363

December, growing houseplants in, 20

dehydrated plants, 98–99, 101–102. *See also* watering

deionization units, 44, 46

designer houseplants, 32

designing with houseplants, 56–59

dibbles, 38, 127

Dieffenbachia genus (dumb cane), 243–244

Dionaea muscipula (Venus flytrap), 281

discount stores, buying houseplants at, 22–23

diseases
    affecting African violets, 330–331
    fungal and bacterial infections, 151–152
    handling sick plants, 153–154
    overview, 141
    preventing problems, 142–143
    surgery to cut out infections, 154
    throwing out sick plants, 144
    viral infections, 151–153, 330–331

disinfectants, 101–102

Disocactus genus, 197–198

displaying houseplants, 56–59, 65–66, 122–124. *See also* containers; growing environment

dormant plants, 96

Dracaena genus, 244–245, 260

Drosera (sundews), 281

dual band LEDs, 79

dumb cane (*Dieffenbachia* genus), 243–244

Duranta erecta (golden dewdrop), 299

dwarf date palm (*Phoenix roebelenii*), 248, 249

E

earth star (*Cryptanthus zonatus*), 255, 256

Easter cactus (*Schlumbergera* or *Rhipsalidopsis gaertneri*), 207–208

east-facing windows, 69

Echeveria genus, 171–173, 178, 185

Echinocactus genus (barrel cactus), 198–199

Echinocereus genus, 199

Echinopsis genus (hedgehog cactus), 199–200

egg crate louvers, increasing humidity with, 82–83

Egyptian star flower (*Pentas lanceolata*), 310–311

'Elatior' begonia hybrids, 351, 352

elephant bush (*Portulacaria afra*), 186, 187

environment. *See* growing environment; lighting

epicuticular wax, 161

Epiphyllum genus (orchid cactus/climbing cactus), 200–201

Epipremnum or *Scindapsus* genus (pothos), 271–272

Episcia genus, 326, 327

equitant (variegata), 236

'Escargot' begonia, 348

Euphorbia genus, 173–175

Euphorbia pulcherrima (poinsettia), 299–301

evaporative-pad humidifiers, 47, 82

eyelash begonia ('Tiger Paws' begonias), 349, 350

F

F_1 (first generation) seeds, 132–133

fans, 48, 80, 83–84

Fantasy streptocarpus, 340, 341

farina, on succulents, 161

Fatsia japonica (Japanese aralia/figleaf palm), 245–246

Faucaria genus, 175–176

February, growing houseplants in, 14–15

fern arum (*Zamioculcas zamiifolia*), 253

ferns, 260–263

Ferocactus genus, 201–202

fertilization
    death of houseplants, avoiding, 361
    fertilizer types and uses, 106–108
    keeping things in balance, 91
    for orchids, 210
    overview, 93, 103
    preventing fertilizer deposits on pots, 108
    with siphon mixer, 45
    for succulents and cacti, 161
    what to look for in fertilizers, 103–105

fertilizer beads, 116

fertilizer burn, 104

fertilizer injectors, 44

Ficus genus (rubber plants), 246–247

Ficus pumila (creeping fig), 276–277

figleaf palm (*Fatsia japonica*), 245–246

firecracker jatropha (*Jatropha podagrica/Jatropha peregrina*), 307

firecracker plant (*Crossandra undulifolia*), 297–298

first generation (F_1) seeds, 132–133

P

Pachyphytum genus, 184, 185

Pachystachys lutea (lollipop plant), 310, 311

Pachyveria genus, 185

palms, 248–249

Paphiopedilum 'Asian Lady's Slipper', 232–235

Parodia genus, 205–206

passion vine (Gynura sarmentosa (procumbens)), 277

pasteurized seed starting potting mix, 137

Pearcea genus, 329

peat moss, 117

pebbles, increasing humidity with, 82

pedestals, displaying plants on, 58, 59

Pellaea (Hemionitis) rotundifolia (button fern), 262

pelleted seeds, 133

Pentas lanceolata (Egyptian star flower), 310–311

Peperomia genus, 266–268

peppermint phalaenopsis, 218, 219

perlite, 116

Persian shield (Strobilanthes dyerianus), 272–273

pesticides, 141, 150–151, 153–154, 362

pests
  affecting African violets, 330–331
  aphids, 144–145
  applying treatments, 150–151
  cockroaches, 147
  death of houseplants, avoiding, 361
  identifying, importance of, 143
  inspecting purchased plants for, 29
  mealybugs, 145
  mice, 148
  need for regular inspections, 143
  overview, 141
  pollinating insects, 147
  preventing problems, 142–143
  safe and effective control measures, 148–150

scale, 146

slugs and snails, 146–147

spider mites, 146, 147

starting with least toxic solution, 141

on succulents and cacti, 161

in summer months, 18

thrips, 145–146

throwing out sick plants, 144

Phalaenopsis genus. See moth orchids

Philodendron genus, 249–250

Phoenix roebelenii (dwarf date palm/ pygmy date palm), 248, 249

phosphorus, fertilizer containing, 104

photosynthesis, 103

Pilea genus, 268–269

pincushion cactus (Mammillaria genus), 202–203

pinwheel flower (Tabernaemontana divaricata), 314–315

pitcher plants, 279–280

plant identification apps, 30, 373

plant shows, buying houseplants at, 23

plant sitters, 18

plant societies, 371–372

planting sticks, 38

Platycerium bifurcatum (staghorn fern), 262, 263

Plectranthus ciliatus (Indian borage/ Swedish ivy), 269

Pleiospilos genus, 186

Plumbago auriculata (cape plumbago), 311–312

Plumeria genus (frangipani), 312–313

poinsettia (Euphorbia pulcherrima), 299–301

poisonous houseplants, 31

polishing leaves, 20, 55

polka dot plant (Hypoestes phyllostachya), 263–264

pollinating insects, 147

pollination, 132

polymer gels, moisture-retaining, 116

Polyscias fruticosa (Ming aralia), 250

poor performers, getting rid of, 85

poquito banana plant (Musa acuminata 'Poquito'), 247–248

portable greenhouses, 90

Portulacaria afra (elephant bush), 186, 187

pot feet, 122

pot hangers, 91

pot-bound plants, 95, 332

pothos (Epipremnum or Scindapsus genus), 271–272

Potinara Burana Beauty 'Burana' HCC/AOS (Rhyncattleanthe Burana Beauty), 228

pots. See containers

potting mixes
  for African violets, 332
  for begonias, 345
  choosing, 118–119
  comparing to soil, 115
  components of, 116–118
  creating, 119
  for growing plants from seed, 137
  for orchids, 210
  overview, 115, 369
  peat moss, 117
  for rooting stem cuttings, 126
  for succulents and cacti, 158–159
  watering, relation to type and age of, 95
  when repotting plants, 121

potting tools, 37–41

pot-weighting method, 96–97

powdery mildew, 331

prayer plants (Maranta genus), 264–265

preservative for cut flowers, 62

preventing problems in plants, 142–143, 152–153, 359–363

prickers, on cacti, 194

prickly pear cactus (Opuntia genus), 203–204

propagation. See also seeds, growing plants from
  of African violets, 331
  overview, 31, 125
  understanding, 32
  vegetative reproduction, 125–131

Prosthechea genus, 231–232

About the Author

Steven A. Frowine has been a passionate grower and lover of plants since he was a kid. He has tended indoor and outdoor plants professionally as a horticulturist when he worked in Hawaii at the National Tropical Botanical Garden and at the Missouri Botanical Garden, where he was chairperson of indoor horticulture and managed one of the largest indoor plant collections in the United States. However, Steve's greatest pleasure comes from plants has been growing them in his home under lights, on windowsills, and outdoors, which he has done for more than 50 years.

Steve has a BS and an MS in horticulture from The Ohio State University and Cornell University, respectively. In addition to his long and rich career as a professional horticulturist for premier botanical gardens in the United States, he was an executive at top horticultural businesses, including W. Atlee Burpee & Company and White Flower Farm. Steve is sought out as a speaker and has delivered hundreds of lectures throughout the country. His presentations are noted for his excellent photography, knowledge of the subject, and sense of humor. He has appeared on various national TV shows and writes extensively, authoring many articles for horticultural trade and consumer magazines. He has written several books, including *Gardening Basics For Dummies* (1st and 2nd editions), *Orchids For Dummies* (1st and 2nd editions), *Miniature Orchids, Fragrant Orchids, Moth Orchids: The Complete Guide to Phalaenopsis,* and *Complete Guide to Orchids* (Miracle-Gro).

Steve now resides in the beautiful mountains of Asheville, North Carolina, with his wife and adorable and spoiled Weimaraner, Sophie.

Dedication

To my late mother, Janet, and my late father, Samuel, who encouraged me to pursue in my life and work what I love and believe in.

To my loving wife, Sascha, who shares my passions and tolerates my obsessions.

Author's Acknowledgments

Many thanks are extended to Teri Dunn Chace, who served as the technical editor for this book. It's reassuring to have someone with Teri's extensive experience as a highly accomplished author and editor of gardening books to pore over my manuscript and lend her constructive, helpful criticism, as well as make sure the information I've presented rings true. To my project editor, Charlotte Kughen, who must receive full credit for guiding me through the *For Dummies* process and making this a much better book. Thank you for your editing expertise and patience. To Kelly Brillhart, a talented copy editor, thank you for making my copy more readable. And to this book's behind-the-scenes editors, I also thank you for your contributions.

Thanks to the worldwide community of amateur and professional plant growers, societies, and breeders who educate all of us about the plants they love, put on plant shows, and continue to produce new and exciting plants for us to enjoy.

Lastly, I want to thank my wife, Sascha, for her patience in putting up with me pounding away at the keyboard for seemingly countless days, evenings, and weekends, and to my dog, Sophie, who always provided pleasant company and never complained (unless I didn't feed her on time!).

Publisher's Acknowledgments

Executive Editor: Steve Hayes

Project Editor: Charlotte Kughen

Copy Editor: Kelly Brillhart

Technical Editors: Teri Chace

Sr. Editorial Assistant: Cherie Case

Production Editor: Tamilmani Varadharaj

Cover Images: © Sladic/Getty Images